ELECTRONIC MEDIA AND LIBRARY INFORMATION TECHNOLOGY

ELECTRONIC MEDIA AND LIBRARY INFORMATION TECHNOLOGY

By

Dr. B.J.Ankuya

In-charge
University Librarian & Head of Dept.
Library & Information Science
Veer Narmad South Gujarat University
Surat (India)

DPH

DISCOVERY PUBLISHING HOUSE PVT. LTD.
NEW DELHI-110 002

Published by:
Tilak Wasan
DISCOVERY PUBLISHING HOUSE PVT. LTD.
4383/4B, Ansari Road, Darya Ganj
New Delhi-110 002 (India)
Phone : +91-11-23279245, 43596064-65
Fax : +91-11-23253475
E-mail : discoverypublishinghouse@gmail.com
sales@discoverypublishinggroup.com
parul.wasan@gmail.com
web : www.discoverypublishinggroup.com

***First Edition:* 2013**

ISBN: 978-93-5056-364-9

Electronic Media and Library Information Technology

Printed at:
Dynamic Printers
Delhi

Contents

Preface

The information technology has changed the way that information is stored and disseminated and has threatened the traditional approaches to the library and its services. The digital revolution has taken on the world of publishing also. Now paperless publishing or electronic publishing is gaining more prominence. In the changing scenario, libraries and librarians will have to play a crucial role in handling conventional and electronic resources. Thus the era of electronic publishing has begun affecting library and information professionals. The ultimate goal of electronic publishing is to provide fast and easy access to the information contained in the objective publications with simple, powerful search and retrieval capabilities. Thus, e-publishing can be used effectively in the context of Dr. S.R. Ranganathan's fourth law *'Save the time of user'* for many purposes.

—Author

1

The Evolution of Electronic Publishing

INTRODUCTION

The scope of the term 'electronic publishing' can be interpreted in many different ways. For example, it could be considered to include all forms of electronic aids to authors, from simple word processing capabilities to actual typesetting and/or mark-up tools as well as networking support to collaborative authorship and electronic communication among authors, editors, referees, and other participants in the publishing process.

Since, 'publishing' implies production and distribution, however, the term refers most obviously to the generation of publications in electronic form or, at least, with the aid of electronics. In this more restricted sense, electronic publishing can be considered to have evolved gradually over a period of about thirty years, the evolution having the following manifestations. Use of computers to generate conventional print-on-paper publications. This development can be traced back to the early 1960s.

The use of electronics to print on paper is not a completely pedestrian application since, it allows new capabilities such as printing on demand and even the production of customised publications tailored to individual needs:

- The distribution of text in electronic form, where the electronic version is the exact equivalent of a paper version and may have been used to generate the paper version. For secondary publications, electronic distribution began early in the 1960s. For primary journals, the development occurred somewhat later. Today there is considerable activity and interest in projects that make electronically accessible the text and/or graphics of journals that are also sold in print-on-paper form. Major projects of this kind include ADONIS, Red Sage, CORE, and TULIP. Moreover, the full text of a significant number of journals is now made accessible online by vendors such as DIALOG.

- Distribution in electronic form only but with the publication being little more than print on paper displayed electronically. Nevertheless, it may have various 'value added' features, including search, data manipulation and alerting capabilities.
- The generation of completely new publications that exploit the true capabilities of electronics. This phase of development can actually be subdivided into:
  - The presentation of existing text and graphics in innovative ways, and
  - The production of publications designed *ab initio* to exploit full electronic capabilities.

ELECTRONIC PUBLISHING

For the purposes of this resource guide electronic publishing is defined as:

- Making the content of the journal available online.

This chapter will also address the use of electronic tools to facilitate the processes of, publication, for example online electronic editorial processing.

WHY DO ELECTRONIC PUBLISHING AT ALL

Many journals around the world struggle to attract authors and readers, and frequently suffer from a lack of resources—both human and financial. In addition, research habits are changing and researchers increasingly expect any information to be found online, which means that a journal which cannot be located on the web may be effectively invisible. Online publication can help to address some of these issues. At the same time, many readers still seem to prefer print so you may not feel you can stop producing a print edition as well.

Publishing a journal electronically sounds very attractive. There are a number of good reasons for doing so, but it does have disadvantages too. Before committing yourself and your organisation to the effort and expense involved, it is sensible to look carefully at both the advantages and disadvantages. In the end, the decision will depend on what your main objectives are, so it is important to be clear about why you are publishing, or planning to publish, in the first place: what information you want to disseminate, and to whom. Electronic publishing is often considered to have six advantages over print: international reach, speed, additional capabilities, lower cost, new publishing opportunities and sustainability.

INTERNATIONAL REACH

If a journal is available on the Internet, it is true that readers all over the world can obtain and read your journal; you do not have to arrange for printed copies to be mailed to different parts of the world, which can be both expensive and slow. However, if readers are going to obtain and read your journal they need to know of its existence, and they must want to read the articles you publish. To enable readers to discover your articles/journal, you need to be visible on the main search engines and to encourage use, you really need to carry out some international promotion to raise awareness and trust in your publication.

SPEED OF PUBLICATION

An online journal has a great advantage over a print journal, as it is possible to publish an issue as soon as it is ready, and not wait for it to be printed and bound, then despatched. What is more, you do not need to wait until you have enough articles to make up a complete printed issue. You can, if you wish, publish articles individually as soon as they are ready.

These time savings can be very helpful to authors, particularly in fast-moving subjects such as some of the sciences where speed of publication is extremely important. Many of the important processes of publication, however, cannot be speeded up if you want to produce a quality journal. If it is a research journal, you will still need to arrange for peer review to be carried out—and peer review is often the most time-consuming step between submission of an article and its eventual publication.

The transmission of papers to referees, and of their reports to the editorial office, can be done instantly by electronic means, and make some time savings, but the reading, thinking and writing of reports will take exactly the same amount of time. It is also important to recognise that even online publication is not instantaneous; preparing the files correctly, loading them online and maintaining the online service all take time—further time is inevitably introduced if you are working with a third party host.

ADDITIONAL CAPABILITIES

The online environment offers the potential to provide readers with more functionality. One key feature of online publications is the ability to search for articles—at a minimum within one journal, and frequently across multiple journals Another feature commonly added to online journals is that of linking. This refers to the ability to go from one place online to another, at a click of a button—the most common example being the link from a citation within the body of an article to the relevant reference at the end of the article, and from there to the actual article which is being referenced.

Reference linking in scholarly journals is now increasingly being undertaken using DOIs, which are unique identification codes assigned to online articles, and which provide permanent links for the user. This is one of the international standards being developed to assist different systems to communicate and link with each other, to help with visibility and discovery of online material. The methodology of using DOIs in scholarly journals is being managed by an organisation called CrossRef. Electronic publication also makes it possible to include material which you would not include in a print journal, either for space reasons or because the material is difficult, costly or even impossible to print.

Research articles online can be accompanied by the full data-sets from which the results were reached—ideally in a form which readers can manipulate for themselves. Colour illustrations may be prohibitively expensive in a printed journal, but present no such problems in an electronic journal. Moving images, sound, or animations may also be included, although relatively few authors automatically think of providing such material at present and the technical complexities may outweigh the benefits. Before introducing any additional features within the online journal, you must consider whether your readers are likely to have the necessary software to make use of the additional material.

It is also worth noting that linking is generally rated very highly by readers, who find it an invaluable way of enhancing their research; however, other additional features are much less highly valued. It may, therefore, not be worth spending a great deal of time and money on these. One final consideration is that the additional capabilities which online publishing can offer may be of particular relevance to you, as the publisher, and not so much use to the user. These may involve the ease with which you can upload your content, and streamline your working practices.

One particularly important new facility which online publishing can provide you with, is a tool to measure and monitor online use. Most commercial hosts will automatically offer sophisticated usage statistics, and most of these will be COUNTER compliant, which is another increasingly important international standard which online publications should comply with.

REDUCED COSTS

It was originally assumed that publishing online introduced immediate cost savings. However, this is only true if the journal is no longer printed at all; continuing to print even a few copies removes most of the cost savings.. If you decide to cease printing altogether, you may save a significant percentage of your total direct costs, although many costs will be unchanged—however, most readers still seem to want print copies. The cost of administering an electronic version will also be considerably lower if you are able to make it available to everyone, free of charge.

Depending on the way the journal is funded, however, you may need to replace subscriptions income by raising author-side charges; this will require an administration system, which will reduce the savings. The costs of publishing a journal can be split into direct costs and indirect costs. Direct costs are those where an invoice is received from an external supplier, and the journal needs to find the money to pay them. Indirect costs are those costs which are covered by the parent organisation, and the journal may be unaware of them. Introducing online publishing may provide an opportunity to reduce direct costs but is likely to increase indirect costs.

NEW PUBLISHING OPPORTUNITIES

It is perfectly possible for an online journal to work in all respects exactly like a print journal. However, the online medium does make possible new ways of doing things—new ways of publishing, new ways of covering costs, and new processes—which may help to address the problems of a struggling journal.

New Ways of Publishing

Publish Often, Print Infrequently

This approach may be particularly attractive if you have difficulty publishing issues on time, whether this is due to lack of funds to pay for printing and distribution, or to a shortage of articles. Online issues would be published regularly and frequently, but you might only produce one, archival, print issue per year. This can help to improve regularity of publication, whilst at the same time saving some of the print and distribution costs.

Article-by-article Publication

This approach may be even more attractive if rapid publication is important to authors in your subject area. Articles would be published online individually, as soon as they are ready. In addition to offering fast publication for authors, this will bring readers back to the online journal frequently, thus increasing usage.

Separate Online and Print Content

Some journals have separated their print and online publications so that they are almost different journals—an example of this is 'electronic long, paper short' used in the British Medical Journal. This model publishes the full article online, but only publishes a shorter version of the article within its print journal. Some journals include additional sections within their online journal, and some exclude some materials from online version that appear in the print journal. However, if you decide to publish different content in the print and the online publication, this brings extra complexity into the way of dealing with your content, which is likely to increase your editorial costs overall.

New Publishing Processes

Open Peer Review

The Internet makes it easy for readers to comment on papers after they are published by the journal. This may be done once papers have gone through the normal peer review process, or it may precede or even replace it. Some journals then allow authors to modify their articles in the light of feedback. However, this makes for considerable extra complexity, and makes it essential that readers know which version of the article they are actually reading; this approach may not be welcomed in all disciplines, as scholars differ in their willingness to expose their unfinished work to their colleagues, so it is important that you know your reader/author community before making a decision.

Index

You may be able to do without an index if the web site allows searching of the full text of articles, particularly if it also allows searching by specific fields. However, human indexers add considerable value-electronic searching will only find the exact word you are looking for, whereas an indexer can think of synonyms, and will not index irrelevant occurrences of the word. If you can afford it, many publishers believe that a human-compiled index is still worth having.

CHALLENGES

Although publishing online presents many opportunities for journals, it can also present some challenges. Two of the most important challenges are presented here.

PERPETUAL ACCESS AND ARCHIVING

This is an issue which is worrying publishers and libraries the world over. In the print environment, a library which has subscribed to a journal in the past will always have the copies to which it subscribed, even if one day it has to cancel its subscription. However the same may not be true in the electronic environment, where the library does not 'purchase' the online journal, but merely 'rents access' for a specified period of time. Thus the library never holds the content locally, but relies on third-party servers to deliver the content.

Many publishers have now changed their agreements with libraries so that the library has perpetual access to any journal issues to which it subscribed; however, this means that the publisher needs to ensure good records and administration of online access to make sure that this works smoothly over time. Print journals are relatively easy to archive but there is no easy way of archiving an electronic-only online journal. Even if the archiving library makes backup files of the journals, these may need to be updated over time as technology changes.

Links to other sites—one of the most attractive features of online journals—may become inactive due to the impermanence of World Wide Web addresses. Some publishers have signed an agreement with archiving organisations to preserve their journals permanently; this has the advantage that they can also provide ongoing access to customers after they have ceased to subscribe, or even in the event of the publisher's own service failing, or of the journal or publisher going out of business.

Much work is going on in various countries to extend their legislation to provide for legal deposit of electronic materials in the same way as is currently required for print. For example, the UK law was updated in 2003, and in 2004 the British Library started a pilot project to test deposit of online journals. Another related consideration is the digitisation and online publishing of your historical print content. Although it is costly, there are benefits to placing all issues of your journal online so that they can be searched; there is evidence that usage of older issues increases. Some organisations will fund the digitisation on the condition that subsequent access is free.

CITATION AND DEFINITIVE VERSION

Electronic publication gives rise to a whole range of new questions, such as: How do you cite a reference in an electronic-only journal? Or to an article pre-published online? What do you give as the publication date for an article which is published online before the print issue is available? What is the definitive version of the journal—the online or the print? There are more fundamental issues, too, about what counts as 'publication' in an environment of potentially continually updated documents; these are all difficult and, so far, largely unanswered questions.

One issue that has been problematic for journals wishing to move to online-only publication has been the way that these journals are perceived by the research and academic community. In the past they have not always been recognised as credible publications by the relevant authorities when considering tenure and promotion based on publication. Fortunately this attitude is changing, and it has been assisted by the acceptance of online-only publications within indexing services, giving them recognition within the journal publishing community.

Citations can be made far more useful, in online journals, by linking directly to the cited item. This is facilitated by the Digital Object Identifier which provides a much more permanent link than a URL. The DOI/CrossRef system is now being used extensively; it does not in fact require sophisticated publishing although there are charges, these are relatively small.

An illustration of how DOIs may be used in citations can be found on the BMJ web site, in the area called 'Online First' which contains articles that have been accepted, but are not yet published, or assigned an issue. On this web page, the readers are instructed to cite the articles using their DOIs and the date of publication online. In some communities this has become an accepted method of citation, but it is early days and it is still to gain acceptance in many areas of academic publishing and research.

HOSTING ISSUES

Where a journal is published online can affect its success or failure as the online site can help or hinder the journal by the technical facilities and visibility that it offers. The price of online hosting is another important consideration. There are various options open to the journal publisher.

OWN/ORGANISATION WEB SITE

The benefit of publishing your journal on your own web site is that you have complete control over the web site—the design and the 'look and feel' of the site. Although there are, of course, costs associated with this option, no external supplier is involved. However, there are also disadvantages to publishing online this way. These may include a lack of technical skills and support for the journal, and a lack of current awareness of online publishing standards and compliance with new protocols.

In addition maintenance and updating of the web site may not receive enough attention if it competes with the other requirement of the institution's own web site. In addition, the journal may suffer from low visibility, since, it may be difficult to locate within the institution's web site, and visitors will not be attracted to discover it.

COMMERCIAL HOST

Several commercial companies are now hosting scholarly journals on behalf of their publishers. They also frequently provide value-added benefits, for example file conversion, and supply of metadata to abstracting and indexing services, as well as all the benefits of a sophisticated system which is continually being developed. They are also experienced in dealing with subscribers and access-controlled environments, and ensuring security of the online journal from hackers and unauthorised access.

Against this, there are some disadvantages. The prime one, for a journal with little access to funding, is that they charge for their services, and although most of them offer a price which is reasonable within the budgets of western journals, they may be too costly for journals from the developing world. It should also be remembered that commercial hosts may only provide a hosting service; although they can offer advice on matters relating to online publishing, they are unable to take on the role of a publisher. However, some do offer marketing services—for additional payment—to help increase subscriptions and visibility through promotion.

SUBSCRIPTION AGENTS

Some subscription agents also now offer to host online journals on behalf of publishers. Again, they offer a high level of technical competence and value-added benefits. However they are unlikely to take your online journal unless they feel able to earn sufficient revenue from sales. They will deduct the fee for their hosting from revenues that they obtain, in which case you would not have to find the money up-front.

Another potential disadvantage is that they may not be effective at increasing the journal's visibility outside their own customer base.

AGGREGATORS

A number of companies will put your journal content online as part of a large package which they sell in its entirety to libraries.

OTHER ONLINE HOSTS

There are a number of organisations set up specifically to support the online hosting of journals from developing and transitional countries.

Further information about online hosts can be found on the web site of the Association of Learned and Professional Society Publishers, and the International Network for the Availability of Scientific Publications:

- African Journals OnLine (AJOL) is an initiative originally established by INASP, and now managed within South Africa, to host African-published journals. The web site contains abstracts only for most journals, but in addition it has been developed to host full-text journals where required. Currently there is no provision for charging for access but this is likely to be offered in future for journals which require it.
- Bioline is an initiative set up by the Electronic Publishing Trust to host online versions of journals from developing countries around the world. They will convert print journals into electronic format; however, Bioline also supports training to help publishers prepare their own e-files. Bioline only supports journals that are willing to publish under the Open Access model.
- CLACSO provides support for a digital library of social science journals from member institutions within Latin America. Its digital library site hosts the full text of journals and other publications from the member organisations; the site currently operates under the Open Access model.
- Hrcak is a project of the National and University Library in Zagreb, Croatia, to host Croatian journals online.
- Sabinet is a South African company which hosts and sells African-published journals as a single package–access is thus restricted to subscribers, but this model does provide some revenue to the journals.
- SciElo is another Latin American initiative which hosts full-text, Open Access journals within the

biomedical and applied sciences. This platform only accepts journals which are judged to be of high enough quality—so it provides both support for publishers and also quality assurance for users.

MULTIPLE HOSTING

You can–of course–host your journal on multiple web sites, using different hosting services. Although full-text hosting on more than one web site is unusual and probably unnecessary, a common model is for your own web site to host a homepage for the journal, with detailed information about the journal, the editorial board, guides for authors, etc., but to use a commercial host for the full text content. You may, however, wish to consider also including your content in the collection of one aggregators as well.

CHOOSING AN ONLINE HOST

Choosing an online host is an important decision for all journals, and although it is quite possible to change hosts, the decision of which to go with should not be undertaken lightly.

There are many considerations to be taken into account, which are described more fully in a recent publishing Guide Sheet from ALPSP but the first two questions to be asked are:

- What technology and resources do you have within your organisation, and what do you need to buy in from external companies/suppliers.
- How much can you afford to pay for online hosting.

WHAT CHANGES DO YOU HAVE TO MAKE TO YOUR PROCEDURES

Whether you decide to do it all yourself or not, electronic publication will require you to change the way you do things. It is important not to overlook this aspect. You may need to re-examine all your processes—from receipt of submitted manuscripts to final publication—in order to make sure they are as streamlined, and in as logical an order, as possible. In fact, this exercise is often highly beneficial in improving both cost and time-efficiency!

EDITORIAL

The peer review, revision, and editing of articles, as already pointed out, does not become any less important if they are to be published electronically. In addition, editors may need to add electronic links within the article, within the journal, to other publications and to additional material. The majority of authors may be able to submit their articles in electronic form, and should be encouraged to do so, as this will facilitate the editorial processes. Electronic editorial processing software is available to manage the entire editorial process from online author submission to article acceptance. These software packages can help to streamline the editorial process, but are not essential to online publishing.

They have several advantages:

- There are no postal delays for authors submitting articles, or for the editorial office, editors and reviewers during the editorial processes, since, everything is managed and held online.
- The systems automate much of the correspondence, which can assist the editorial office.
- Most systems maintain and generate records of article progress, which may be accessible to authors as well as the editorial office. In addition, systems generally provide for a database of reviewers; this assists the editorial team in choosing the most appropriate reviewers for each manuscript.
- Since, the packages operate online, the editors, reviewers, and authors can all access the database and upload or download articles from any Internet connection worldwide, thus facilitating work when they are not in the office.

However these systems also have some disadvantages:

- They require everyone involved in the journal to have online access.
- They only save the time spent in postal delays—they do not reduce the time required to review, correct or finalise the articles.

- They require the authors, reviewers and—especially—the editorial team to be competent in using online systems, since, they are not always very user-friendly.
- They require reviewers and the editorial team to have adequate computer equipment, and either to work entirely online, or to be able to print out articles locally for reviewing, etc.
- Unless the majority of authors, reviewers and editors do make use of the software, such systems can actually increase the workload of the editorial office, who will need to load articles online themselves.
- And of course, most of them also cost money—usually in the form of a software licence fee.

Copyright

It is essential that, when acquiring copyright or the right to publish from your journal contributors—which you should always do—you make sure that you have also secured the electronic rights. It is also important to double-check that you or the author have obtained electronic rights for any other material you wish to include, such as illustrations or quotations from other publications. Examples of appropriate agreements have been produced by ALPSP and INASP.

PRODUCTION

Your methods of production are unlikely to be entirely suitable for publishing in the online environment, and this area of your activities is the one to be most affected by the introduction of online publication. It is sensible to get the articles into electronic form as early as possible; all the subsequent processing should then be done on the electronic version, and both print and electronic version should be output from the same file at the very end of the process. It is highly inefficient to work on a paper version, and then convert it to electronic at the very end.

The first change is that the final articles will need to be in suitable format for online as well as print publication. The most efficient approach is to process all articles in a 'neutral' format from which both print and electronic outputs can be produced. PDF files are adequate for straightforward journals, and of course this does preserve the appearance of the printed page; some systems may require the header information in other formats to enable searching and indexing. For more sophisticated electronic publication, PDF files are not sufficient—HTML or XML will be needed.

To produce appropriate files, you will need either to train staff and purchase appropriate software and computer equipment, or to identify and recruit suitable external suppliers to undertake this work; if it is done in-house, you will need to adapt the existing journal production system to ensure that the correct files are produced. If you decide to introduce additional functionality within the online version, you will also need to introduce production systems to implement this. Illustrations may cause problems if authors cannot supply them electronically, since,—at some point–they need to be converted into digital files for electronic publication. If the authors cannot supply e-files for all artwork, either you or the printer/typesetter/designer need to be able to scan the artwork so that the appropriate e-files can be created for online publication.

The electronic files must be carefully checked for accuracy, as it is surprisingly easy for errors to creep in when they are converted. You will need to devise—and stick rigourously to–a system for naming the electronic files for each article, and for every table or illustration associated with that article; it is sensible to include a version numbering/dating system so that you do not use an earlier version by mistake. When deciding to publish online you need to consider carefully whether your existing staff have the necessary level of skills to undertake the work required, and whether you have the hardware and software needed.

To produce the files required you may need to outsource the work that was previously done by departmental/journal staff, or you may need to change your existing suppliers if they do not have the skills, experience and equipment to provide what you need. Alternatively, the online host may undertake some or all of the file conversion work. If you decide to have different content in the print and online versions you need to ensure that the production set-up takes this into account, and that you are able to manage the administration of different versions.

MARKETING AND PROMOTION

Marketing, in the true sense of discovering what your market wants and then providing it, is every bit as necessary for electronic journals as it is for print journals. Many journals are not sufficiently visible—*i.e.*, not enough people know about them, or are able to discover them—and although publishing online may help, it is vital that some promotional activity is undertaken if online publication is to achieve the goal of making the journal more visible, and thus more used. For any journal—in print or online—conducting market research to identify what readers and authors want is essential.

In addition to talking to as many potential authors and readers and possible, try to carry out systematic surveys by questionnaire. If you see electronic publication as being a way to make your journal more international, your market research should be international too. This may cost money, but not as much as you could lose if your journal fails. An electronic journal will not sell itself, any more than a print journal. You will need to make sure that those who should be interested in reading it, and writing for it, are aware of its existence. This is not simply a matter of mailing a leaflet.

If you can obtain suitable lists of e-mail addresses, this is much cheaper than a postal mailing; be careful, however, about sending 'promotional' messages to e-mail discussion lists, as this is considered unprofessional, and may generate a strong negative reaction, although straightforward information about journals is welcomed on many lists. You should always check the 'rules' for posting to a listserv with the listserv manager.

In addition, you could involve the editorial team in promoting the journal by, for example:

- Referring to the journal within their e-mail signature;
- Handing out leaflets at relevant meetings, and

- Ensuring that their institutional library is not only aware of the existence of the journal, but also makes it visible to users.

Online publication relies on readers coming to the web site, rather than sending the print journal to their library or their desks. Bringing people back to a web site is particularly important if the journal is published infrequently or irregularly. E-mail alerts are a good way to tell people about the latest issue when it becomes available online, and can be set up manually or you could offer the facility to sign up to an automated alert on the journal's web site.

Linking to and from abstracting and indexing databases, and citation linking using DOI and CrossRef are also important ways to bring readers to your content. To ensure visibility to researchers and librarians you must make sure your journal is covered by the major Internet search engines. Another very important way of ensuring visibility to your community is to make sure your journal is included in secondary databases. The major services used to be resistant to including electronic-only journals, but this is no longer the case.

The one often considered most influential is ISI although their acceptance procedures are quite stringent and the number of journals they include is restricted. However, you cannot include your journal in too many such databases; identify as many as you can which are relevant to the subject matter. You may be asked to provide a free subscription, but this is a very small price to pay. If you can supply 'headers'—bibliographic details and, ideally, abstracts—in electronic form, so much the better; unfortunately, however, there is as yet no standardisation about the format in which they require them.

You should also make sure that your journal is listed in Ulrich's International Periodicals Directory, which is the major reference source for librarians. Some abstracting and indexing databases—such as Medline—require the journal's header information in XML format. If you are unable to obtain these files from your supplier, INASP have a template available for use which simplifies generation of these XML documents. Once a journal is made available online, the process of gathering feedback from readers and authors can be much easier than for a printed title, as the Internet facilitates two-way communications. Online feedback forms, direct links to e-mail addresses, and discussion forums all permit much more effective exchange of information.

SALES

Printed journals need little or nothing in the way of salesmen. Libraries decide which journals they want, and then choose their preferred channel for buying them. However, site licensing of electronic journals does require detailed discussion and negotiation with each customer; this is time-consuming, and if you decide to do it yourself you are likely to need extra staff with the appropriate skills. The alternative is to have someone else, such as a subscription agent, do it for you—but you need to be willing for someone else to negotiate prices on your behalf.

Bear in mind that the price for a single library may represent several subscriptions; if libraries join together to form consortia, this is even more likely to be the case. Selling to library consortia is a particularly difficult and time-consuming process, and the publisher with only a small number of journals can easily get squeezed out.

Initiatives are, however, being developed to help smaller publishers work together to sell a single, larger collection of journals in these circumstances. It may be beneficial to try to work with other publishers, whether internationally or in your own country or region, to overcome these problems. In some countries, the tax situation will be made more complicated if you are selling electronic journals; they may attract tax where printed journals do not. You will need expert local advice on this.

SUBSCRIPTIONS ADMINISTRATION/CUSTOMER SERVICE

If you decide to restrict access in any way you will need to administer this process, providing passwords or other access controls to new users, disabling those which have come to an end, and ensuring that your system can identify authorised users when they try to access the system. All of this will entail even more complicated administration than is required for a printed journal, and will require considerable technical expertise. Customers do not need any help to use print journals; however, the situation is different with electronic journals. Some customers will forget their passwords and you will need to reissue them.

Others will be unable to get access even though apparently using the correct password. Even if you make your journal available free of charge, you will find that some of your customers have technical problems in accessing or using it.

Thus you will need to provide some kind of helpline for customer support, whether on the telephone, on e-mail or both; customers will become very frustrated if help is not available at the exact moment when they need it, so the helpline should ideally be manned full-time during working hours, even if not for 24 hours a day. Of course, if you decide to use an intermediary to provide access to your electronic journal, all of these problems will be taken care of, although naturally at a cost.

WHAT MIGHT IT COST

It is impossible to put precise figures on the cost of publishing a journal electronically; however, it is vitally important to work out your own probable costs in full detail, and not to underestimate either the time or the money that will be required. A summary of the cost differences between print-only, online-only and online-plus-print is given in the table. However, indirect costs should never be ignored!

Item	Print Only	Online Only	Online Plus Print
Editorial costs	Yes	Yes (no change)	Yes (no change)
Copy-preparation costs (*e.g.*, copyediting, typesetting, design and proofing)	Yes	Yes–plus additional costs for e-file preparation	Yes–plus additional costs for e-file preparation

(Contd...)

Printing and binding	Yes	No	Yes
Distribution	Yes	No	Yes
Marketing and promotion	Yes	Yes	Yes
Sales	Minimal	Yes–sales and negotiation of licences	Yes–sales and negotiation of licences
Customer support	Minimal	Yes	Yes
Long-term archiving and maintenance costs	Yes (warehousing and some file archiving)	Yes (e-file and online maintenance)	Yes (including print and e-file archiving)
Financial management of subscription/licence payments	Yes (if charge for subscription)	Yes (if still have subscribers to online content)	Yes (if still charge subscription for print– possible additional costs if online subscriptions are sold separately)
Financial management of author charges	Yes (if charge author fees)	Yes (if charge author fees)	Yes (if charge author fees)

TIME

Someone will need to be responsible for thinking through all the questions raised in this document, and making the necessary decisions. This is not a one-time process; your electronic journal will need to be continuously monitored and managed to an even greater extent than a print journal. There will be additional complications to your production processes and new skills and procedures to be learned. If you do it yourself, your subscriptions administration and customer support will also be more labour intensive.

MONEY/PEOPLE

While, taking the 'electronic only' route will save costs on paper, printing, warehousing and despatch, these savings can very easily be offset by new costs.

The areas in which you will incur costs are as follows:

- *Hosting:* Whether you undertake to build and host your own journal web site, or to pay an external provider, you will have start-up and then ongoing costs.
- *Equipment:* You may need to purchase new equipment to manage the electronic processes.
- *Online Costs:* You may need to increase your access to the Internet.
- *Staff and Training:* You may need to devote some funds to building skills within existing journal staff, and perhaps to also recruit additional staff.
- *Production Costs:* If you reduce or eliminate print you may make savings on costs such as postage, printing, warehousing and distribution. Further postage savings may be made in the editorial office if you introduce an electronic submission and peer review system. However, you may incur additional costs if you need to outsource more work or to pay for additional services from your existing providers.

It is impossible to give definite guideline costs, as there are so many variables—the number of articles received and published, the number of subscribers, the number of other journals handled by the same system, not to mention local variations in equipment, service and labour costs.

Depending on the accounting principles followed by your organisation in dealing with overheads, your journal's finances may appear to benefit from a reduction in direct third-party costs; some organisations may not allocate a share of internal overhead costs to the journal.

However, it is misleading to ignore these overhead costs altogether in arriving at a realistic appraisal of the journal's financial health. Of course, if you decide to charge for access, some of the additional costs could be offset by increased revenues; however, you need to be realistic in your expectations.

SALES MODELS FOR ONLINE JOURNALS

SELL IT YOURSELF, AND/OR GO THROUGH INTERMEDIARIES

Making the journal available electronically is only half the story. If you rely on subscription revenue, you then need to sell the journal, which includes not only making the sale, but also arranging electronic access and managing whatever access control mechanisms you have selected. In addition, you would be wise to consider the licences which you want your customers to have; unlike print journals, electronic journals provide users with a wide range of possible uses, some of which you may not want to allow.

It is possible to have one or more intermediaries handle online sales for you; many subscription agents are now offering this service, for a fee, for electronic journals. This can make very good sense, as most libraries already deal with subscription agents for their printed journals. Furthermore, most subscription agents' systems offer the user the ability to obtain access to all their electronic journals through a single access mechanism; this is obviously preferable for the user, as the alternative is having to use different web sites, with different passwords, for each journal.

It is obviously easiest if the agent is also acting as host for your journal; if they are not hosting your journal, you will need to provide them with basic 'header' information for each issue in electronic form so that their users can search these on the subscription agent's site, and from there gain access your journal web site. Taking this route will increase your overall costs, since, you will need to pay the intermediary, but it is very likely also to increase the accessibility, and thus the use, of your journals.

DIFFERENT SUBSCRIPTION SALES MODELS

Singly or 'Bundled'

If you are fortunate enough to publish a number of journals, there may be benefits in selling them as a single package. The evidence shows that usage of titles to which customers did not previously subscribe can be unexpectedly high. If you also publish books or other content related to the journal's subject, an even richer package could be created; you could also include links to material on other sites. Another possibility would be to collaborate with one or more other publishers to create a larger package.

Electronic Version Free to Print Subscribers

You may want to do this either permanently, or for an initial period as a form of promotion. It will require an access control system, and you will need to assign a password or other form of identification to every subscriber. Be careful not to increase the print subscription price too steeply, or subscribers will feel—with some justification—that they are being asked to cover the cost of the electronic version, whether they want it or not; this could lose you print subscribers.

Electronic Version Sales

You may decide to set a separate subscription price for the electronic journal. If there is a parallel print version, it is sensible to consider the relationship of this price to the print subscription. Should it be the same? Or more? Or less? You might want to offer a discount for combined print-plus-electronic subscriptions.

Electronic Version Sold to Print Subscribers for an Extra Charge

A number of publishers are making an additional charge to include the electronic subscription; the supplements range enormously, from 10 per cent to 50 per cent or more. An alternative is to consider the print subscription to be the 'add-on', charging a substantially reduced rate to those who subscribe to the electronic version only.

Individual Subscriptions

The majority of print journal subscription income usually comes from libraries and institutions, but many publishers also sell at a lower price to individuals. You might want to consider offering individual subscriptions to your electronic journals, on one or more of the models. It is indeed arguable that the real benefits of electronic journals are more attractive to the individual reader than they are to the library.

However, you should also bear in mind that if you offer library subscriptions, particularly on the basis of site licences, individuals may already have good access to the electronic journal through their place of work. On the other hand, low-priced individual subscriptions may be the most practical way of permitting users to access the journal when they are not at their place of work. If you offer more than one kind of electronic subscription, and if the privileges or permitted uses differ, remember that your system will need to be able to distinguish the different kinds of subscriber at the point when they access the system.

Member Subscriptions

For those societies and associations which get much of their income from membership subscriptions, and who provide members with their journal free or at a very low cost, electronic journals can present something of a problem. If members see access to their own personal copy of the journal as one of the main benefits of membership, but have access at their own desk through a library subscription at their place of work, there is a risk that they will be inclined to discontinue their membership. Society and association publishers will need to think carefully about this, perhaps offering additional electronic benefits or services only to members.

Annual Subscription or Any-time Start

It is possible to sell a subscription based on either an annual basis or any-time start. With an annual basis, regardless of when the subscriber pays, they will be provided with the journal issues published within the calendar year; this is generally preferred by libraries as it is easiest for them to manage. With an any-time start, customers will receive 12 months' subscription starting from the date of payment. This may be attractive for users, but may also cause complications and additional work for the person who has to manage the subscribers. You may also find it more difficult to work out how much journal revenue to allocate if your organisation's financial year does not coincide with the subscription year.

Site Licences

Universities, companies and other institutional journal subscribers are always very interested in obtaining site-wide access to electronic materials. Access which is only possible from one or more specified computer terminals in the library is very much less attractive than being able to provide it to each faculty or departmental library and office. It is therefore a good idea to work out a licensing policy, and an access system, which permits this. Defining the 'site' may be quite difficult, particularly for a multi-site organisation such as a large company.

Pricing is a particular problem, since, organisations vary greatly in size and in the potential or actual number of users. If you simply have a price based on the print subscription price, then large and small organisations will pay exactly the same, while at the same time none of them will need multiple subscriptions—so you may end up losing revenue. Some method of pricing based on number of users might be more equitable, although it will be more complicated to work out the appropriate price for any given customer.

Although pricing for a set number of 'simultaneous users' has worked well for computer software and databases, it has not proved a popular model for e-journals. Different publishers have looked at the funding of the institution, the total number of faculty and students, or just the numbers in the most relevant department. In most cases, publishers have found it simplest to establish a relatively small number of 'price bands' based on these measures.

Consortium Licences

It is becoming increasingly common for institutions, particularly universities, to band together in order to make better use of their limited budgets, and to share the availability of the materials to which they subscribe. This can be a very effective way of getting your journal content to a much larger community, while still only necessitating a single negotiation. Combined institutions, however, make very powerful negotiators and you need to be careful to make the right pricing decisions and not to allow yourself unintentionally to do business at a loss. It is also difficult for a publisher with only one or a small number of journals to sell to large customers and consortia—and equally difficult for the customer.

The process is no less time-consuming for one journal than for a hundred, and it requires specialist skills and knowledge. Some organisations are trying to act on behalf of many small publishers to overcome this problem. For example the Association of Learned and Professional Society Publishers, in partnership with subscription agent Swets, has established the ALPSP Learned Journals Collection which acts on behalf its smaller member publishers to sell their journals to libraries and consortia throughout the world—it does not, however, offer hosting for online journals. Similarly Project Muse in America, and SABINET in South Africa offer publishers a service both to host their journals and to sell them to libraries.

SINGLE ARTICLE SALES

It is often argued that, since, a reader will only be interested in some articles, it would be better if he or she could buy those articles separately. While the costs of administering such a system might be prohibitive in the print environment, it is in principle much easier electronically, although the publisher does need a suitable journal system which can provide access to individual articles and collect payment, whether by invoice or by credit card.

One of the problems of this system is that individual readers are often unwilling to pay for articles that they think the library should obtain on their behalf. Publishers have feared that single article sales could reduce the demand for subscriptions, but in fact studies so far do not bear this out—if anything, this seems to tap an additional source of revenue sold in excess of 2000 articles to non-subscribers during 2005, and a survey by ALPSP in 2005 showed approximately 25 per cent of the publishers that offered this service found it was becoming a significant source of revenue). Most commercial hosts and numerous other intermediaries and specialist document suppliers are set up to manage such transactions; the reader needs to be able to pay by credit card online, and the intermediary will retain an amount of the payment to cover its costs.

OPEN ACCESS

The traditional publishing model restricts access to the publication by requiring payment by or on behalf of the reader. However, some argue that in the online environment scholarly information should be free to the reader. It is also possible that Open Access journals will achieve higher visibility and use, since, anyone can read the journal content.

Open Access publishing does remove the cost and complexity of access controls, although it may introduce the requirement for a system to handle author-side payments, and, of course, as with any other electronic publishing model, if the publisher wishes to maintain some form of print version then the costs associated with print will be retained. In general, Open Access simply means 'free access to online research information'. However, there are a number of formal statements which associate various other conditions with this basic idea. It is important to stress that Open Access does not require any specific commercial model—the key point is that the user does not pay to view the material.

There are also various models of Open Access that are designed to minimise any impact on subscription revenue:

- *Delayed Open Access:* Offering free access after a specified period. The length of time after publication which is necessary to avoid loss of subscriptions is likely to vary depending both on the subject area and the frequency of publication of the journal.
- *Short-term Open Access:* Providing free access to articles for a short period after publication, after which they are only available to subscribers. The argument for this is that this provides immediate

impact and raises citation of the articles and visibility, but does not affect subscription revenue, as people are still willing to pay for ongoing access. This may not give sufficient protection, however, for all journals.

- *Selected Open Access:* Some journals make selected articles freely available whilst the rest remain behind an access control system.
- *Hybrid Open Access:* Increasing number of journals are experimenting with Hybrid Open Access. This means that the author can choose to pay the publication charge to make his or her article Open Access immediately on publication. Articles by authors who choose not to pay remain behind the access barrier. Depending on the proportion of articles paid for, the publisher can gradually reduce the subscription/licence price for the remaining content. This model enables a publisher to test the author demand for OA without putting existing subscriptions/licence income at risk; many publishers are currently experimenting along these lines.
- *Partial Open Access:* It is possible to make the journal's primary research content available under an Open Access model, but to make a charge for other value-added content such as editorials and review articles, and/or for additional services. For example, several of BioMedCentral's journals charge subscriptions to cover non-primary material—so does the British Medical Journal.

It is important to remember that the Open Access model only works for online publications. Many Open Access journals still sell a print version on subscription; in addition to covering the costs of printing and distribution, this may also help to defray the journal's other costs.

WHO PAYS FOR OPEN ACCESS

If the user does not pay, any money required to produce the journal needs to come from somewhere else.

Common sources for OA journals include:

- *Funders:* Many journals in developing countries already rely on funders, whose aims may be best satisfied by making the content freely available.
- *Organisations:* Many parent organisations already support their journals 'in kind' by not recharging the cost of accommodation, support services, staff, equipment, etc. Some also provide direct financial support by paying for third-party costs.
- *Government Funding:* Some countries provide support for journals out of government funds, and governments may prefer the funding to be used to ensure greatest access to their content.
- *Author-side Payments:* Some subscription journals, particularly in the USA, already charge authors, although this is becoming less common; some journals in Western Africa, particularly in Nigeria, also charge authors. A number of Western OA journals rely on author-side charges: the authors pay a publication charge on acceptance. A recent study shows that this is in fact a less common funding model for OA journals than it is for subscription journals.

These fees are unlikely to come from the author's own pocket. More likely sources are:

- *Research Funds:* Some research grants already include publication fees, and this may become more common in future.
- *Libraries:* Some publishers encourage institutions to make a single annual payment, in return for which they waive or reduce publication charges for authors based at that institution.

SELF-ARCHIVING

Another way of achieving widespread free access to journal content is for the author to post a freely accessible version of his or her article online. This may be a pre-print or a post-print. It may be deposited on the author's or his or her institution's home page, or in a subject-based or institutional repository. In the last decade the number of online repositories of articles—both subject-based and institution-based—has grown.

Subject-based Repositories

These are most common in disciplines where researchers are accustomed to distributing their work to each other informally before publication, or see a need to make their research available quickly. The longest-established is arXiv, which was established in 1991 and covers some disciplines of physics and related subjects. Initially, publishers in other disciplines often refused to consider for publication articles which had already been posted in such repositories; however, these days most publishers accept this.

Institutional Repositories

A relatively recent development has been the introduction of institutional repositories. These are similar to the subject-based repositories, but are being developed to preserve the intellectual output of an institution, which often includes theses, working papers., lecture notes and teaching materials. The number of institutional repositories is growing, but the majority contain little content so far and even less in the way of journal articles. The cost to the institution of establishing, maintaining and archiving the repository also has to be taken into account.

Support for Repositories

Some research funders, such as the National Institutes of Health (USA), the Wellcome Trust (UK) and the Research Councils UK, are introducing new rules for the researchers whom they fund, requesting or requiring them to deposit copies of their published articles within subject or institutional repositories either on or at a specified time after publication. In the absence of a specific mandate, few authors have so far complied—it remains to be seen whether making this compulsory will have the desired effect.

Impact on Journals

It is sometimes argued that pre-prints are not a threat to publishers, since, the publisher has added value to the published version. The threat to the business of the journal is even more obvious when the final published articles are posted in repositories; this enables readers to bypass the journal entirely. It seems possible that, if all or most of a journal's content became freely available in this way, subscriptions to that journal might be adversely affected.

If that happens, what will happen to the peer review and quality filtering mechanism currently provided by journals? However, at present many publishers' policies do allow authors to deposit a version in such repositories; there is, though, growing concern about the dangers of this and some publishers are changing their policies, for example to specify a period of time from publication before which the author may not deposit his or her article. Ideally, a research funder's policy should respect these embargoes. publishers only institute them in order to ensure the continuing survival of their journals.

LICENSING CONSIDERATIONS

When you sell a printed journal, it is fairly clear and well understood what your customers are and are not permitted to do with the material. However, in the electronic environment there is much less agreement about what is allowed; abuse is also far more risky for the publisher, since, it is far easier to make a perfect copy of an original item in the electronic environment and distribute it widely. It is therefore sensible to draw up a statement of what customers may and may not do, which they will be asked to accept formally. This should be done whether access is paid for or not. There are different ways of bringing the licence to the attention of the user.

The individual user may be presented with a short summary on screen of what is permitted and forbidden, and you might even want to configure your system so that they have to click on a button marked 'I agree' before they go any further. When a sale is made to an institution, the customer might be asked to sign a more detailed printed licence as part of the sale. The latter approach does allow for a certain amount of negotiation if necessary, although obviously you would wish to design your licence so that it was acceptable to most of your customers without involving both them and you in the time and cost of individual negotiation.

Some of your terms and conditions of use would depend on whether or not the electronic version is free or not, but others would be applicable in any case. You would undoubtedly want to permit users to search, retrieve, and print articles from the journal; you might or might not also allow them to save individual articles electronically on their own computers. You should think about the best policy on allowing users to re-send articles, particularly electronically, to other people outside the subscribing institution—a number of publishers do allow this on a small-scale, personal basis.

It is unlikely that you would want users to sell articles or redistribute them systematically on a large scale, or to mount all or possibly any of the content on other web sites. While you will probably want a signature or other indication of acceptance of the terms and conditions when a sale is made to an institution or consortium, it is not always easy to enforce these. Within the academic and scientific communities, a culture of trust and honesty generally prevails and evidence of misuse is infrequent.

Some very useful work has been done to produce 'model' licences, or licensing frameworks, which will help you to devise a suitable licence for your own journals. All have been produced in discussion between publishers and customers, and thus try to address the concerns of both. While you may not wish to use any of them as they stand, without considering carefully the implications of the various alternatives they present, they may save you a great deal of time in working out appropriate wording, and they will also help you to make sure that you don't leave anything out of your licence.

One such example was devised in the UK by a group of university librarians and publishers. The LibLicense site also provides much useful information about licensing and licences.

Some publishers have stopped requiring their customers to sign a licence at all—instead, they have a clear statement on the journal site of what is and is not permitted. So far, no problems have been reported with this approach, and of course it saves everyone a great deal of time and expense.

CREATIVE COMMONS

The Creative Commons provides a simple guide to drawing up licences for the Open Access environment. These licences grant the user wide-ranging rights to re-use the content, whilst still protecting the copyright in that content. The copyright owner can select the most appropriate version of the licence. For example, all INASP materials are published under one of the range of Creative Commons licences, which allows re-use for non-commercial purposes, but requires that the re-user must always credit the author.

2

Standards for Electronic Publishing

TERMS AND DEFINITIONS

DEFINITIONS

We do not believe that it is necessary in a report of this kind to provide a glossary or definitions of commonly used technical terms and acronyms like SGML or PDF. It is assumed that all of our readers will be sufficiently familiar with the technology to understand such technical terms as suggested, unavoidably use. However, some initial definition of certain terms is necessary to avoid misunderstanding. These are terms where there may be some ambiguity of meaning, because of the lack of precision with which these terms are sometimes used.

As suggested, talk about the following categories of publication:

- Offline electronic publications, by which we mean those issued on discrete physical digital media such as tapes, diskettes or, more commonly, optical disks of some kind, such as CD-ROM.
- Hybrid electronic publications, by which we mean offline publications which contain links to online material.
- Online electronic publications, by which we mean published resources accessible on the Internet or on proprietary networks.

Online publications can be further characterised by the 'fixity' of their publication.

We use the following terms to describe fixity:

- Static resources, those whose form and/or content is recognised as substantially fixed throughout at the point of publication and throughout its lifecycle.
- Cumulative resources, those whose content is being added to throughout its lifecycle; these are probably the most common online resources that are of interest in this report, since, they are broadly the equivalent of serial publications.
- Dynamic resources, those whose form and/or content change continuously or 'dynamically' throughout its lifecycle. Dynamic resources will be addressed very little in this report, since, the issues relating to their deposit are not primarily standards related.

We excluded e-books from our definition of offline publications deliberately; they do not fit easily into any category, since, they are typically distributed online but consumed offline. Current publishing-community efforts to define e-books are proving complex.

The latest working definition of an e-Book from the AAP e-Book initiative is:

- "A Literary Work in the form of a Digital Object consisting of one or more standard Unique Identifiers and Monographic body of content, intended to be published and accessed electronically."

This definition is further qualified by definition of most the terms used. Most importantly, 'literary work' is defined by reference to copyright legislation and 'monographic' is used to distinguish an e-book from an e-serial. It is this definition that as suggested, use in our report. The difficulty of naming and definition in this particular area of electronic publication should serve to alert us to the generic problem of unambiguous communication between libraries and publishers in the electronic publishing arena. Clear definition of terms is essential. The final definition as suggested, introduce at this point is metadata. We use the term in the broad sense of 'descriptive data', encompassing what we commonly understand to be 'bibliographic information' and also the more complex technical data that is essential to the management and preservation of electronic publications.

PRESENTATION OR CONTENT

For as long as we can remember, there has been a fundamental division in electronic publishing between an approach based on logical content mark-up and an approach based on form. In print-on-paper publishing, these two approaches are so intimately bound together that we rarely think about them. However, typographic conventions prove to be unexpectedly opaque to computer interpretation. The more sophisticated manipulation of text that is possible if it is marked up for logical content is much more difficult to achieve using presentation-based electronic formats.

Nevertheless, following the PDF route has some substantial advantages to publishers. PDF is extremely inexpensive and easy to produce as a by-product of the traditional print-on-paper publication process. PDF also provides publishers with a suitable format for managing content for print-on-demand applications, which are of growing commercial significance. Producing text that is marked up for form has traditionally been significantly less expensive than producing the same text marked up for content. Although the additional cost of producing 'neutrally coded' text is now much less than it was, the number of suppliers able to produce SGML of a sufficiently high quality for reliable and consistent publication remains restricted.

On the other hand, there is self-evidently something of a mismatch between online publication and the use of the 'printed page' presentation metaphor. PDF pages often present information rather badly on the standard computer screen and the page metaphor is arguably entirely unnecessary in an electronic environment. However, by publishing in PDF, publishers have been able to maintain complete control over the format of their electronic publications. They can also ensure complete conformance in content between print and electronic versions. There is another advantage to publishing in PDF that may reduce over time. PDF allows the publisher easily to represent arbitrarily complex text in a way that standard methods for rendering marked up text cannot easily match.

Although there are developments that may ultimately overcome these problems, publishers that have followed the 'full text SGML' route to online publication currently have little option but to present complex text either as graphics or by using proprietary technology. This question of 'presentation or content' remains essentially unresolved in much electronic publishing. It has reappeared once again in the e-book domain. It seems unlikely to be resolved in the near future, and publishers are likely to have to maintain multiple parallel formats for the foreseeable future.

PUBLISHING—SOME BACKGROUND ISSUES

A HETEROGENEOUS COMMUNITY

It is almost always misleading to talk about 'publishing' as if it were a single industry; there are many different publishing industries, loosely grouped together by their use of a common medium for dissemination—print on paper. 'Publishing' is conventionally broken down into major sub-categories—newspapers, magazines, books, journals. Even at this high level of granularity, some significant problems begin to appear at the margins—in defining when a magazine becomes a journal. Our major focus in this report is 'book and journal' publishing—but this categorisation masks considerable differences between different sectors.

There are at least four major categories of book publishing: consumer; educational; professional; and academic. Each of these has very different business models and very different businesses. As we move further into the network environment, various aspects of our approach to categorising publishers must start to change. There is considerable convergence between different types of content as they come together for the first time in a common distribution environment. However, the differences between the different markets to which each of these types of publisher disseminates are in some ways further highlighted by the different ways with which different communities of users are adopting electronic dissemination. There are, for example, some interesting sectoral differences already beginning to emerge in attitudes towards e-books.

The publishers to whom we spoke for this report are primarily in professional and academic publishing; however, we included some publishers who publish educational content and some who publish for general consumers. As suggested, draw out such differences as we observe between these groups, although we must again stress that our sample size in insufficient for drawing statistically significant conclusions.

PUBLISHING AND THE PRODUCTION PROCESS

We often observe a tendency to equate 'the publishing industry' with the process by which an author's raw material is converted into a consumable product; this is the aspect of publishing that we mean when we talk about the 'production process'. Although the origins of publishing and printing may have been very closely linked, for the greater part of the twentieth century at least, the majority of publishers took very little interest in their production process. Production was a relatively unimportant part of their activity; most or all of it has been subcontracted to external suppliers, and the technical aspects of the process are of little interest to publishing management.

In recent years, those publishers who have felt the greatest impact of the digital revolution—particularly those in professional and STM publishing—have greatly increased their technological expertise. The type of larger publisher to whom we spoke for this report now employ people who can speak with some degree of confidence about SGML, for example. This would not have been uniformly the case five or ten years ago. Nevertheless, publishers themselves emphatically do not equate publishing and production.

What is more, we have spoken to a somewhat non-representative sample of the publishing industry as a whole. Most publishers do not have the kind of expertise that exists among our target group, and have no desire to acquire it. They will publish in digital formats as the market demands that they do so; but they will continue to depend entirely on outsourcing for all the technological aspects of the production process.

The significance of this, from the point of view of libraries with an interest in digital deposit and preservation, is that the people with whom they will find themselves dealing will not have much understanding of the technology involved. They will not manage their own content, but will depend on third parties. In an era of increasing globalisation, those third parties are as likely as not to be elsewhere in the world. This is likely greatly to complicate dealings relating to the management of digital deposit.

PUBLISHERS' MOTIVATION FOR ADOPTING STANDARDS

As suggested, introduce immediately here one theme that will be–implicitly if not explicitly—recurrent throughout our report. Publishers' motives in adopting standards are the same as those that drive all of their decision-making; they are strictly commercial. The decision on whether or not to adopt a standard will be driven entirely by perceptions of their own commercial advantage. In general, publishers do not produce their publications with an eye to their long-term preservation. They produce publications to sell them at a profit; long-term preservation may become significant to them, but only when the failure to accommodate its requirements in some way looks likely to have a significant impact on their commercial interest.

As one publisher revealingly said to us:

- "I am not particularly optimistic if you take the long-term view. I don't think publishers are well equipped or even well motivated to manage the long-term availability of their material—any material is only going to be cared for if it's financially viable. Once we can't get any money for something, we're not likely to worry about it. We should deliver whatever we can to the preservation libraries, but then it's over to them."

Several of our other respondents explicitly stated that they considered long-term preservation to be 'someone else's problem'. In the recent history of print-on-paper publishing, we can observe the direct analogy of the adoption of 'acid-free' papers. When publishers of scholarly monographs were first asked to produce books on acid-free paper, the response from larger academic publishers was generally slow and uninterested. Acid-free paper tended to be more expensive and difficult to source.

This remained the case until competition in paper manufacture eliminated the price premium from acid-free stocks. At that point, when it became entirely painless to make the transition, publishers were happy to adopt acid-free paper and to earn whatever public relations value there was from being able to advertise the fact that they had done so. There was no commercial disbenefit and possibly a small commercial benefit. The decision became an easy one to make. Commercial motivation is now driving publishers of one specific type of content—scholarly journals—to think harder about preservation issues. Major publishers have made a commitment to moving their primary publication platform from print-on-paper to electronic publication in the very near future.

It has been widely posited that a possible reason for academic authors' reluctance to publish in 'electronic-only' serials is their concern for the long-term preservation of the academic record. Certainly, there is anecdotal evidence that such a concern stands behind some academic librarians' reluctance to move to an 'electronic only' strategy for their serials collection. This has pushed some publishers of journals publicly to acknowledge that the development of an active policy relating to the deposit of their journals with national libraries is becoming an essential element of their long-term commercial strategy.

In this context, it is notable that major journal publishers in the Netherlands and Germany are already depositing electronic versions of their journals on a voluntary basis with their national libraries. At this stage, it seems to us to be unlikely that in any other sector of the publishing market either authors or customers will be found to be so concerned about issues relating to longterm preservation; this is likely to be reflected in publishers' attitudes towards the deposit of many of their digital publications. While they may be entirely happy to deposit their publications they are unlikely willingly to take on substantial additional cost or effort in order to facilitate long-term preservation.

The adoption of standards for electronic publishing will be driven by other factors. Any benefit that this may bring to the business of long-term preservation will be purely serendipitous. Some specific examples may deserve exploration here. A simple one relates to the adoption of standard identifiers. The near universal adoption of the ISBN was driven by the commercial demands of the channel of distribution. A significant subset of the STM journal publishing community has recently found a similar commercial driver for the widespread adoption of the Digital Object Identifier (DOI) at the individual article level, in reference linking. However, a recent conversation with an electronic publisher in another sector suggests to us that some publishers see common identification standards as being at odds with their commercial interests.

It will be a long time before that sector adopts a similar solution. A more significant example may be the adoption of PDF. Despite fierce competition between proprietary page description languages during the 1980s, Adobe's success in establishing PostScript as the *de facto* standard in the graphics arts industries has been complete. The close relationship between PDF and PostScript allowed a few publishers quickly to adopt PDF as an electronic publishing platform very simply and at comparatively low cost.

The 'network effect' rapidly created a community of producers and consumers that has increasingly expected PDF to be used for the dissemination of page-based electronic publications. Despite the claimed superiority of other formats, it is very notable that all but one of our respondents who are delivering page-based images are using PDF to do so. Where information from multiple sources has to be combined into a single resource, the drive towards standardisation is strongest. The recent announcement of NewsML, an XML-based standard for managing and interchanging multimedia news, is an obvious case in point. NewsML will allow the easy distribution of syndicated news in conformance to a standard XML DTD. For the time being, we can foresee no similar developments in other areas of content, since, the need to interchange content has not proved strong enough to generate real enthusiasm for the adoption of standards.

PUBLISHERS AND METADATA

The generation of bibliographic data by publishers has been notorious for its inaccuracy and inconsistency. Publishers have generally depended on third-party bibliographic agencies for the maintenance and dissemination of information about their products—and indeed have often re-purchased information about their own products. However, recent developments are making it increasingly clear—to some publishers at least—that accurate and consistent metadata is an essential aspect of their business in the network environment.

One element of BIBLINK, a European project that involved several deposit libraries as partners, tested the principles of the interchange and 'improvement' of simple metadata records between publishers and libraries. Dialogue between libraries and publishers during the course of that project revealed that many publishers—particularly the smaller and 'newer' ones—are becoming increasingly aware of the fact that their metadata is inadequate. They are actively seeking appropriate standards for the management and interchange of metadata. Libraries involved in the project, aware of the proven difficulties involved in cataloguing electronic publications, made considerable efforts to raise the awareness among publishers of the need for 'electronic title pages' to be included in their publications.

In the electronic publication of academic journals, publishers realised from the outset that article level metadata would be an essential element of any online delivery service; as a result, even where the primary delivery format has been PDF, article 'headers' have consistently been provided in SGML. These now have the benefit of being produced as part of the production workflow and should therefore be consistent with the published document.

The most significant current driver of metadata developments in the book publishing community is the pressure from online booksellers for more extensive descriptive information. The development of the EPICS data dictionary and even more so its subset, ONIX International, have been strongly motivated by the need to provide information in a consistent form to the online bookselling community. ONIX International provides a data dictionary and a standard XML DTD as a mechanism for the electronic interchange of a limited bibliographic metadata record. Although the initial release is focussed on conventional print on paper books, future releases are expected to cover not only e-books but also other media.

The extent to which all publishers will prove able to manage their metadata to a sufficiently high standard to meet market requirements remains to be seen. However, it is notable that a growing number of publishers, certainly in the US and the UK, are making significant systems investment in this area. The adoption of the ONIX International standard appears to be moving ahead with surprising speed in the US and the UK; and there is a real possibility that it could move towards rapid global acceptance in the publishing industry. We believe that publisher-generated metadata will be particularly significant in the whole area of deposit of electronic publications; otherwise the conceptual and technical difficulties of cataloguing will be extremely difficult to overcome.

To what extent does ONIX International meet libraries' cataloguing needs? A forthcoming conference presentation by Priscilla Caplan suggests that libraries should:

- "...Begin thinking about basic bibliographic metadata as a commodity, produced and exchanged by a number of communities in order to serve a number

> of purposes.... As suggested, soon be in an environment where most metadata is exchanged in XML: the publishers have already adopted it, and library systems are moving in that direction. In this context it makes very little sense to think that libraries, publishers, booksellers, distributors and vendors will all be creating incompatible, non-reusable bibliographic metadata...I do urge librarians to take a serious and objective look at the metadata schemas emerging in the publishing community with the long-term goal of maximising the interchangeability of data.".

Caplan goes on to suggest that libraries should "work proactively with publishers to establish enough commonality between respective rule sets to allow meaningful exchange and reuse of metadata." This co-operative approach was also endorsed during a workshop on digital preservation and deposit held in London in July 2000. For example, it became apparent during the conference that the technical data that publishers are gathering for the management of their own internal content repositories is essentially identical to that required by libraries for the long-term preservation of the same resources. There is nothing to be gained from recreating essentially identical data.

The EPICS data dictionary is designed to be extensible in ways that will encompass the necessary technical description of resources and it is anticipated that co-operative work between publishers and librarians will enable the development of such an extension. However, it is important to remember that only a small minority even of large publishers currently have sophisticated digital content repositories; most are continuing to outsource their content management requirements. This can only make the protocols for metadata exchange more complex to manage.

PUBLICATION MEDIA

OFFLINE PUBLICATIONS

In the offline category, as suggested, consider only CDROM publications: only one of our respondents mentioned any other offline media in their publishing. Seven of our respondents are publishing 'stand alone' CDROMs. For us, perhaps the most striking response to our questionnaire is the very rapid decline in interest in CDROM publishing among most of the publishers in our sample. Several of those we spoke to have established very satisfactory CDROM-based publishing businesses and some publishers use CDROM as an adjunct to online publication.

Most did not expect to be publishing many if any new products on CDROM in future. Increases in the available bandwidth are simply rendering this style of publication, dependent on a physical supply chain, unnecessary and rather clumsy. Most publications previously published on CDROM seem likely to migrate primarily to online publication, although some migration to ebook publication must be a possibility. This decline in offline publication seems to us in general terms to represent good news from the point of view of libraries managing digital deposit. Although protocols for the physical deposit of offline publications may be a great deal easier to manage, the process of managing the long-term preservation of their content seems to us to be likely to be rather more complex.

This is partly because of the lower degree of standardisation of their content, when compared with web-based products. CDROM products deliver their content through proprietary user interfaces. Our respondents named a number of such interfaces; of these, only FolioViews and DynaText received more than one mention. Many, indeed most, CDROM user interfaces are specific to a particular product. All of these CDROMs are typically Windows products; only four of our respondents produce products for Macintosh; two specifically mentioned that some of their products also run under UNIX.

The other complication with the preservation of offline publications is that, frequently, the content is encrypted. Publishers themselves, because they do not manage the production of their own CDROM publications, often do not have easy access to non-encrypted versions of the content.

ONLINE AND HYBRID PUBLICATIONS

All fourteen of our respondents publish either online or hybrid publications. All twelve of the larger publishers publish products that are entirely online. Seven of the fourteen publishers publish hybrid products. Among almost all the publishers we spoke to, the trend is again away from hybrid products towards pure online delivery. As we mentioned in respect of the offline publications, the requirement to deliver 'high band width' content offline is seen to be of decreasing importance as available bandwidth increases.

All the online publications in our sample are delivered using standard Web browsers for their user interface; many, though, require users to have additional software for access to some content. Commonly, this is a requirement for the PDF Reader plug-in, but the lack of standardisation of formats for sound and audio-visual means that a variety of interfaces are needed for these elements. One publisher in our sample is also, for example, using a specific ASCII-based format for rendering chemical structures. Publishers often provide supplementary material in their online content; it appears that the commonest file formats for such material are mainstream Microsoft applications.

Among academic publishers, there is very rapid growth in the publication of author-supplied supplementary material, alongside journal articles; this is seen as a significant value added of electronic publication and is typically published in whatever file format the author may provide. Access to this supplementary material therefore requires the user to have a copy of the specific application. While these may most frequently be in the form of research data, published as mainstream Microsoft application files, this is not controlled. For example, two publishers mentioned that raw PostScript was used for some supplementary material.

Two publishers mentioned TeX, and we are aware of audio-visual materials also being submitted for publication in this way. Standardisation of this supplementary material is therefore only achieved only to the extent that standard applications are adopted within the author community at large. Security of content in online applications is usually achieved through access control, rather than encryption. Although the content may be inaccessible to Web harvesting techniques, it is very much easier for publishers and libraries to manage deposit processes with essentially unprotected content.

CONTENT AND CONTENT FORMATS

CONTENT TYPES

The following diagram indicates the content types our respondents include in their products:

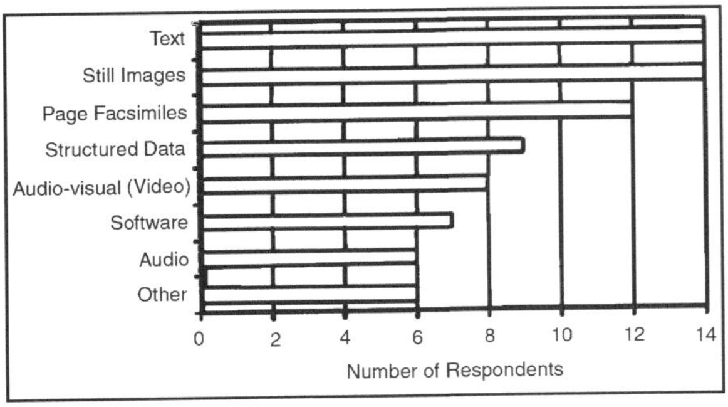

Unsurprisingly, all fourteen include both text and still images. Perhaps more surprisingly, twelve of the fourteen include page image facsimiles. Structured data is the next most common content type. Video is included in products by more publishers than audio. None of the publishers in our sample is making extensive use of either audio or video.

CONTENT FORMATS–TEXT

Again, unsurprisingly, HTML is the common factor—all of our respondents deliver text in HTML to end-users. However, there is a distinct difference in approach between different publishers, in the use of 'hard coded' HTML. About two-thirds of the publishers in our sample are generating HTML 'on the fly' from SGML or XML coded text. This brings us to what was perhaps the next most unexpected result in our survey—ten out of the fourteen publishers have repositories of SGML-encoded text, a much higher proportion than we might have expected. Online publishing has clearly pushed the adoption of SGML-based workflows in the publishing industry. One publisher is also making extensive use of RTF.

CONTENT FORMATS—GRAPHICS

The following diagram shows the use of different graphics formats by our respondents. It should be noted that most respondents are using more than one format. EPS is used as an intermediary format, not for final delivery to end-users. One respondent mentioned to us the possibility of using SVG for future online products.

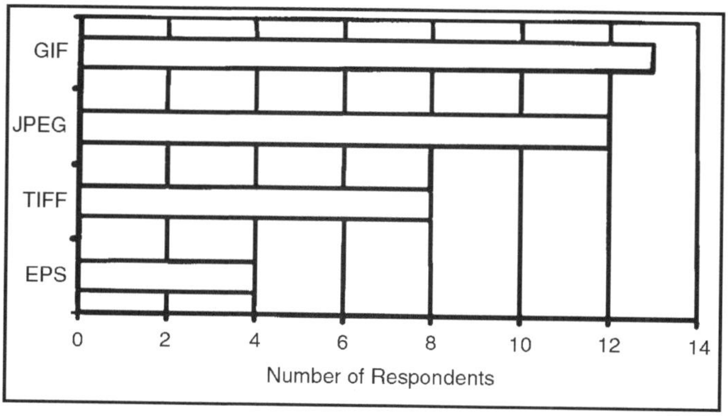

CONTENT FORMATS—PAGE FACSIMILES

All except one of our respondents who are delivering page facsimiles to end-users are using PDF to do so. The odd one out uses EPS. One publisher is also delivering PostScript pages to a specific scientific community that has expressed a preference for this format. Two publishers told us that their supplementary material also contains raw PostScript.

CONTENT FORMATS—STRUCTURED DATA

As we have already discussed structured data is usually provided in either spreadsheet or database formats. Some online structured products are being held in proprietary database formats, with results of queries converted on the fly to HTML. This sort of product is typically dynamic and therefore creates rather different challenges relating to deposit and preservation.

CONTENT FORMATS—AUDIO, VIDEO AND MULTIMEDIA

There was very little consistency from our respondents in terms of their approach to formatting multimedia content. One specifically mentioned attempting to avoid proprietary multimedia solutions through the use of Dynamic HTML and JavaScript but this does not seem to be a uniform approach. For audio, the formats that were mentioned by respondents were MP3, WAV, RealAudio. WAV was most frequently mentioned. For video, respondents are using QuickTime, RealVideo and Lotus QuickCam–QuickTime was most frequently mentioned. One respondent mentioned that they are using VRML.

SOFTWARE

Software is most frequently included in computer science products. These are often supplied on CDROM. The software may be provided either as an executable or as source code.

OTHER

Respondents mentioned various other types of content. These include: Microsoft Word templates; PowerPoint presentations; TeX for mathematics. A number of publishers control the presentation of their content through proprietary stylesheets. A small number of publishers include fonts with their content, but most appear content to rely on default fonts available on end-user machines.

DEPENDENCE ON MIDDLEWARE

A large number of products as delivered are dependent on middleware of one sort or another. Most commonly, this provides SGML/XML to HTML conversion. Search engines are also essential components of products, and these are often provided by a hosting intermediary rather than by the publisher. One publisher of educational content also mentioned the significance of third party educational middleware. Their content is developed as courseware for integrated learning systems. This content would be largely meaningless without preservation of the appropriate middleware.

OTHER FORMATS

A small number of publishers are managing their published content in specific application files. However, there is general agreement that these are inappropriate for long-term archiving even by the publishers.

THE E-BOOK REVOLUTION

SHOULD DEPOSIT LIBRARIES BE INTERESTED IN E-BOOK TECHNOLOGY

Essentially, this question can only be answered by another question. Will e-books have a major impact on publishing? Although the timing of consumer acceptance of the reading of books on portable electronic devices may remain uncertain, there appears very little doubt that the e-book is set to have a fundamental impact on the dissemination of what we might call 'book-like content'. Some publishers have already made major commitments to the conversion of part or all of their backlist to e-books; many of these are trade publishers, but the recent announcement from Taylor and Francis in the UK that they will digitise the whole of their backlist of 17,000 academic books cannot be ignored.

However, despite much publicised initiatives from Stephen King and a few others, today the greater part of e-book activity is focussed on backlist titles. Several publishers have told us that this immediate emphasis on the conversion of backlist is not accidental. There is so much uncertainty about the impact that e-books may have on frontlist sales that publishers are unwilling to add to the considerable uncertainty that already exists in their sales projections. Conversion of backlist provides the potential of revenue from an otherwise dormant asset, without creating significant risk. However, if ebooks become a significant medium for the consumption of backlist titles, it can only be a matter of time before market demand drives publishers in the direction of publishing their frontlist in e-book formats. 'e-book-only' publishing may currently be largely confined to what many dismiss as an enhanced form of vanity publishing in the US; this is unlikely to remain the case for long.

For this reason we believe that libraries cannot afford to ignore developments in e-book publishing, but should begin to think about the implications for deposit. While it may be several years before their impact becomes very significant, we believe that it is unlikely that e-books will not be having a major impact on publishing by the end of this decade.

ARE OUR RESPONDENTS INTERESTED IN E-BOOKS

Half of our twelve larger publisher respondents are either already publishing in e-book formats or expect to start doing so shortly. However, only one has already published anything solely in e-book format; and of the other five, three have no plans to publish only in e-book, and the other two say they regard it as premature to do so in 2001. In terms of their commitment to e-book publishing, the five publishers already involved range from the very tentative and experimental to the fully committed—one of them is expecting to have their complete trade frontlist in e-book in 2001. The other publishers told us that they currently have no plans for publishing in e-book formats.

E-BOOK CONTENT DELIVERY FORMATS

The same 'content and form' division that we discussed in our introduction is also being played out in the e-book arena. ebook devices are divided between those which use content marked up for form and those which use page-based content. The following table sets out the formats used by each device and the current distribution channel for these formats in the United States.

Primary Format	Derivative Format	Current distribution channel (in the US)
OEB	Microsoft Reader Rocket eBook (originally HTML) SoftBook Peanut Press Acrobat Reader Glassbook Reader	bn.com Lightning Source bn.com Powell's, etc. SoftBook Press Peanut Press Adobe PDF Merchant bn.com Glassbook, etc
PDF	Print-on-Demand SoftLock Systems	bn.com Lightning Source Replica Books Sprout SoftLock Systems

One of our respondents referred to the OEB standard as "little more than HTML expressed as XML'. He went on to say that, as a result, the existing version of OEB, although theoretically extensible, is more suitable for novels than for more complex text. More complex ebooks can currently only be delivered using PDF-based formats. The OEB standard is also undergoing revision, and another of our respondents expressed concern about version control.

It is also important to recognise that each of the different derivative formats are different file formats, to a greater or lesser extent. Although we expect to see the different devices becoming more conformant with standards as time passes, there are significant divergences today. Publishers who wish to provide content to multiple devices need to maintain multiple electronic versions of the same title. This is even the case with PDF-based formats, where the text layout for one device may not be suitable for another.

PRODUCING EBOOKS

For the time being at least, ebook production has not been embedded into publishers' standard production workflows. e-books today are typically being produced by scanning of printed products—we are told that this is often the case even for newly published titles. Publishers' workflows for books in the print on paper environment are typically much less standardised than they are for serial publications. Except in the case of major structured reference works, neutral coding of text is rare or non-existent. It is likely to take some time for ebook production to become a settled part of publisher's production workflows. Meanwhile, production workflows will remain somewhat *ad hoc*. It has also been suggested to us that vendors of tools for production of ebook formats may have a strong commercial interest in obstructing the adoption of stable, capable, neutral formats.

E-BOOKS AND OTHER CONTENT TYPES

For the time being, e-books are generally restricted to fairly straightforward text and still images. We would regard it as unlikely that this will remain the case for very long. The OEB standard allows for arbitrary external technology to manage other content types and it may be some time before there is any general agreement on the optimum file formats. In the meantime, in the same way as we have seen in online resources, there will almost certainly be many different proprietary approaches.

E-BOOKS AND METADATA

The OEB 'package' incorporates a simple Dublin Core (DC) metadata record in Version 1. We understand that is has been recognised that the DC set is not adequate for the purpose, and a significant revision of the metadata structure is expected in future releases.

E-BOOKS AND ENCRYPTION

An essential element in the marketing of all e-book devices is security, because of the 'distributed' model of distribution. The content on ebook devices is encrypted to prevent it being passed along to other users. There is an industry grouping, EBX, which is defining a standard approach to rights management and encryption. The different approaches used for encryption need not detain us here. However, the fact that the content is encrypted does create a particular problem for libraries, not least in managing long-term preservation. If e-books are to be deposited with libraries, it will clearly be advantageous if these are non-encrypted versions. However, publishers will be very reluctant to allow libraries to provide any public access to unencrypted versions.

MANAGING E-BOOK CONTENT

Only a small number of publishers are currently planning to manage their own ebook content in house. Most will be happy to see their ebook content managed by outside vendors. Since, this means that publishers will not be in direct control of their content, it is likely to complicate the process of deposit, particularly deposit of unencrypted versions of content.

PUBLISHERS AND CONTENT MANAGEMENT—AN EXPLANATORY NOTE

We have made a number of references in the text to publishers' attitudes to content management, and it seems appropriate to draw together here some explanation of the issues involved.

HISTORIC ATTITUDES

Traditionally, the great majority of publishers have not been closely involved with the technical aspects of their production processes. Although most books and journals have been produced using digital technology for typesetting for over twenty years, the management of the digital files used for their production has not—until very recently at least—been a high priority for publishers: the cost of managing the content has not been matched by any measurable commercial gain from doing so.

To the extent that anyone managed the digital content, it was seen as a job for the outside suppliers—typesetters—on whom publishers depended for their text preparation. The 'DTP' revolution of the mid 80s did not, in most instances, lead to a major change in the approach of book and journal publishers. Some publishers—particularly those preparing highly integrated educational textbooks, or books with similar design requirements—successfully brought their text formatting in house. But most continued to depend on external suppliers for the majority of their requirements.

They simply found that managing the text preparation and formatting processes in house was too expensive and too difficult to manage. The decision not to bring the work in house was supported by the collapsing price of buying-in services from outside vendors, whose adoption of much lower cost, PC-based systems has brought about extraordinary cost reductions in typesetting in real terms. Of course, there was some waste in this system.

Often, when new editions had to be typeset, files for the old edition could not be found or were incompatible with a new generation of equipment. But the overall system itself was efficient—the difficulty of guessing which files you might need again would have made it essential to manage all files; and the cost of doing this was prohibitive.

THE ARRIVAL OF ELECTRONIC PUBLISHING—THE e-*JOURNAL*

Publishers therefore arrived at the dawn of the electronic publishing revolution with little or no experience of managing their own content. There is a fund of stories about journal publishers who believed that they had access to their digital archives because their typesetters held years of typesetting tapes. Unfortunately, these tapes proved entirely inappropriate for conversion. As a next step, PDF appeared to offer a simple solution to the problem—it could be produced easily and cheaply enough as a by-product of the current print production process.

There was a rapid recognition among journal publishers that they would have to produce SGML-encoded 'headers' but this was typically tacked onto the side of the existing production workflow. One or two journal publishers recognised very early that full text SGML would, in the end, prove to be essential to journal publishing and moved early to full SGML workflow for their journals. However, the difficulty of managing SGML workflows on this scale is tremendous, the costs involved high, and the quality assurance issues raised difficult to overcome. There are many difficulties in managing content from multiple sources.

These can be as simple as enforcing file-naming conventions and ensuring control of fonts and character sets. Most journal publishers set out on this process around a decade ago, and have learned many very difficult lessons along the way. Some publishers have worked their way fairly successfully through these issues—others have still barely started on the process of moving to 'full text' SGML. It will be several years before all mainstream journals are available in a neutrally coded form, and the content sufficiently well managed for its straightforward transfer from publisher to deposit library.

Most of the major journal publishers are now managing their completed content in house and are also hosting their own content online. Many of the smaller journal publishers depend entirely on outsourcing for text preparation, content management and online hosting. This is unlikely to change, since, few smaller publishers will be able to justify the systems investment required. It is extremely hard to predict whether the trend in future among larger publishers will be a return to outsourcing or the continued development of ever-greater technical resources in house. Publishers have in the past tried to outsource as much of their operations as they can, and we believe that ultimately this may prove to be the overwhelming instinct.

THE DIGITAL REVOLUTION AND BOOKS

Journal publishers had a significant advantage over their book publishing colleagues—the relative uniformity of their content. Journal publishers have found very considerable problems in arriving at uniform DTDs to cover all of their journals, and have often found this to be unmanageable; a uniform DTD to manage all of a publisher's book output is unlikely to be attainable. Publishers have not therefore looked to manage their books in SGML, but some of the very large publishers have recently started to look instead at ways of managing their content in the multiple formats that they already have—in the word processor format supplied by the author, in the native file format of the formatting software used by their typesetter, in PostScript, in PDF. Available technology for managing digital content on this scale, with all the implicit version control for example, is expensive and mostly ill-suited to publishers' needs.

The technology comes either from the print industry or from online content management—whereas publishers, for the foreseeable future, require a combination of the two which proves very difficult to achieve. While a small number of large publishers have now taken the plunge into managing their own book content repositories; most have looked at the scale of the task and backed away from it. Now comes the challenge of managing yet more multiple formats, for e-book publishing. While this may theoretically involve holding only a single master format and generating the content for different application formats as required 'on the fly', it seems likely to be more complex than that, at least for the immediate future.

In these circumstances, it is perhaps unsurprising that many book publishers appear to be making the decision to outsource their content management, at least for the time being. It may well take five years—as it did for the journal publishers—for patterns of e-book publishing to settle down sufficiently to allow many book publishers to make the major investments in content management that their journal publishing colleagues have now made. Even then, they may choose to outsource.

As we have earlier discussed new publishers, established to take advantage of electronic publishing from the outset may make the transition more easily. But the potential for a proliferation of new, small publishers will lead to its own problem from the viewpoint of deposit of electronic publication.

IMPLICATIONS FOR DEPOSIT LIBRARIES

There is a plethora of companies involved in the processing and storage of published content. These include:

typesetters; specialist online hosting services like CatchWord; content-management technology companies like Versaware; e-book and print-ondemand intermediaries like Lightning Source; and many more. The roles they play and the services they provide are different for different publishers. The processes and relationships are far from standardised at this point.

The services provided by these companies in electronic publishing may have a direct impact on the content that might be delivered to deposit libraries; on file formats and protocols, for example; and on metadata relating to the content. However these companies are typically operating simply as agents of the publishers and other rights owners. It is neither appropriate nor possible for these companies to develop direct relationships with deposit libraries. Deposit libraries will have no option but to deal with these suppliers through the publishers—any attempt to establish a direct relationship would be regarded as entirely unacceptable by publisher and supplier alike. However, it is vital to recognise that there may often be greater technical expertise the ends of the chain than in the middle, which may create some barrier to effective communication.

THE PUBLIC WEB

PUBLISHING AND THE WORLD WIDE WEB

When we speak of 'the public Web', we mean that part of the Web that is publicly and freely accessible to any user of the Internet. Despite extraordinary growth in many other published media during the 1990s, the World Wide Web represents the easily largest single explosion in the volume of publishing in the last decade, with estimates that the total number of pages on the 'public web' worldwide has now passed one billion.

Most of those who post content to the Web probably do not regard themselves as 'publishers'—although we would contend that they most certainly are, even if their published output occasionally reveals some lack of real publishing expertise! This explosion of publishing activity has been built on the rapid and universal adoption of a standard, and proves the power of the network effect on the adoption of standards.

CONTENT STANDARDS ON THE WEB

Experiments in 'Web harvesting' for archiving in both Scandinavia and the Netherlands have demonstrated that the overwhelming majority of files harvested have been in common formats. This would suggest that this is also true for the public Web as a whole.

Year of Collection	**1998**	**2000**
Country of Collection	**Sweden**[45]	**The Netherlands**
Sample size (number of files harvested)	179,784	79,879
File type		
HTML tagged text file	56 %	66 %
GIF image file	20 %	24 %
JPEG image file	10 %	6 %
Plain text file	9 %	2 %
All other file types	5 %	1 %

Without more data than is available to us, we cannot immediately suggest reasons for the marked variance in the data between 1998 in Sweden and 2000 in The Netherlands. It may suggest some difference in sampling methods. It is also impossible to extract from this data the 'average complexity' of a Web page—although clearly there must be a very high proportion of Web pages that are simply HTML tagged text. It is unsurprising to us that the public web should be relatively simply structured. For obvious reasons, harvesting operations of this type are unable to access content that is protected, or content that is dynamically served.

DIGITAL PRESERVATION AND THE WEB

The low cost of becoming a 'publisher' on the Web has been the major facilitator of all this activity, and has significantly lowered the barriers to entry. This lowering of the significant investment barrier to becoming a publisher raises a number of new problems for all users of information—not least the deposit libraries. In the past deposit libraries were content to allow the commercial hurdle of publication to provide a primary filter in determining what should and what should not be deposited. With the Web, that primary filter is no longer in place.

Most of these 'publishers' are not very prolific: in the Netherlands harvesting exercise to which we have already referred, over 80 per cent of the domains harvested had fewer than 10 pages of content—and fewer than one per cent had more than 500. Much of this 'publishing' is at the level of personal home pages, which are almost certainly of only passing interest—the ephemera of the digital age. However, some of what is published has lasting value—even though it may be distributed for nothing. Because of the negligible cost of distribution, the Web provides a mechanism for the publication of some content that would never have justified publication in print on paper form, including for example doctoral theses and a growing number of conference proceedings.

At the same time, it allows Governments to provide free access to information that was previously difficult to find. It will not be at all easy for deposit libraries to separate that which has value from that which does not in the absence of the commercial 'cues' which are available in the print world. The primary issues concerning deposit and preservation of this content are not related to file formats and similar technical production issues; rather they relate to the amount of human intervention that is required in selection, identification and description of the content.

Most of these publishers will not have heard of the term 'metadata'; nor will they have given thought to issues of unique identification. There are other issues to be considered, like identifying the 'boundaries' of a publication in a hyperlinked environment. Where does one document start and another begin? Can you only usefully preserve a document if you preserve all the documents to which it links? Although the purely technical issues relating to preservation of the Web may be difficult, particularly as the Web becomes more technically complex, it seems to us that finding answers to some of these other questions may ultimately prove to be more difficult.

CONCLUSION

REASONS FOR OPTIMISM

In our research, we found a number of reasons why libraries with an interest in the long-term preservation of electronically published content might be optimistic about trends in publishers' production.

These included:

- The very rapid trend in the direction of full SGML/ XML mark up of text, particularly among journal and professional publishers. It seems to us that SGML/ XML mark up come closest to providing a format that is susceptible to long-term preservation of content.
- The near universal acceptance of PDF for page facsimiles.
- The small number of formats in use for still images.
- The trend away from 'offline' publication towards online and e-book publication.
- The drive towards standardisation of e-book file formats.
- The increased sophistication in some publishers' approach to content management, which means that their electronic content is being stored in a more consistent and coherent form than has been the case in the past.
- The increased interest and investment by publishers in the generation of metadata, both bibliographic and technical.

REASONS FOR REALISM

This optimism needs to be tempered with realism.

- SGML and XML, while apparently 'neutral' in their application, are never entirely neutral. Publishers develop their DTDs to meet their own specific needs and workflows. Publishers using SGML amend their DTDs, if not frequently at least occasionally, to overcome deficiencies on one kind and another. This implies major tasks for libraries in managing SGML-encoded text, in terms of version control of text and the DTDs that accompany it.

- It is highly unlikely that any time in the near future their will be a trend towards standardisation of DTDs even by publishers in the same sector, except where there is a real market requirement to share syndicated content from a number of sources. We do not see this happening in the near future in any other sector.
- At the moment, at least, the SGML and XML archives that are available do not constitute the 'published product'—the product is dependent on middleware to deliver it to the end user. This middleware may or may not lie within the publisher's control. This situation may become a little easier as XML-capable browsers become standard, and publishers can use the full capabilities of XML.
- An increase in the use of SGML or XML will prove to be a double-edged sword. Greater sophistication in a publisher's ability to 'slice and dice' content is likely to lead to a proliferation of new units of delivery. Publishers are already talking about using their SGML/XML-based archives as a means of extracting more granular pieces of content for new kinds of commercial exploitation. Individual chapters might be sold, or even smaller chunks in combination with material from other sources. If this becomes a significant practice, it will represent a new type of dynamic publishing model in which the content itself is static but the number of products increases by an order of magnitude.
- Although a small number of formats may be used for text and still images, there is still a proliferation

of formats used for other types of content. This is likely to remain particularly significant in the case of author-supplied supplementary material to academic journals. The 'standardisation' of the format of this content will depend on the standardisation of the applications used by the author community. Again, we do not anticipate that this will happen in the near future.

- We have long been promised the coming together of technology for managing 'content and presentation', it seems unlikely to us that any significant breakthrough either in more effective 'on the fly' formatting of structurally-marked-up content or more flexible management of page-formatted text is likely in the very near future. Publishers are likely to need to continue to publish in parallel forms for a considerable time to come. PDF will not disappear as a format for some time to come, and may indeed remain the format of choice for some types of publication.
- Security mechanisms, particularly encryption, are likely to continue to create a barrier to straightforward long-term preservation, at least in e-books.
- We have been speaking to a group of technically sophisticated publishers. Many publishers still do not employ personnel who would understand the issues raised in this report. This is unlikely to change; technical issues will continue to be outsourced. This will make communication between publisher and deposit library more difficult.
- The problems relating to understanding of content issues relate equally to understanding of metadata issues. One publisher we spoke to recently told us that he was appalled by the continuing lack of understanding he had found of the significance of metadata to the future of publishing. Without better publisher-generated metadata, the management of

deposit of electronic publications will be extremely difficult if not impossible.

- The new economics of publishing seem likely to lead to a considerable increase in the volume of publishing and the number of publishers. Many of those publishing will not recognise themselves as publishers. We believe that the significance of this for the deposit of electronic publications cannot be overstated.
- Even in a straightforward technical survey of this kind, publishers continue to express some reservations about the deposit of electronic publications with libraries, particularly with respect to the provision of access. It was suggested to us more than once that deposit should wait until the commercial life of the content has been exhausted. Very close co-operation will be required between librarians and publishers to allow digital deposit to work satisfactorily—and it may prove difficult to motivate publishers to become involved in such co-operation. The cost of compliance with library needs will have to be low to publishers—and the difficulty of attracting the attention of publisher's hard pushed technical staff to meeting library requirements should not be under-estimated. In general, there is good will but resources are very stretched.

SOME FINAL THOUGHTS

In general terms, publishers are driven by the market place. With few exceptions, publishers will not develop standards for themselves but will adopt the standards that are widely adopted within their community of customers. This is clearly observable among our respondents. Both online and e-book publishing will see the 'network effect' take greater and greater hold on standards.

The market will enforce standardisation wherever lack of standardisation creates inefficiency for the end user. The Web provides a very good example of the extent to which *de facto* standards can come rapidly to dominate an electronic distribution medium. Despite the limitations of HTML, publishers of all types of content have found 'work rounds' to enable them to deliver content in this format, because of its widespread market acceptance. Inefficiency for the end user and inefficiency for the deposit library are not necessarily entirely congruent. However, the trends are encouraging.

3

Electronic Publishing
Research Issues for Academic Librarians and Users

INTRODUCTION

In the rush to a digital information world we rarely pause to consider the long-term effects on libraries, scholars, and students. Even more rarely considered are the long-term effects that changes in the media of scholarly communication may have on learning and understanding of content. Marshall McLuhan understood the relationship between variations in media and meaning over time and the impacts of these variations on society when he famously declared that the 'medium is the message.' McLuhan was concerned mostly with television, radio, and mass media, rather than with scholarly information sources. It is difficult to know if such concerns are valid for the materials that academic libraries emphasise—scholarly research reports, journals, and other reference and information resources that are used for finding information rather than for entertainment or news.

If the same scholarly information is available in both printed and digital form, are there differences in how it is used and understood? Or, does the content stand separate from the medium through which it is delivered? How can librarians and other information professionals apply their knowledge about how scholarly materials are organised and used to help people make most of the information available to them?

Many research questions can be posed concerning this general issue, including:

- How does the medium of information affect people's preferences, understanding, and use of the content.
- Do people seek for, understand, and use information delivered in digital form differently from that delivered on paper.
- Does the medium of information resources used make a difference in the new knowledge people create from these information resources.
- How does a library's choice of format for information products affect the library users.

These very broad questions need to be answered in the coming decade as libraries continue to move to digital services, but to answer such general questions, many more specific research questions must be addressed. This article explores three of the specific research questions that are critical to the delivery of effective library service to students and scholars.

- *Medium and Student Work:* How is the change to digital information sources affecting the scholarly work of college and university students.
- *New Models for Scholarly Journals:* When libraries select electronic journals, how do the products offered to them or the models they choose influence scholarship and the way journals are used.
- *Librarians as Intermediaries:* Are librarians—as intermediaries to the search process—still necessary in a digital age? What do human information professionals bring to the online research process that cannot be adequately duplicated online.

MEDIUM AND STUDENT WORK
HOW IS THE CHANGE TO DIGITAL INFORMATION SOURCES AFFECTING THE SCHOLARLY WORK OF COLLEGE AND UNIVERSITY STUDENTS

This Includes Several Subquestions, Including: Are there differences in citing patterns, quality of work, and the research process? When faculty assign papers that require students to use the recorded knowledge, what do they expect and how has this changed? How can educators and librarians influence students' work in a positive way?

WHY THIS QUESTION IS IMPORTANT

It is unclear how the move from paper-based library collections to digital collections is affecting scholarly work. In the past when faculty assigned research papers to their students, the expectations of what types of sources would be used and the role of librarians in providing access to these sources were fairly clear. Today, there is much more variety in media and sources available to students and students often do their research without setting foot in a library. Libraries purchase electronic resources and students access the resources from their dormitories, homes, or offices. Students may not seek help from librarians, either because they have confidence in their online searching skills or because they no longer come to the libraries and librarians are 'out of sight, out of mind.' Librarians have always been concerned that college students demonstrate basic information literacy skills, but in today's virtual library environments teaching these skills may be more important than ever.

In 2000 the Association of College and Research Libraries (ACRL) adopted competency standards for information literacy that recommend: students must be able to articulate information needs, know how to search for and access information resources, and effectively use the information they find. Librarians face new challenges in reaching students who only access library resources online and have grown up with the Web. It is difficult to make sure that such students know how to select appropriate resources, evaluate the quality of what they select, and use these resources well regardless of format or medium.

Academic librarians and faculty members would likely agree that most college students today prefer digital resources to print resources. Even within the realm of digital resources, a majority of undergraduate students seem to choose Web sites or digital resources that include the full text often without regard to how appropriate the source is for their assignment. The impact of this is not yet known, but several aspects of this issue need to be studied. Librarians need to know more about how students make decisions regarding what information sources they use for their class assignments, in order to design better library instruction programmes and so librarians can work more effectively with faculty and with students.

If these decisions are based more on the convenience of electronic full texts or affinity for the Web, we need to understand how the change to digital information sources is affecting the scholarly work of college and university students. The prevalence of electronic resources is likely causing changes in students' citing patterns and may be even changing the quality of work and the research process. Ultimately, understanding these changes in the work habits of undergraduate students may help educators and librarians influence students' work in a positive way.

PREVIOUS WORK

Student Preferences

In the late 1990s, Tenopir and Tenopir and Read recorded academic librarians' observations of online use among students in all types and sizes of colleges and universities. These surveys found that appropriate content, recommendations from trusted people, and ease-of-use are all believed to be important factors that influence which research online resources are selected by students. The one factor, however, that was found to be most important was the availability of the full text.

According to one librarian from a small college: 'Students expect to see the full article pop out. Also, full-text greatly enhances our own, small collection.' Another respondent explained, 'The concept of one-stop information shopping is an important factor in using any electronic information resource". Full text often overrides all other preference factors, in particular for undergraduate students. Librarians who have faith in users to pick the best content sometimes change their opinion when full text is the issue, and, increasingly, not just any full-text will do. One librarian summarised the new expectations: 'End users want full text; preferably with graphics and they want it delivered over a Web interface that provides the flexibility for a variety of output and access options".

When more than one full-text database is available, students may choose the resource that is best suited to their research needs, although convenience and recommendations by peers, instructors, and librarians are influential. Librarians reported in the Tenopir survey that when products are recommended specifically by their instructors or by librarians, students generally use them.

Faculty Concerns

Many university faculties are concerned that students choose the convenience of full-text digital resources without regard to quality or appropriateness for their tasks. One recent study found that although faculty respondents feel positive about the Web, they expressed concerns about their students' ability to evaluate Internet resources and questioned the accuracy and reliability of Web resources. Rothenberg attributed a decline in the quality of student term papers—both in quality of writing and originality of thought—to reliance on the Web for research.

In a recent survey of academic research libraries one respondent commented that 'more and more faculty are unhappy with the Internet resources their students are using and have come to the librarians to help instruct students on reliable resources". Some students may not be aware of the need to carefully evaluate Web and other full text sources. Grimes and Boening found that students are using Web resources in English composition assignments without evaluating the quality and reliability of the sources, contrary to the expectations of their professors.

Preference for resources that are convenient and familiar is natural, of course. Not all faculty, and certainly not all students agree that the Web has had a negative effect on student work. McBride and Dickstein saw no decline in quality of student writing in Women's Studies at the University of Arizona, even though the Web was used more often for research.

A 1998 survey by librarians at Duke University found that 20 per cent of undergraduate students interviewed felt the Web had a positive effect on their work, while another 40 per cent felt the Web made a difference to the quality of their work. Over half identified the Web as a time saver. D'Esposito and Gardner found that undergraduate students are aware that quality is an important factor to consider when selecting Web resources to use for schoolwork. Students in their study reported that government, educational, and reputable business sites are the most reliable. Undergraduate students studied by Wei He and Jacobson felt strongly that the Internet was useful for research and seeking information.

Motivation

Motivations of students who use the Web were studied by Ko from the perspective of media uses and gratification. Ko found that students with higher motivation tended to go more to informational sites, but she did not examine the quality or accuracy of the informational sites they visited. Duggan asked students to self-judge 'valuable educational' Web sites. They found that students who keep track of these sites have a more favourable attitude about using the Web for class assignments.

Many of these studies imply that, contrary to faculty belief as measured in other studies, some students are aware of the need to judge quality of Web sites. The problem may simply be that they do not know how to do so. Instruction by librarians on how to evaluate topical Web sites and integrate them into classes may help solve this problem.

It is not surprising that peoples' motivation levels influence how much effort they put into a task and how long they stick with it. It has been well demonstrated that motivation plays a role in what medium users select. The use of digital research materials is no exception, whether the searchers are students, scholars, or scientists. Research by Nahl and Tenopir and Tenopir, Nahl-Jakobovits, and Howard found that time spent online and search strategies varied if faculty or university students were searching for personal or for work-related purposes.

More highly motivated users spent more time on a search and made more changes to their search strategies. Wildemuth found that the search moves used by medical students varied with motivation. Motivation also plays a factor in what resources are selected. Ko discovered that when users are motivated to use the Web by the need to learn new things or to solve problems they are more likely to visit 'personal identity' and informational Web sites. Users who are online a lot are more likely to visit informational Web sites.

Librarians and Recommendations

Librarians are making adjustments to student preferences for the Web. One librarian responded to the Tenopir and Ennis survey: "we have found in the last couple of years that too many students, because they know how to use the Web are using only the Web itself to find materials for their assignments, rather than trying the periodical indexes that we offer via the Web. We've had to change our instruction efforts to address this problem. We don't discourage them from searching the Web for material on their subject in addition to using the indexes, but we talk a lot about the quality of what they find on the Web—the quality and the provenance". A librarian's recommendation is believed by most academic librarians to be very important, although in most libraries trying to reach a large proportion of students and faculty is a constant effort.

A database demonstrated in instruction classes or English 101 will be selected if students remember it when they need information. For those students who are motivated enough to ask at the reference desk, the recommendation of a specific source is believed to be very influential. Tenopir found that one library saw its usage statistics triple for a particular online system when they introduced a separate instruction class and promoted its use with faculty. Recommendations of relevant sources may be most important the first time a student has to choose a database. After that, familiarity often takes over. If students have had success in a previous use, they are likely to select the same source again, even if 'its use in this instance may or may not be appropriate'. Positive encounters are influential. "If their initial instruction and usage has been successful, I feel they keep returning to what is familiar," says another.

Changes in Citing Patterns

Although there are many opinions among faculty and librarians, only a few researchers have studied what impact these choices have had on scholarship, whether positive or negative. Further research on this topic will help librarians make better collection development choices and will help faculty and librarians design optimal information instruction courses. Philip Davis at Cornell University is one of the few to study changes in the citing behaviour of students over time. Davis and Cohen found a significant decrease in the frequency of citing scholarly resources in microeconomics undergraduate term papers from 1996 to 1999. Scholarly materials are cited less often and non-scholarly materials such as newspaper articles and Web sites are cited more.

The prevalence of newspaper article citations can almost certainly be attributed to the widespread availability of full text newspaper databases such as ProQuest or LexisNexis Academic Universe through university libraries. The Web may be used from home or on campus. Disturbingly, Davis and Cohen found that approximately only one-half of the URLs cited in student papers led to the correct Web site. An update to this research found that the number of citations to Web sites and newspaper articles in undergraduate term papers continued to increase in 2000, but papers submitted electronically had a higher percentage of correct URLs.

RESEARCH METHODS FOR STUDYING THESE QUESTIONS

The importance of changes in what research sources are being used and cited is still difficult to judge. Davis found no significant relationship "between grade and total number of citations, number of Web citations, number of scholarly citations, or number of non-scholarly citations". Further research is needed to examine the intellectual products created by students and their performance in relationship to the resources used. Studying student preferences and faculty concerns answers only a small part of this important question. Librarians and faculty members can guide students to high quality resources in digital formats as well as in print.

More important, but more difficult to understand, is how the inherent properties of a medium influence the learning process. Most of the concerns by faculty and libraries are related to the quality and appropriateness of the content of digital resources used by students. Quality of content is likely independent of the medium, but undergraduate students may be willing to accept online sources without question. Increased emphasis on teaching evaluation skills, library created portals to authoritative Web sites, and stricter citation guidelines in class assignments are recommended by Davis and Cohen to help solve this problem in the future. If such suggestions are followed, they should be tested to see if the problem truly lies in the quality of student work or in faculty perceptions of what citations are likely to lead to quality information.

Further studies that look at the link between what is cited and the quality of scholarly output will help reveal if a problem truly exists. Academic librarians should work with teaching faculty to conduct such controlled studies. A related research area is to test the effectiveness of user instruction that emphasises Web site evaluation. Other than course requirements, what truly motivates undergraduate researchers? Is instruction in evaluation methods truly effective or is a more prescribed approach to acceptable resources in assignments necessary? Will student achievement increase after such instruction? Finally, the larger issue of medium and understanding needs more research in the scholarly domain, outside of the world of mass media.

The Web combines components of mass media with a wealth of scholarly materials making interdisciplinary research appropriate. The work of communications research and information science research dovetails well in this research area.

NEW MODELS FOR SCHOLARLY JOURNALS *WHEN LIBRARIES SELECT ELECTRONIC JOURNALS, HOW DO THE PRODUCTS OFFERED TO THEM OR THE DELIVERY MODELS THEY CHOOSE INFLUENCE SCHOLARSHIP AND THE WAY JOURNALS ARE USED*

WHY THIS QUESTION IS IMPORTANT

Faculty are concerned about what resources students use and cite because there is a long tradition of high quality being associated with peer-reviewed, scholarly journals. Scholarly journals provide scholars with a way to convey their own research findings and to keep up with what others are doing in their disciplines. Peer review provides a quality assurance mechanism. The structure of traditional journals has evolved to provide a forum for research, events, and controversies in each discipline.

Through such devices as topic issues, letters-to-the-editor, book reviews, and editorials, journals have evolved to provide more to a discipline that just a body of individual research articles. It can be argued that a journal with a large following in its field, such as Journal of the American Medical Association (JAMA), Reference and User Services Quarterly (RUSQ), or Tetrahedron Letters builds or reflects the community of physicians, or reference librarians, or organic chemists who read it, subscribe to it, and/or publish in it. Traditional scholarly journals continue to be the single most important information source for scientists and social scientists.

Today, journals may still be delivered on paper but they may also be delivered digitally, either directly from the publisher or through an aggregator such as LexisNexis, ProQuest, or OCLC. Collection development policies for journals now often favour online versions of journals over print. Digital distribution does not necessarily mean the end of the traditional journal, but it does provide many alternatives to journal article delivery. Publishers may continue to create their journals in issues and merely make each issue accessible on the World Wide Web to subscribers, individual articles can be separated from the journal issue and be made available in large full text databases that combine articles from many different journals, or authors may choose to post their scholarly work directly on e-print servers or their own Web page and forgo publishing in a journal altogether. Electronic publishing clearly has many advantages for libraries, authors, and readers, including a speedier publishing/distribution cycle, desktop delivery, and the possibility of wider distribution.

The move towards electronic journals is well underway and, while it will move more slowly for some journal titles and some disciplines than others, it is a movement that will continue its momentum. There are several aspects to this research question, answers to which will help publishers, librarians, authors, and readers design the best electronic journals for current and future scholars. We need to know if scholarly journals as we know them contribute more to scholarship and the furtherance of science than separate collections of research articles.

If not, databases of separate articles with a good search engine may be the best way for libraries to provide access to the research literature. If so, the scholarly community needs to put pressure on publishers and libraries to continue the journal model. To understand the consequences of such important collection development decisions, librarians and publishers must understand the contributions of a traditional form of a journal. A traditional journal that provides scholars in a discipline with a regularly issued bundled collection of related articles plus substantial non-article materials such as book reviews, letters-to-the-editor, and an editorial voice includes much more material than a database of articles.

We need to understand the extent to which this additional information is valuable to scholarship. Collection development and reference librarians must ask themselves, if we have a good search engine and separate collections of articles is this sufficient for scholarship? Libraries are cancelling subscriptions to print and electronic journals in favour of the collection of articles model, often without asking if it matters to researchers and to research.

Many times the collection of articles model is offered by a third-party aggregator, while the journal model comes directly from the primary publisher. Choosing aggregate models over journal models may, in the long run, cause smaller journal publishers to cease publication altogether. Perhaps the old model of a journal is obsolete and new models of separate articles distributed through e-print servers, author Web sites, or in databases will replace traditional journals. Librarians now have choices and their choices will help to define the future. These choices should be based on full knowledge of the possible implications of their actions.

PREVIOUS WORK

Models for Access to Electronic Journal Articles

To understand the need for research on these questions, it is necessary to understand the current state of electronic journal publishing. Electronic publishing is still in a state of development and experimentation, with many different variations concurrently available.

Two main models are competing for subscription dollars and readers' attention:

- The journal model; and
- The article model.

The journal model retains the structure and purpose of a print journal, but it is delivered in digital form. It is usually available directly from the publisher as a Web product. The traditional publishing device of issues and volumes may be retained or articles may be put up on the electronic version as soon as they are ready, without regard to issue numbers. Editorials, letters, and short features likely appear with research articles as part of the electronic journal and a table of contents leads readers to the material. Subscription fees may or may not be charged.

All in all, the journal model for electronic publishing retains the sense of community, branding, and editorial voice of the traditional journal, while taking advantage of what electronic distribution and formatting offers. Authors and readers approach an electronic journal much as they do a print journal—by recognition of the journal title as being of interest to them without necessarily knowing what specific information they will find each time they read it. Browsing is the most common method of searching for relevant information and tables of contents with links to the articles are key to browsing. Readers tend to stick to a handful of journals which they consider core to their work.

The 'SuperJournal' research project in the United Kingdom found that scientists tend to favour the journal model more than social scientists. So-called 'journal focussed' users look for specific journals, use them to keep up-to-date in their field, and log on to an online journal system every time new issues of their favoured journals are loaded. The article model is quite different. Aggregators take articles from print or electronic journals and make them available in large multititle full text databases. Readers use a search engine to search for and identify articles of interest to them and they read the specific articles out of the context of a complete journal. Pullinger has called these readers 'topic-focussed' if they search for articles without limiting to specific journal titles or 'article-focussed' if they seek to retrieve known articles from a specific journal title.

Topic-focussed readers likely read articles from a much greater variety of journal titles than do journal-focussed or article-focussed readers, as found by studies conducted by the OhioLink state consortium. A variation on the article model forgoes the first step of publishing in a traditional journal. Authors go directly to an e-print service and post their research papers on this site or post papers on their own or institutional Web site.

As with the more traditional article model, readers may rely on a search engine to locate individual articles of interest to their research and the articles are read out of the context of a bundled collection of material that a journal provides. Adoption of e-print servers varies with workfield, with high-energy physicists notable early adopters. Alternatively, readers may go directly to a known author's Web site to read separate articles by that author or to a university's collection of faculty articles in a standard format such as that promulgated by the Open Archives Initiative.

The Importance of the Journal Model

Research by Amin and Mabe reveals why, in an age that offers both print and electronic publishing, authors choose a particular journal in which to publish. The reputation of a journal within its discipline and its reach to the scientific community are important considerations, in addition to factors such as timeliness and responsiveness to authors. These findings echo earlier studies, in a print-only world, by Kochen and Tagliacozzo and King, McDonald, and Roderer. 'Prestige' of the journal is an important characteristic mentioned in all of these studies. Clearly authors have long considered the journal as a branded bundle, where presence within a high-quality journal title lends cache to a research article. ISI's 'Journal Impact Factors' are another important quality factor for authors, editors, and scholars.

Journal Impact Factors cannot exist without the concept of 'journal title,' as an impact score is calculated for each title in a field based on the number of times articles in that journal are cited, divided by the total number of articles published in the journal each year. Many authors seek to publish in journals with high impact factors and scientists in some countries are given bonuses when they publish in these prestigious journals. Much of the research to date has focussed on the importance of journal articles to researchers' work, rather than the importance of an entire journal.

Exceptions are the periodic studies of the number of personal subscriptions held by scientists. In his 1974 book, Meadows examined the studies through the early 1970s that discussed personal subscriptions of entire journals, concluding that scientists subscribe to major journals they read regularly either in their research field or general periodicals like Nature or Science. More recent studies show a decline in the number of journals that scientists subscribe to on the average, in direct relationship to the increase in journal prices; however, the purchase of full-text separate articles by individuals did not affect their use of print journals.

The number of personal subscriptions has decreased steadily over the last few decades, as the price of scholarly journals has increased. In the past, North American scientists subscribed to an average of six journals each. By the late 1990s this had declined to just over two and the downward trend is continuing. As the number of subscriptions goes down, scientists rely more on library subscriptions and on separates, from electronic full text databases, paper reprints from colleagues or authors, interlibrary loan, or document delivery services. OhioLink, a large library consortium, offers hundreds of scholarly journals to academic libraries across Ohio. They report that many of the journal titles provided electronically as separate articles were never subscribed to by the libraries that now access them. OhioLink research has found that when such journals are available to faculty and students electronically, the number of journal titles from which they read articles goes up.

Beyond those journals considered core to a particular subject, if made readily available, scientists and students read from a variety of sources. Recent data from the NorthEast Research Libraries Consortia, however, suggests that the amount of reading from titles that libraries do not subscribe to in print may be less than that found in the OhioLink libraries, with a majority of electronic readings coming from journals that the libraries already subscribe to.

What Libraries are Doing

Libraries are spending an increasing amount of their overall materials budgets on serials and an increasing amount of their serials budgets on electronic journals. Some of these are journal model products, such as JSTOR, Project Muse, and Springer-Link. Many are article model databases, such as those from ProQuest, LexisNexis, Ovid, and OCLC. Some combine elements of both, such as Science-Direct from Elsevier Science. Since, budget constraints do not allow much duplication, many libraries are replacing print subscriptions with access to electronic journals. Although libraries have always maintained access to both journal and article models in print collections, electronic collections are more heavily weighted towards article models. Some libraries also provide links to e-print servers.

The Pre-Print Network, created by the Department of Energy, Office of Scientific and Technical Information, provides access to many disparate e-print servers. Right now, librarians make the choice whether to purchase a journal model or article model, as both are widely available. If a library changes from a journal model to an article model for electronic journals, will all of the needs of all scholars still be met? Are we, as a recent cover story in Library Journal suggests, in the midst of a revolution in scholarly publishing that means the old models are no longer valid? Many models will be used and tested—only research will tell what the effects will be on authors, readers, libraries, and, ultimately, on scholarship.

RESEARCH METHODS FOR STUDYING THESE QUESTIONS

Studying the potential effects of changes is a challenge and necessarily must include an element of forecasting. Past research into preferences or journal use can provide some insights into possible methodologies for studying this phenomenon.

Two main methodologies have been used to date:

- Surveys to determine preferences of individual scholars; and
- Building prototype electronic journal systems to measure usage and preferences.

Tenopir and King have surveyed nearly 15,000 scientists and social scientists since, the late 1970s to discover a variety of reading variables, including how much they read, characteristics of what they read, what value they get from journal articles, and how much time they spend reading.

Questions in the earlier surveys focussed, of course, on reading of print-onpaper articles, those from the mid-1990s to the present also include questions to differentiate print and electronic journals. Brown and others have surveyed faculty within their respective universities to find out how much they read in electronic journals and their preferences for formats. Surveys can create a statistical picture of current habits and, over time, a picture of how things change, which can provide a basis for forecasting future trends.

They can reveal differences in preferences among work fields and workplaces. They show how things change over time. They can also be used to measure preferences and readers' perceptions of and desires for the future, so both qualitative and quantitative data can be collected. Prototype studies focus specifically on electronic journals and can be used to test preferences for specific search or design features. They borrow methods from both focus group studies and system usability studies. Focus group participants can convey preferences and offer ideas for design features.

When these features are incorporated into the prototype design, use can be observed in a natural or controlled environment. Pullinger's SuperJournal project is the most recent ambitious prototype study; others done in the past include studies by the American Chemical Society and BRS. Several measures can be made in prototype studies, including measures of opinions, preferences as measured by use, and other usage patterns within the prototype system. Both qualitative and quantitative data can be collected as users are studied in an experimental setting. Research methods for studying issues surrounding the impacts of various models for electronic journals include surveys, experiments, and observations.

These methods yield both quantitative and qualitative data. Qualitative data will give a picture of user preferences, opinions, and forecasts of future behaviour. Quantitative data provide information on use, usage patterns, and changes under experimental treatment. Together, qualitative and quantitative studies can provide insights into how journals are now used and will be used in the future. These insights will help us under stand the implications of collection development decisions by librarians and publishing decisions of both publishers and authors on scholarship.

INTERMEDIARIES—ARE LIBRARIANS—AS INTERMEDIARIES TO THE SEARCH PROCESS—STILL NECESSARY IN A DIGITAL AGE

WHY THIS QUESTION IS IMPORTANT

The articles model of electronic journals relies on effective search strategies entered into reliable online systems. Since, the early days of online searching in the 1970s, researchers have studied search strategies, first of expert searchers and later of novices, and observed the interactions of search intermediaries and their clients. These studies have aimed to develop optimal search strategies and procedures that could be incorporated into online systems to make them easier to use and build on the many decades of studying how reference librarians interact with library patrons. It may seem odd to place a phenomenon that has been studied for so long on a list of research topics for the future, but researchers have reached the point with this topic that they are able to build on a firm foundation and compare future research with an accepted body of research from the past.

This is not always the case with library and information science research topics. The ultimate goal of many information retrieval system designers is to create a system that will be so user friendly and 'intelligent' that it can be used independently, so users can answer their information needs with a minimal amount of assistance. The intermediary may not often conduct an entire online search for a user anymore, but even the traditional helping roles of the reference librarian are being questioned in a digital environment.

Many users search online without seeking help from a reference librarian and spend many hours on the Web without ever considering asking for assistance. Even if human assistance is no longer being sought by many users, librarians need to understand what, if anything, a human intermediary or reference librarian contributes to the information search process, which of these contributions can be captured in system design, and which must remain an individualized human process. We need to understand which of these contributions can lead not only to better systems and better library services, but also perhaps to justification for funding librarian services.

PREVIOUS WORK

The literature review here is not comprehensive, due to the vast quantities of articles on this and related topics. Several review chapters in the Annual Review of Information Science and Technology (ARIST) and an early literature review by Fenichel describes in depth related research literature on topics of search strategies, online system evaluation, and expert system design. Lynch studied the reference interview process in public libraries in a mostly preonline era, and Bunge reviewed the traditional reference interview literature in 1984. The current discussion includes only some of the studies that specifically address the contributions of the intermediary in the online searching process.

Seminal Work

Even a limited discussion of this topic must include mention of several seminal studies that form the basis for much of the work that came after them. Most modern studies of the intermediary-client interaction point to Taylor, who, in 1968, differentiated between when users seek information on their own and when they approach a librarian. Asking for assistance usually only occurs late in the search process, and reference librarians are skilled at using questions as filters to elicit the information needed to understand an information need.

Bourne was one of the first to observe strategies of expert online searchers, placing strategies into several broad categories. Citation Pearl Growing, Building Blocks, Successive Fractions, etc., are now recognised general approaches to searching that have been tested and extended by Bates and others. In 1979 Bates developed a set of search tactics that are used to record and measure specific steps used in online searches of standard Booleanlogic based systems. Soon after, Fidel empirically developed a set of operational and conceptual moves used by intermediary online searchers. These specific moves and tactics are still used today to measure search strategies by both novices and information professionals.

Having two accepted measurement scales makes research easier to conduct and to compare, so much of the research on search strategies conducted from the 1980s on uses the work of Bates or Fidel. Borgman examined in depth how individual differences and human characteristics influence choice of search strategies. Borgman found that the time to reach success in computer-related tasks, such as online searching, has a much larger variance than in other types of tasks. Technologically inclined people are able to complete search tasks much more quickly than others and have fewer problems with search techniques such as Boolean logic.

Questioning

The questions asked by both users and intermediaries, and how they are asked, have been shown by many researchers over time to be a crucial factor in the search process and search success. Some early important studies of the human aspects of interaction with information systems show why questions are so important. Belkin observed that users approach a system due to a gap in their knowledge. Belkin expressed this as Anomalous States of Knowledge (ASK) and demonstrated that it is difficult for users to express an information need or ask a question when they have such gaps in their knowledge or understanding. Human intermediaries may, through the reference interview, help users get to the point where the ASK can be resolved, but online systems do not yet do this very well.

Information seeking online involves a range of human capabilities, including the cognitive, affective, and sensori-motor domains. All three domains interact and influence each other. Most systems and documentation confront only the cognitive and sensori-motor domain questions. Human interaction can better address the affective domain than help screens or documentation do. The role of each domain has been identified in studying questions asked during the search process. Nahl and Tenopir and Tenopir, Nahl-Jakobovits, and Howard found that novices ask many questions when they are searching for information online, and, when no intermediary is present, most of these questions are never verbally expressed.

Using the technique of protocol analysis, the researchers tape-recorded novice faculty, undergraduates, and graduate students while they searched for information in a general interest full-text periodicals database. Participants were instructed to 'think aloud' as they proceeded, voicing their internal thoughts. Analysis of the transcribed recordings revealed that, on the average, novices had many questions per search, an average of eleven moves per search. If a reference librarian had been nearby, at least some of these questions would likely have been asked and answered. Questions may get verbalised when a human intermediary is present. Wu recorded the many questions asked of intermediaries by search clients both in the presearch interview and, more frequently, during the search.

Although no one session contained all categories of questions, Wu observed nine categories of questions, including questions related to: search terms, search procedures, databases, output, and other information services. Both Wu and Nahl and Tenopir observed a high percentage of reassurance questions—questions that needed no answer but are basically part of the affective side of human interaction. The interaction between an intermediary and a client can take on many dimensions. Spink, Goodrum, and Robins studied interactions both in the presearch interview and during the search session.

They found that intermediaries requested fifteen different types of information from their users, including requests for information about search strategy and terms, output domain knowledge, and database selection. Spink studied interactive feedback between intermediaries and academic clients during presearch interviews and online searching sessions. Data collected and analysed included videotapes, transcripts, online searching logs, and relevance judgements by the users. This gives a good picture of the various types of interaction that occur between an intermediary and a client during a search and shows how rich that interaction can be. Spink discovered a total of 885 interactive feedback occurrences in 40 mediated online searches, with a mean of 22 per search. She further categorised these occurrences into five types: content relevance feedback, term relevance feedback, magnitude feedback, tactical review feedback, and term review feedback.

White has studied the reference interview over time. In her 1998 study she found that the information specialist dominates the presearch interview, but both clients and intermediaries tend to ask shortanswer questions that are mostly focussed on the subject, search strategy, the service, and the output. The most common types of questions were verification questions. Verification questions are similar to the echoing or rogering questions so commonly held by users, in that the questioner already knows a supposed answer, as opposed to questions that elicit totally new knowledge. Several researchers have studied how different types of questions posed by reference librarians influence the satisfaction and perceptions of users. Findings show that, although both open-ended and closed questions are asked during the interview process, users are more responsive to open-ended questions and questions that probe into why something is needed, rather than close ended or simply factual questions.

Spink observed 'complex interactions' between users and intermediaries throughout a search session. Whether the questions are posed by an intermediary to a user or from a user to the intermediary, the online research process is one in which numerous spoken and unspoken elicitations occur. Robins found that the mediated online search process is highly interactive and that intermediaries and users work together in a non-linear interplay both during the presearch interview and during the search. The search topic even changes focus on the average approximately every seven utterances. Systems today do not yet recognise this important interaction. More research is needed on the effect question asking and question answering have on the success of online research and on the satisfaction levels of users. Most of the studies tape-recorded interactions, with the researchers working from transcripts of these recordings. Transaction log analysis is another method for gaining insights into the searching behaviour of novices. Many researchers in the past decade have analysed the transaction logs from searches of library catalogs, commercial online systems, or Web search engines.

Wallace, for example, examined transaction logs of the online catalog from public access terminals at the University of Colorado libraries. She found variability in the amount of use the search aids available on the system. Quick search and express search features were used rarely; search history and searching other databases were used more extensively. Catalog users prefer to search for natural language keywords and then scan lists of titles.

Information Overload

These studies show that intermediaries help answer factual questions, provide reassurance to affective questions, and help users clarify their information needs. Another role that librarians as intermediaries play is to help users select the best resources and overcome information overload. Information seekers today are much more likely to find too much on their topic rather than too little because most of our online systems are better at locating lots of information than locating only the best information. Extensive studies of Web search behaviour by Spink, Wolfram, and Jansen found that average users of a Web search engine enter only a little over one term per search and review only the first page or two pages of the results.

This either means that the relevance ranking algorithm in the Web search engine works so well that the users find everything they need on the first screen or, more likely, they are overwhelmed by the thought of going beyond twenty or so items and decline to delve more deeply. Many librarians have called for reference librarians to help end users sort through the vast quantities of information to locate the best sources for their needs. Hopkins suggests several possible ways this might be accomplished, including quality filtering by ranking by citation counts or citations in review articles, structured guides to the literature that include quality judgements, and better information literacy instruction.

Teaching Search Strategies

User instruction is another traditional role of reference librarians. Many librarians have commented on the increased need for instruction with the prevalence of independent end user online searching. Mercado surveyed how instruction programmes have changed and recommended that library users need to be taught not only how to search, but critical thinking skills. Beyond the specific techniques of systems, librarians are finding that students need to know overall search approaches and how to choose which databases to search. Developing search strategies is not a natural skill. Taylor and Penhale, for example, found that, even after instruction, students at Earlham College still needed librarians to help them devise and refine complicated searches. Students may have unrealistic expectations of their searching ability and what information they can find on their own. Librarians, through instruction and real-time assistance can help inject some reality as well as skills. Searching is more of an art than a science, however.

Saracevic and Kantor studied search strategies used by experienced searchers on the same topics. They found much variation in the terms selected for searching and the search formulations. Critical thinking skills, rather than the one best way to search, will help make more independent searchers, but intermediary assistance can help users think about alternatives.

RESEARCH METHODS FOR STUDYING THESE QUESTIONS

Information professionals play many roles in the search process, not only that of an intermediary conducting a search for a client. The roles of question-answerer, affective reassurer, instructor, presenter of alternatives, and quality filter have all been found to be a part of search success. Most of the research into these roles and the effect on search success can fit under the general heading of 'user centered' research.

The methods and methodologies of user-based research are well defined and described by Wang. Observations, protocol analysis, and transaction logs together provide a baseline of mostly qualitative data. In the future, additional observational studies will build on past research, but observations should be combined with experimental techniques. Observational studies generally rely on qualitative data and are often described as 'preliminary' or 'exploratory.'

This is appropriate when a topic is new, but now that specific factors and behaviours have been observed and measures developed, traditional experimental techniques can explicitly test these factors. In the future, we need to discover in more depth how search behaviours vary with different intermediary behaviours and with systematically introduced variations in help screens, real-time online help by librarians, and documentation. Similarly, user satisfaction and the effect on the intellectual output of students and scholars should be measured against the introduction of different treatments in the mediation process. With such a rich baseline of exploratory studies, it is now time to produce more definitive experimental work.

4

eBooks

INTRODUCTION

eBooks are increasingly occupying a large portion of any discussion that involves publishing or publishers. While many of us are told that eBooks are an inevitable part of the future landscape of publishing and, therefore, must receive due attention from publishers that do not wish to be driven to extinction, very little information about it is readily available. Some questions persist: What are eBooks? How are they developed? What are the formatting guidelines, if any? What might be the costs involved? What are the returns on investment? How do they reach customers? These questions have no easy answers. This chapter attempts to answer these questions so that the publisher can make an informed choice when it comes to decisions regarding e-publishing and eBooks.

THE CASE FOR E-PUBLISHING

e-publishing is gaining acceptance among publishers for a variety of reasons and it can be argued that e-publishing, or at least examining its feasibility, is now a necessary step every publisher must take.

Some of the reasons why e-publishing has become so important are:

- *Proliferation of Reading Devices:* If the numbers are anything to go by, it seems like publishers can ill afford to ignore e-publishing. These past few years, e-Readers of all shapes and sizes have introduced into the market, each time at a lower price, and are selling in large numbers. With the proliferation of mobile handsets and the increasingly large screen size available on them, these mobile devices too provide sufficient e-reading capability to its many owners. Thus there is no dearth of e-Readers available to readers. Publishers are therefore scrambling to offer their books as eBooks to these readers. Reading devices, and tablets, have found favour with readers primarily because they are portable devices that allow their owners to work on the move. This means books can be read during a stopover or while waiting to meet someone. Because eBooks can easily be accessed via the Internet, one does not have to be prepared with something to read during an emergency.

- *Availability of Cheap Internet Connectivity:* Internet connectivity, especially broadband connectivity, is becoming increasingly cheaper and, thanks to government and private initiatives, available in many remote locations. eBooks, being electronic files in nature, can be easily distributed over the Internet much like files are sent through e-mail. The easy availability of Internet connectivity thus allows eBooks to be transferred to customers no matter how remotely they might be situated. Thus distribution costs are rendered negligible and the location of the customer does not prove to be a barrier to accessibility of eBooks.
- *Media Assimilation and Content Creation:* eBooks in its most basic form consist of PDF files that the reader can read on a PC or a laptop. However, these eBooks can also be 'enhanced' to make them engaging and entertaining. This is done by incorporating voice and visuals within the context of the eBook. A medical textbook may, thus, explain a disease using a video clip or a children's book may contain a series of animations to depict a situation. eBooks thus become more attractive to the average reader.

- *Access to Distant Markets:* As already explained, eBooks are distributed as files over the Internet. That means that the geographical boundaries that deter sale of physical copies are removed making it possible to sell to readers all over the world. This makes eBooks an attractive proposition especially while addressing small, geographically dispersed markets that cannot be efficiently served with printed books.
- *Always Available:* Given the fact that eBooks do not occupy any shelf-space and can be easily reproduced, publishers need not worry anymore about limited shelf exposure or an out-of-print backlist. eBooks have allowed publishers to have greater visibility for their entire list. From the customer's perspective, readers can access eBooks with great ease and speed so not having a book to read isn't an issue because one can be downloaded and read.

THE CONS

Among the few factors that have discouraged publishers from taking the 'e' route, the primary one is the threat of piracy. eBooks can be easily duplicated and disseminated and can easily lend itself to unauthorised copying and distribution. The development of eBooks does cost money and publishers must carefully examine the returns they hope to achieve on such an investment. Development of eBooks therefore must be a choice one takes after examining all costs involved and the ability of the market to 'consume' the eBooks. Since, the next eBook costs next to nothing to produce, readers expect eBooks to be priced much lower than their printed counterparts. The jury is still out on this one but discussions on the Internet point towards growing resentment in cases where the paperback and the eBook have been priced equally.

THE NUTS AND BOLTS OF E-PUBLISHING

This section attempts to explain what is involved in e-publishing. Before that, let's understand more about e-Readers and eBooks. eBooks need e-Readers to render them useful. However, e-Readers, or platforms as they may be commonly referred to, are not similar. They are tuned to recognise eBooks that appear only in a certain form, or format. If the eBook is of a format that is different from the one that the e-Reader recognises, the eBook will be rendered incompatible. Think of it as the inability to play vinyl LP records on a CD player. Different e-Readers are tuned to read different eBook formats. The format of an eBook is recognised from the extension of its file name. Prominent eBook formats are.mobi and.azw, which are recognised by the Amazon Kindle, and.epub which is recognised by the Sony e-Reader, the Nook, the Wink and many others.

It is also important to note that some e-Readers do not recognise some eBook formats. Publishers must therefore take care to see that their books are published in more than one format if they wish to reach out to a larger readership. In most publishing processes, PDF files of the entire content of the book are already produced before the book goes into print. PDF files can themselves be distributed as eBooks or can be converted into.mobi or.epub files for distribution to a larger number of e-Readers.

The costs of producing an eBook will depend on whether or not the process was outsourced and on the quantum of books being converted to the electronic version. Some publishers have chosen to convert their entire list and make them available as eBooks while others have adopted a cautious approach, choosing to produce just a few titles as eBooks and tracking the return on investment before converting the other books. Some publishers choose to convert only their out-of-print back lists into eBooks. Publishers are advised to choose an option that fits their budget and their appetite for risk.

While deciding which books should be converted to eBooks, publishers must also bear in mind the technological constraints imposed on certain types of books. Graphic-intensive books, for instance, are labouriously displayed on e-Readers and need processes that might be expensive to develop. Similarly, books written in other scripts besides the

Roman script have encountered problems related to the font that renders them incomprehensible, especially when converted into formats such as.epub and.mobi. Publishers are advised to discuss these issues with their eBook developers before they invest in the process. Since, eBooks are available primarily on the Internet, it is important that they can be searched and located easily. This is achieved through the use of what is called metadata, data regarding the book such as its title, the names of its authors, its ISBN and other such related data. Publishers should make sure that the appropriate metadata is generated for each book.

COMPARISONS IN PROCESS

The development of eBooks has witnessed a large number of authors being able to self-publish. Besides, many publishers, most of whom are based in the US and in Europe, have launched eBook-only lists. This can be attributed to the fact that the production of eBooks does away with most processes traditionally associated with the production of books. A close examination of the illustration shows that in the case of e-books the publisher can do away with the pre-press and printing stages and, in some cases, with the distribution stage. This allows the publisher to bring the book to market in a relatively short span of time. Books can therefore be launched with relatively greater ease and speed.

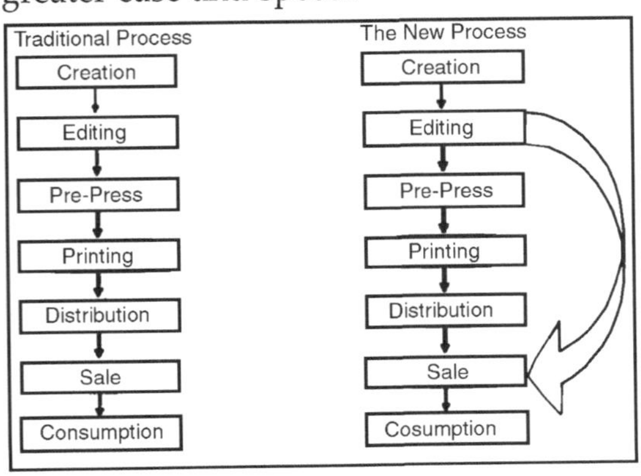

Fig. 4.1

COMPARISONS IN ENGAGEMENTS

Similarly the advent of eBooks has rewritten the rules of engagement between the authors, publishers and other players in the supply chain. As depicted in the following figure, authors can directly reach out to readers. The need for publishers is therefore being questioned and their role as content curators has become more important now than before.

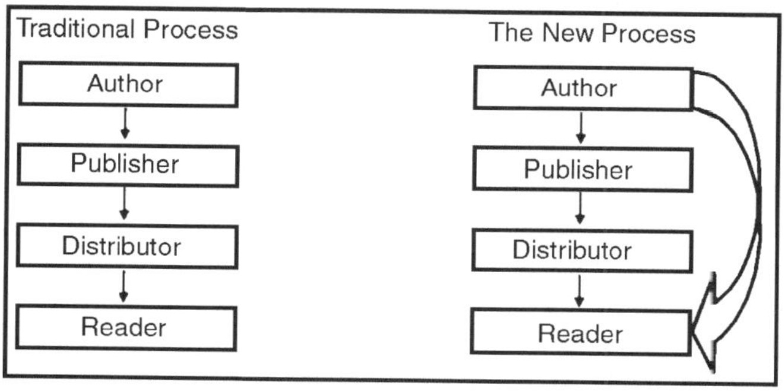

Fig. 4.2

DIGITAL RIGHTS MANAGEMENT

The main concern most publishers have regarding eBooks is that related to piracy. If eBooks are indeed electronic files that can be transferred over the Internet, there seems to be nothing that will stop readers from sharing these files much like music is shared. That should, theoretically, result in a loss of sales for the publisher. This threat has been recognised and addressed in the form of what is called Technical Protection Measures (TPM). These TPM primarily safeguard the 'digital rights' of the owner of the intellectual property, the publisher in this case, and is therefore also sometimes referred to as 'digital rights management' or simply DRM.

One may find that TPM and DRM are used interchangeably. DRM is currently mostly managed by the manufacturers of e-Readers. These e-Readers possess the 'key' to a 'lock' on the eBook. So if the eBook is 'locked' for reading on the Kindle, only the Kindle will possess the 'key' to it. The user will therefore not be able to read it, for instance, on an iPad because the iPad will not have the key for that file. Many times, the key is unique to each device implying that two users of the Kindle will also not be able to share an eBook. The argument is that if a reader has purchased an eBook then he/she should be able to read it only on his/her own device. Another device implies another user and hence, the argument goes, evidence of unauthorised sharing. No doubt effective, this kind of DRM has also caused angst among readers who might have multiple devices and cannot read their books on all of them because the books have been rendered device-specific.

Many publishers who have opted to protect their books through the use of DRM have experienced a backlash in the form of readers refusing to buy their books. The emphasis has, therefore, shifted to what is called 'Social DRM', a less-intrusive type of DRM. This advocates the use of information, usually in the form of a line of text, which uniquely identifies the author and can be used to detect whether the file has changed hands. Publishers have, in fact, been quite innovative in the use of Social DRM, using text such as 'Presented to Kate for her reading pleasure' or a customised bookplate developed uniquely for each buyer. Although piracy remains a large threat to the profitability of publishers and the integrity of their content, publishers must approach the issue of DRM after examining all the issues concerned.

NEXT STEPS

The publisher must have an idea of how eBooks will be sold after they are produced. The channels of distribution that will be employed must be determined before the eBooks are produced so that the eBooks can be immediately put up for sale. While the publisher may choose to sell these eBooks on their own web sites, they may choose to do so also on other web sites that aggregate books by many publishers and facilitate their sale.

This is much like having distributors for your book and also choosing to sell your book yourself. They must be extremely cautious about the terms of your agreement, just like they would in the case of printed books. As in all cases, sales must be tracked and returns on investment calculated. If eBooks are indeed the way books will be traded in the future, publishers must be wary of adopting another's way of doing things and devise a method of developing and distributing eBooks that suits it best.

ENVIRONMENTAL IMPACTS OF e-BOOKS

With the growth in the number of e-readers and sales of Ebooks, many have begun to question the environmental impacts of e-readers and e-Books. Currently e-Books make up a relatively small portion of the overall book market and about 9 per cent of the trade book market. However, sales of e-Books are rapidly increasing, as are the number of devices capable or displaying e-Books. With the rapid adoption of e-Books many have questioned what effects e-readers will have on the environmental impacts of the book industry.

At the time of this was written, none of the major manufacturers of dedicated e-readers have published information about the environmental impacts of their devices, however Apple has released an environmental report on its iPad, a tablet computer with a built in e-Book application, and the ability to download applications to read e-Books from other suppliers. Additionally others have estimated the environmental impacts of Amazon's Kindle, and other e-reader devices and attempted to compare them to the environmental impacts of paper books.

This report will summarise some of the information found in these reports and compare the environmental impacts of e-Books to those of paper books. While e-Books can be read on personal computers and smart phones this report will focus primarily on dedicated e-readers and tablet computers.

e-BOOK SALES

Since, Amazon launched its e-reader the Kindle in November of 2007, sales of e-Books have grown rapidly and more companies have released devices capable reading e-Books. The Amazon Kindle still leads the e-reader market, though a recent study indicates that the Kindle is rapidly losing market share to Apple's iPad. Together the Kindle and the iPad make up the vast majority of the e-reader market. A recent survey of e-reader owners showed that 47 per cent owned a Kindle and 32 per cent owned iPads. The Sony Reader and the Barnes and Noble Nook respectively accounted for 5 per cent and 4 per cent of the respondents e-readers.

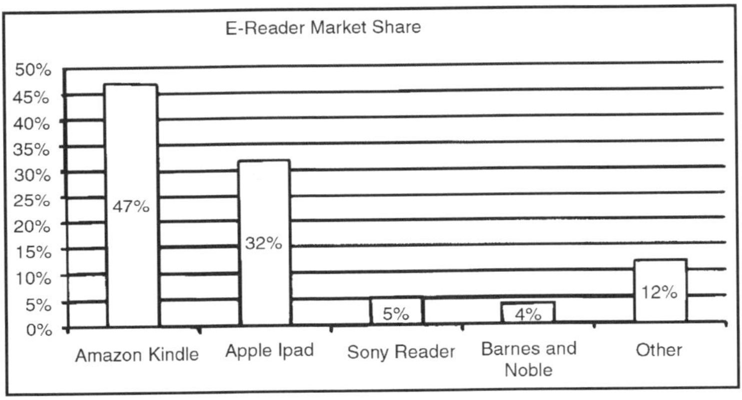

Fig. 4.3 Market Share of E-readers

The rate at which e-Book sales have increased in recent years is impressive. In 2009 sales of e-Books totaled over $169.5 million and e-Books accounted for about 9 per cent of all trade book sales from January through August of 2010. It appears that the shift towards e-Books is only picking up steam. In January to August of 2010 e-Book sales were 193 per cent greater than they were for that same period in 2009.

The Book Industry Study Group's 'Survey of Consumer Attitudes Towards e-Book Reading' suggests that we may just be seeing the beginning of the shift in how people choose to read books. According to the study, which was released in January of 2010, 37 per cent of e-Book buyers had purchased their first e-Book in the past 6 months. Furthermore, the data from the BISG survey suggests that consumers of e-Books will purchase fewer printed books. 25 per cent of e-Book owners surveyed said they would buy fewer printed books, 15 per cent said they buy no printed books and 9 per cent said they would not buy a printed book even if the book they wanted was not available as an e-Book.

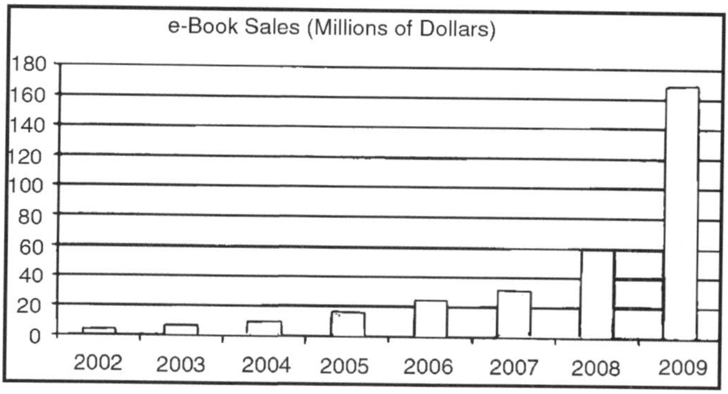

Fig. 4.4 E-book Sales by Year

E-READER LIFECYCLE

Since, the data suggests that sales of e-Books are likely to increase while sales of printed books are likely to decrease, it is logical to question the environmental implications of this transition. In 2008 Green Press Initiative and the Book Industry Study Group commissioned a report on the environmental impacts of the U.S., book industry which included a lifecycle analysis of printed books. That report concluded that in 2006 the U.S., book industry consumed approximately 30 million trees and had a carbon footprint equivalent to 12.4 million metric tons of carbon dioxide, or 8.85 pounds per book sold.

Determining the environmental impacts of an e-Book presents a challenge that does not exist in estimating the impacts of a paper book. That challenge is the fact that user behaviour will significantly influence the impact of an e-book. This is due to the fact that the manufacturing of the e-reader device accounts for the vast majority of an e-books environmental impact. Because of this, on a per book basis, a reader who reads 100 books on an e-reader will have almost 1/100th of the impact of someone who reads only one book on the same device.

Additionally, two readers who each read the same number of books per year, can have a very different per-book environmental impact if one buys a new e-reader every year while the other keeps his for four years before replacing it. Because of the impact that user behaviour can have on the environmental impact of e-books, any analysis will either have to make assumptions about the behaviour of a 'typical" reader of e-books, or else identify a break-even point in terms of the number of books that must be read on an e-reader to offset the environmental impacts of a corresponding number of paper books.

However even this can be confused by the fact that it is not clear that reading one e-book offsets one paper book. For example, the ability to instantly download any book at any time may encourage e-reader owners to read more books in which case each e-book read would not necessarily correspond to a printed book that would have been read. Additionally someone who buys a printed book and later lends it to a friend to read would in effect halve the environmental impact of reading that book.

As such any analysis should strive to account for this and determine a break-even point in terms of 'printed books offset' rather than e-books read. Additional complexity is added by the fact that most e-readers can be used for a variety of tasks other than reading books. For example, most can read newspapers and magazines in addition to books and some e-readers can also read blogs and surf the internet. Tablet computers can allow a user to check e-mail, play games, view photos and videos, listen to music and surf the Internet in addition to other things. Thus for the owner of a Tablet computer, who only spends 10 per cent of his time using the tablet to read books, it would seem reasonable to assume that only 10 per cent of the manufacturing impact of the tablet should be counted towards the impact of that users e-books.

APPLE iPAD

Apple is the only manufacturer that has completed an environmental report for its e-reader device. According to Apple's report, over its lifecycle, the iPad will be responsible for 130 kg of carbon equivalent greenhouse gas emissions. 130 kg is equal to about 287 pounds. Using the carbon footprint of the book industry in the Environmental Trends Report, the average printed book is responsible 8.85 pounds of greenhouse gas emissions.

This means an iPad owner would need to offset 32.4 printed books during the iPad's lifetime to break even in terms of the carbon footprint of reading those books. If you are also offsetting printed magazines and printed newspapers with the iPad then the number of books you would need to offset to break even could be much lower.

Daniel Goleman and Gregory Norris conducted their own lifecycle comparison of the iPad with printed books in an article printed in the New York Times titled 'How Green is My iPad' Their analysis concluded that it would be necessary to offset 100 printed books to make up for the carbon footprint of the iPad, however it is not clear if their analysis included the books impacts on forest carbon loss or not. Of course greenhouse gas emissions are not the only environmental impacts of producing e-readers or printed books. Printed books require wood fibre which needs to be harvested from forests while e-readers require plastic metal and glass as well as other mineral resources to make up the various electronic components and battery. Norris and Goleman mention that some materials that are in e-readers, such as columbite and tantalite, are often mined in wartorn regions of Africa and sourcing these minerals can have negative social impacts.

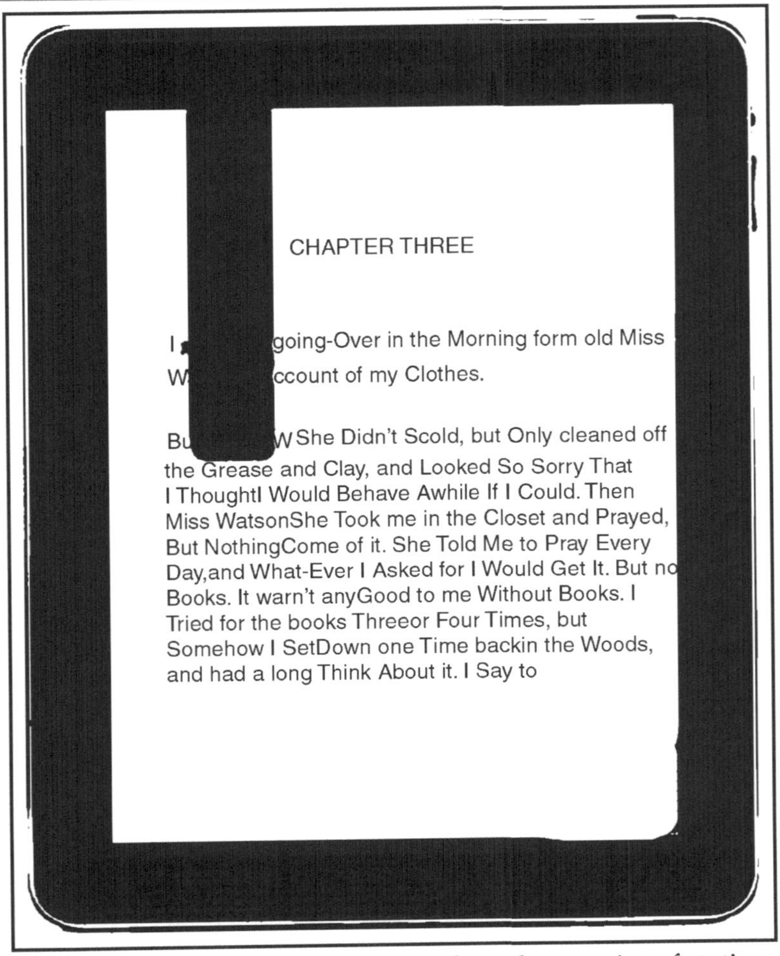

In its environmental report, Apple makes a point of stating that the iPad has a mercury free LED display, that the glass is free of arsenic and that the iPad is free from Brominated Flame Retardants (BFRs) and Polyvinyl chloride (PVC). Norris and Goleman conclude that "With respect to fossil fuels, water use and mineral consumption, the impact of one e-reader payback equals roughly 40 to 50 books".

In terms of health Impacts Norriss and Goleman conclude that in terms of impacts on human health, one e-book has 70 times impact of one printed book, with the primary impact being particulate matter from energy use and production.

AMAZON KINDLE AND OTHER DEDICATED e-READERS

A report by Cleantech estimated that the lifetime carbon footprint of Amazon's kindle is approximately 168 kg of carbon dioxide equivalent emissions. This is equal to 370 lbs. or the emissions of about 42 paper books, which is very much in line with the greenhouse gas estimates for the iPad, however it should be noted that the estimates used in this report have been criticised by some. As with the case of the iPad there are other impacts associated with e-readers besides the carbon emissions.

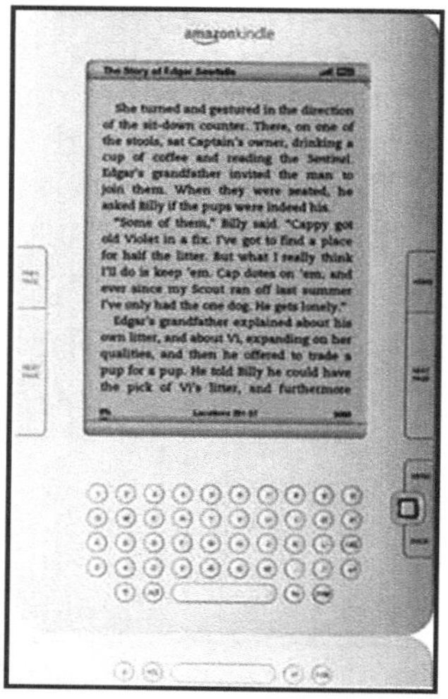

A recent study by Asa Moberg *et al.,* compared the impact of a daily newspaper to that of an e-reader and concluded that for a wide variety of environmental issues the impact of the e-reader is lower. This study is of limited importance because it is comparing newspapers, and using Swedish and European figures for electricity consumption, but it does support the idea that when an e-reader offsets a large amount of printed material there can be significant environmental savings. This study also suggested that more information is needed with respect to toxic materials that could potentially be in e-readers.

OTHER FACTORS TO CONSIDER AND ADDITIONAL RESEARCH NEEDS ENERGY CONSUMPTION

Unlike a printed book, an e-reader requires energy consumption during the 'use' stage of its lifecycle. In most of the estimates, this energy consumption used while the reader is reading is baked into the final estimates. Additionally, this number is likely to be relatively small compared to the energy used in manufacturing the device. For the iPad consumer energy use is equivalent to 30 per cent of the tablet's total carbon footprint.

This number is likely to be much lower for dedicated e-readers that use e-ink technology which only requires energy to change the words on the page and does use power while the user is actually reading. Even the iPad uses very little energy when someone is just reading on it. And Norris and Goleman point out that reading at night with a light on can use more electricity than charging an e-reader.

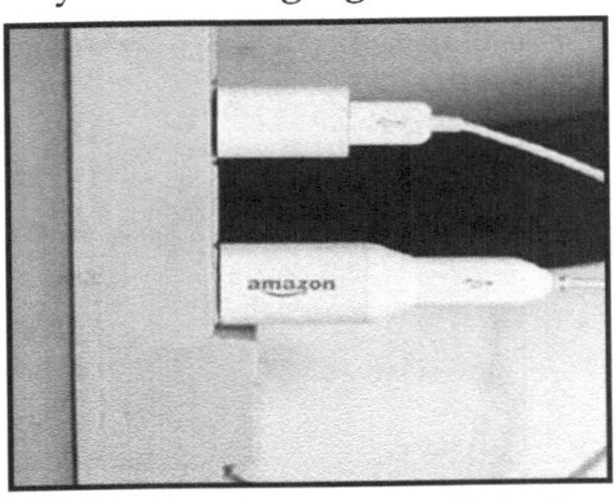

What is not clear is the degree to which the studies address the impact of the servers, modems and infrastructure that makes the delivery of e-books possible. To be certain energy demand for storing and transmitting data over the Internet is increasing rapidly and poses a very serious environmental challenge. However the total portion of data storage that is associated with e-books, while unknown, is at this point assumed to be quite minimal compared to the total content of the internet. Additional research should be conducted to determine the environmental impacts associated with data storage/transmission for e-books.

e-WASTE AND RECYCLING

Paper books can be recycled, though at this point not much data is available regarding the percentage of books that are recycled at the end of their useful life. Electronic equipment can also be recycled, however consumers should make sure they understand exactly what a manufacturer means when they say the will recycle a product. In some cases this simply means the item will be shipped to a developing country where in some cases children will dismantle the product removing only the most valuable components under unsafe working conditions.

The rest of the 'recycled' product is then landfilled or incinerated sometimes exposing workers and the community to toxic materials. It should also be noted that not all e-book manufacturers have recycling programmes.

CALCULATING BOOKS OFFSET

The image to the right is a good way to visualise the environmental impacts of an e-reader. As the number of printed books that the e-reader offsets increases, so do the benefits of that e-reader. At some point these gains offset the impact of manufacturing and using the e-reader. This 'breakeven point' will be different for different metrics of environmental performance but for most it is likely somewhere between 30 and 70 printed books that are offset over the lifetime of the e-reader. For greenhouse gas emissions this number is probably between 20 and 35 books while for measures of human health impacts the number is probably closer to 70 books.

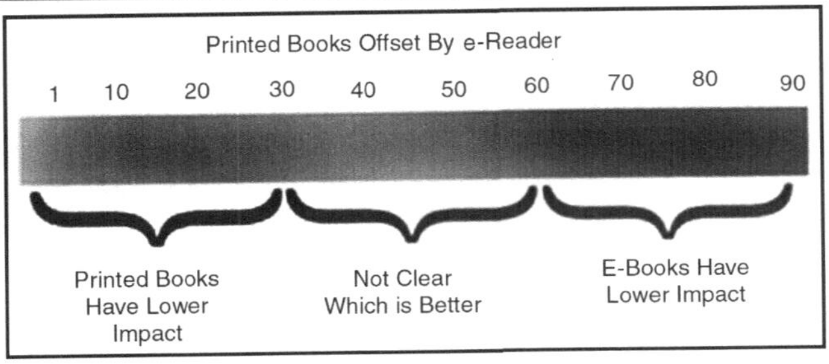

Fig. 4.5 Environmental Benefits of an e-reader by Printed Books Offset

In assessing the impact of an e-reader the idea of printed books offset must be carefully considered. If the owner of an e-reader reads more books because of the ease and convenience of downloading a new title, then every book read on the device does not necessarily correspond to a printed book that is offset. Additionally the numbers in the figure are based on a very simple comparison that is not likely to be replicated in the real world. The assumption is that the reader would either purchase a new printed book once and not share it with anyone else or that the reader would read the books on an e-reader and only use the e-reader for reading books.

If a person would normally share a printed book with others, buy some used printed books, or borrow many of the printed books from the library then the numbers would need to be adjusted to account for that. Additionally, if the e-reader is used for other activities such as watching video, browsing the Internet, checking e-mail, or reading magazines and newspapers, it is unfair to assign the full impacts of producing the e-reader to e-books. More research is needed on typical user behaviour in terms of time spent reading e-books verses other activities on e-readers and Tablet computers in order to make a more accurate comparison.

If the trend of the iPad stealing market share from the Kindle continues, it seems likely that users will spend more time on the other activates that tablets like the iPad are optimised for. Additionally, if someone already owns a tablet computer or an e-reader, the marginal impact of downloading and reading an additional book is quite small. Thus for someone who already owns a device capable of reading e-books, the best choice from an environmental perspective would likely be to read a new book on that device.

e-BOOKS AND e-AUDIO BOOKS

e-BOOKS AND e-AUDIOBOOKS FROM THE LIBRARY

Medicine Hat Public Library pays a company called OverDrive to provide access to copyrightprotected eBooks and eAudiobooks for Library patrons. Anyone with a valid library membership and a PIN number can access these resources from home. Currently, patrons can have up to 5 electronic titles checked out at once and each title can be kept for a maximum of 3 weeks. At the end of the lending period, each title will automatically expire. There are no late fees! While the file will still be visible on your computer or portable device, you will not be able to open it and it can be deleted. Due to restrictions imposed by book publishers, only one person may have an electronic title checked out at once. So when someone checks out The 9th Confession by James Patterson, that book is unavailable to everyone else until it is returned.

A FEW THINGS TO KNOW ABOUT e-BOOKS

Library eBooks come in two formats: ePub and PDF. The main difference between the two formats is that ePub books have reflowable text: as you increase the text size, the words automatically shuffle to fit your screen. PDF books do not have this feature, so when you increase the text size you may need to scroll from left to right to read everything on the page. Both formats are compatible with PCs, Macs, and most portable eReaders like the Sony Reader, Kobo and Nook. The iPad, iPhone and iPod Touch are also compatible with ePub files when downloaded directly to the device using the OverDrive Media Console App. In order to read an eBook on your computer or to transfer it to an applicable eReader, you must first install Adobe Digital Editions which is freely available from the Library to Go web site.

A FEW THINGS TO KNOW ABOUT e-AUDIOBOOKS

eAudiobooks from the Library come in two formats: MP3 and WMA. Both formats will work on PCs and most portable audio devices. Unfortunately, WMA files are not compatible with Mac computers. Depending on the type of software your Apple device is running you may be able to transfer a WMA file through a PC. In order to download an eAudiobook and transfer to a portable device, you must first install OverDrive Media Console which is freely available from the Library to Go web site.

LIBRARY TO GO

Library to Go is the library's catalogue for finding and downloading eBooks and eAudiobooks.

BEFORE YOU START BROWSING: DOWNLOAD THE REQUIRED SOFTWARE

In order to read and transfer eBooks you must first download the Adobe Digital Editions software. For eAudiobooks you must first download OverDrive Media Console.

Both are freely available on the Library to Go web site below the green menu on the left-side of the page:

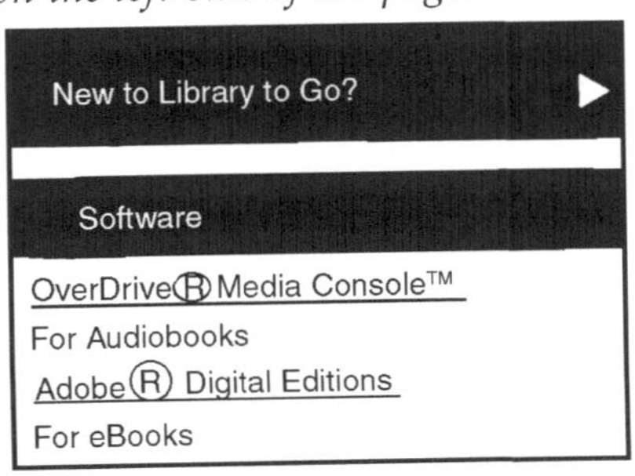

ACTIVATING THE SOFTWARE

After you have installed the software, you need to take steps to activate it before downloading digital materials.

Adobe Digital Editions Requires Activation

You must create an Adobe ID in order to transfer eBooks from a computer to an eReader. When you open Digital Editions for the first time click 'Get an Adobe ID online' and follow the prompts to create your Adobe ID. You can then enter your Adobe ID and password in the relevant boxes in Digital Editions to activate.

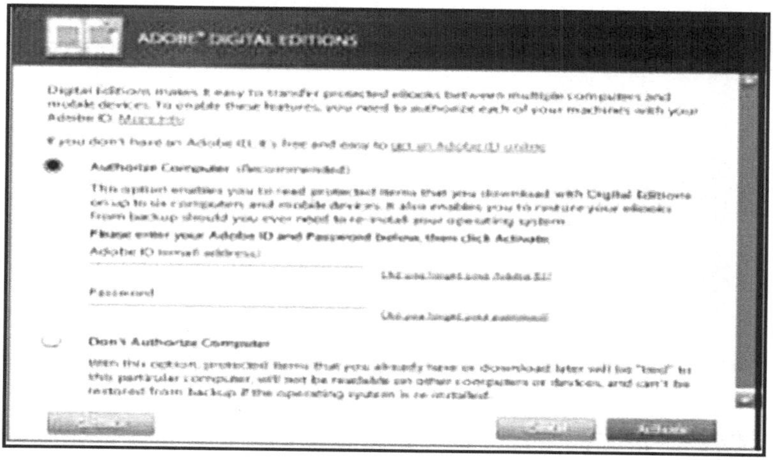

OverDrive Media Console Requires a Security Update

The first time you open an eAudiobook with OverDrive Media Console, a message will appear saying that a security upgrade must be performed before the file can be opened. Simply follow the on-screen instructions to perform the quick upgrade.

FINDING TITLES USING LIBRARY TO GO

You can search for a particular title or author using the 'Quick Search' box near the top of the Library to Go page.

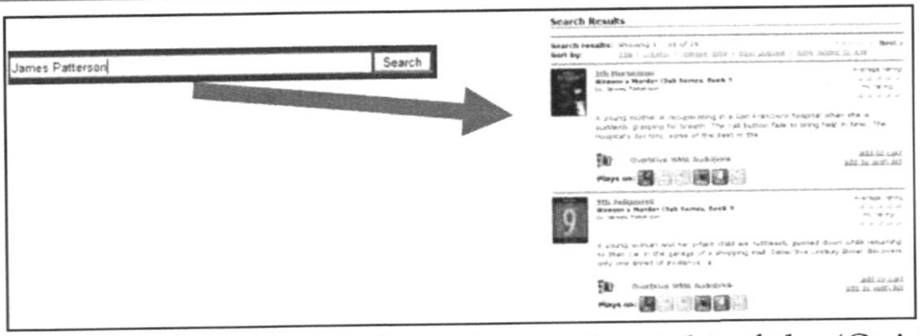

The 'Advanced Search' option to the right of the 'Quick Search' box can be used to perform a more specific search. You can also browse for titles using the green menu on the left side of the page or the categories in the centre of the main Library to Go page.

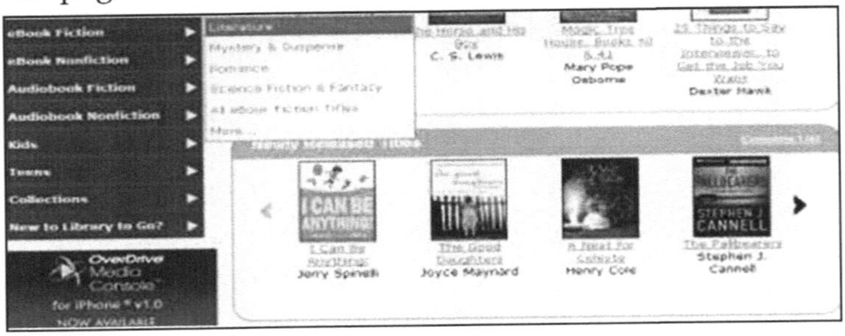

DOWNLOADING AN e-BOOK

When you have found an eBook that interests you, simply click on its title for more information:

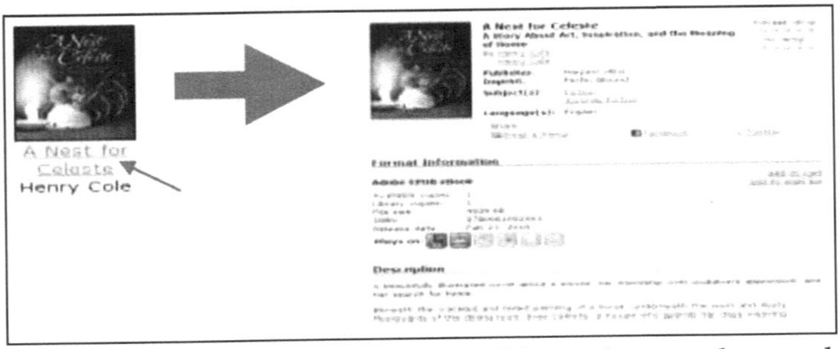

If the 'Add to Cart' option is visible in the grey bar under 'Format Information', then the book is available to download and you can click to move to the next step. If you see 'Place a

Hold' instead, then the item is checked out by someone else and you can click to enter your e-mail address and receive notification when the item is available. Once the item is available for download, you will have three days to complete the checkout. After you click 'Add to Cart' you are given the option to 'Continue Browsing' or 'Proceed to Checkout'-if you 'Continue Browsing', your items will stay in your cart for 45 minutes.

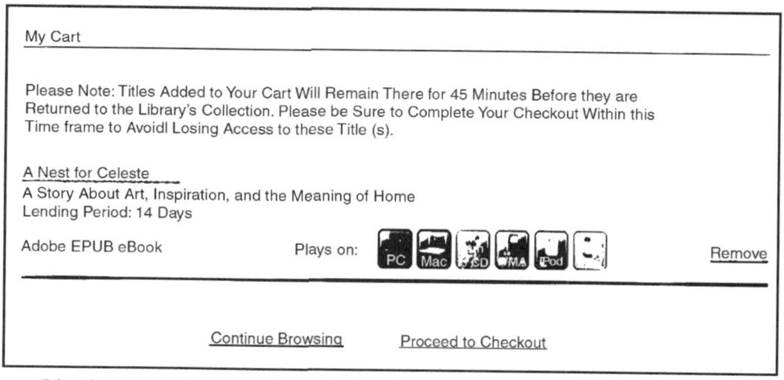

Clicking 'Proceed to Checkout' brings you to a screen asking for your Library card number and PIN number.

When you have entered this information, you will be brought to the Check Out screen:

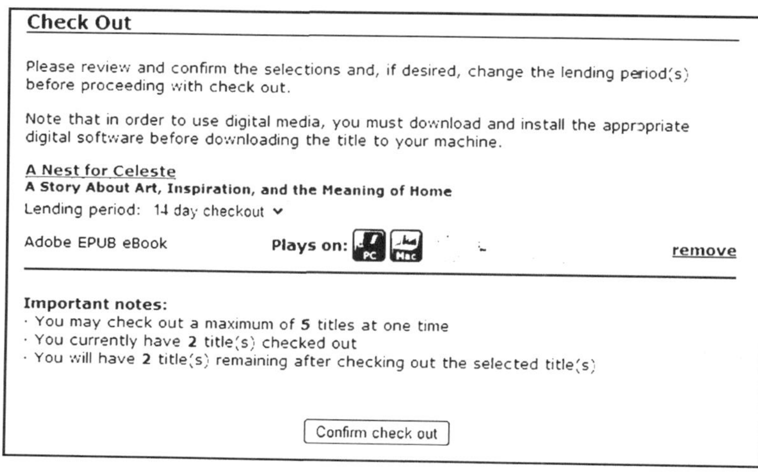

From here you can choose your lending period and see how close you are to your 5 item limit. When you're ready to download, click 'Confirm Checkout' and then the 'Download' button on the next screen that appears.

**If this is the very first time you have downloaded an eBook from the Library, you will need to tell your computer which programme it should use to open the file.

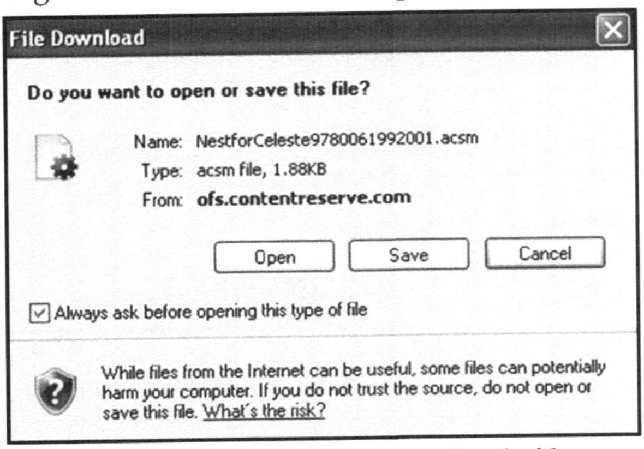

To select the programme to open eBook files, you must click the 'Save' button, choose 'Desktop' as the destination and then click save.

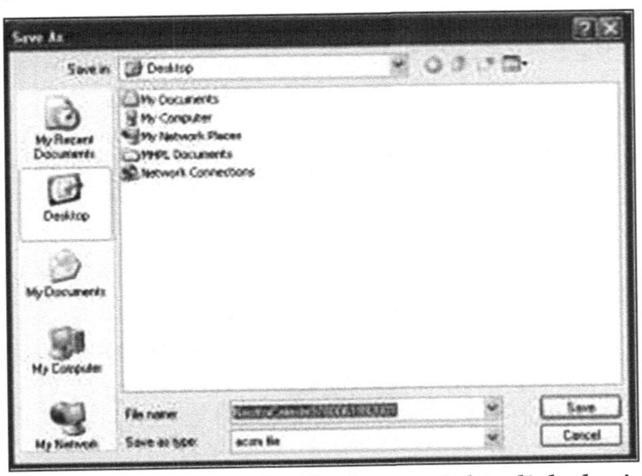

Next, find the file on the Desktop, right-click the icon, go to 'Open With' and click 'Choose Programme'.

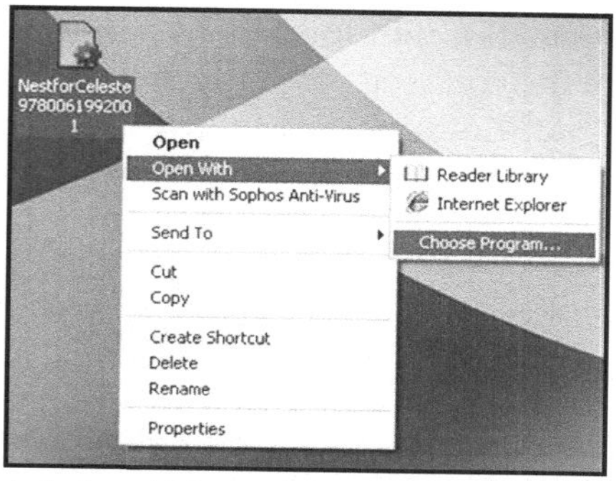

Choose Adobe Digital Editions from the list of programmes, click the box next to "Always use the selected programme to open this kind of file' and click 'OK'.

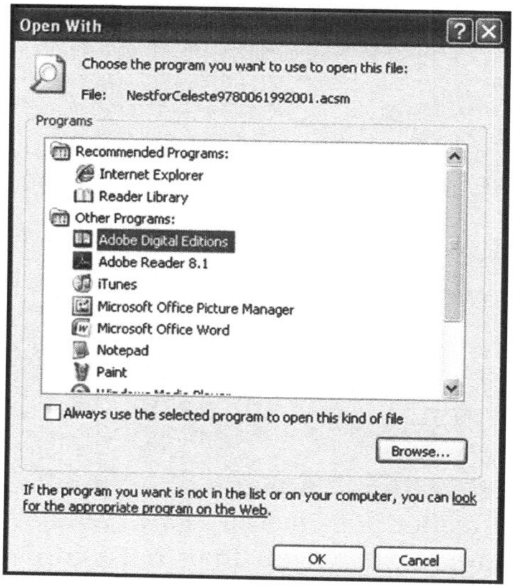

If Digital Editions does not appear in the list of programmes, you will need to find it using the 'Browse' button. Usually, it is saved under Programme Files \ Adobe \ Adobe Digital Editions \ digitaleditions.

TRANSFERRING AN e-BOOK TO AN e-READER

To transfer an eBook from Digital Editions to an eReader such as the Kobo Touch, you must first connect your eReader to your computer. If a window opens asking what Windows should do with the connected device choose 'Take No Action'. Then open Digital Editions and follow the steps to authorise your reader if you are using it for the first time. Click on the icon for Library View in the top-left corner of the screen.

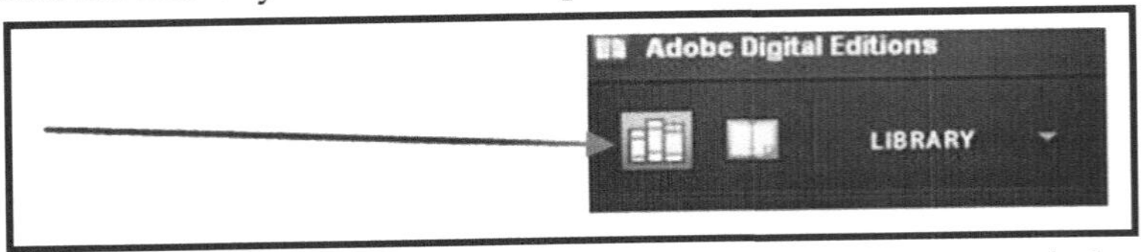

Your eReader should appear at the bottom of the Bookshelves area on the left side of the screen. Simply drag and drop the title you wish to transfer onto your eReader.

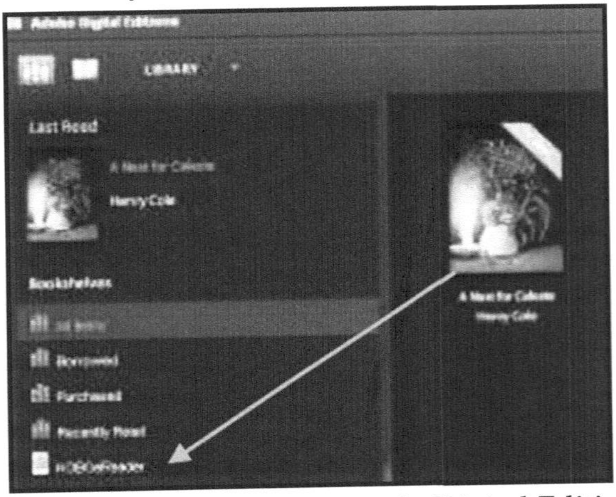

If your eReader does not appear in Digital Editions after you have plugged it in, you may need to download your eReader's software before your computer will recognise it.

RETURNING YOUR e-BOOKS EARLY

Any eBooks you borrow through the library system will automatically return themselves at the end of your borrowing period but if you finish an eBook early, you can also return it yourself.

In the Adobe Digital Editions software on your computer, click the 'Go to Library View' button in the top left corner:

Next, click the 'Item Options' button for the book you wish to return:

Finally, click the 'Return Borrowed Item' in the Item Options menu:

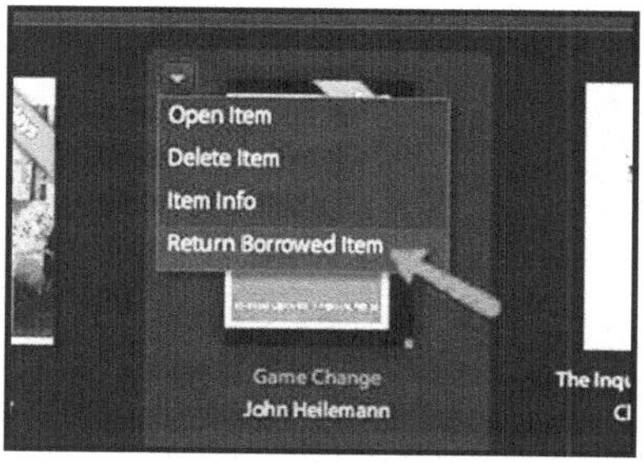

DOWNLOADING AN e-BOOK DIRECTLY TO A SONY WIFI e-READER

The Sony WiFi eReader will allow you to borrow eBooks from the library directly on your device without the use of Adobe Digital Editions or any external applications.

To download books onto your device, use the following procedure:

- Turn on your device.
- Go to page 2 and select the 'Public Library' icon.
- If you are asked to set up an account in the Sony eReader store, follow the prompts to do so. This will authorize your eReader to open the library books you borrow.

- In the 'Public Library' section, select the option to 'Discover More' or 'Find a Library'.
- Type in 'Medicine Hat' into the search area and press the small magnifying next to it.
- Select the 'Medicine Hat Public Library System' and then select the 'Library to Go' option—this will take you to the Library to Go homepage where you can login, search for, and download your eBooks.

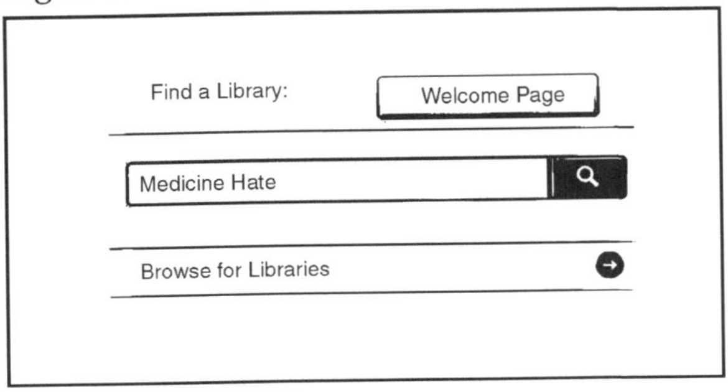

RETURNING e-BOOKS DIRECTLY ON A SONY WIFI e-READER

To return your eBooks directly from your Sony Wifi eReader use the following procedure:

- Select the 'Books' icon on your eReader screen.
- Press the Menu button.
- Select 'Return Books.'
- Select which books you'd like to return by checking the appropriate boxes.
- Press 'Done'.

Overdrive Media Console Mobile is a free app available for most iPad/iPhone/iPod Touch, Android, Blackberry and Windows Mobile devices. This app allows you to download titles directly to your device over Wi-Fi or 3g. However, not all file formats are currently compatible. Apple devices, for example, only support eBooks in ePub format and eAudiobooks in MP3 format. You can download the app from the app store for your device or the Library to Go web site. You must register your Adobe ID with the Overdrive Media

Console Mobile app and you will be prompted for your library card number and PIN before you can download an eBook or eAudiobook.

HOW TO DOWNLOAD e-BOOKS AND e-AUDIOBOOKS WITH OVERDRIVE MEDIA CONSOLE MOBILE

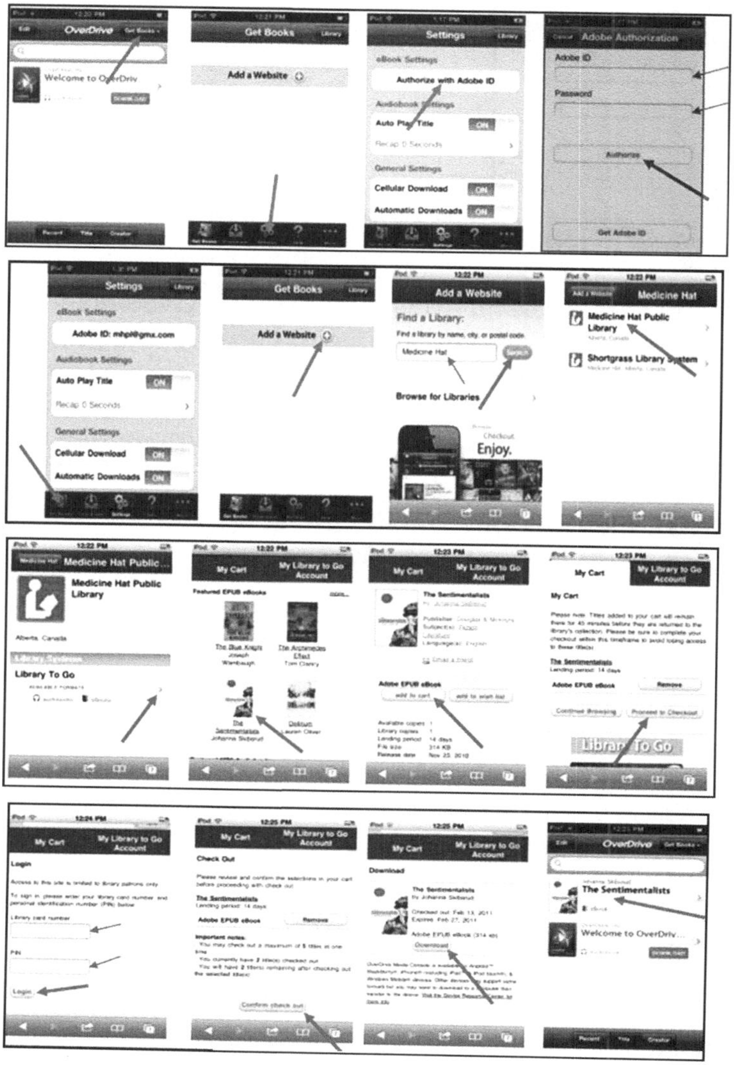

Note

Library books borrowed through the OverDrive Media Console app will always be found by opening that app on your device. For example, if you downloaded a title on your Kobo Vox using OverDrive, the next time you wanted to go and read it, you would open the app instead of looking for the title in your library.

RETURNING e-BOOKS DIRECTLY FROM YOUR PORTABLE DEVICE

You can also return your eBooks directly from your portable device by using the OverDrive Media Console app. By swiping your finger across the title on the main page you will be shown a button to delete the book. When you click that button, you will then be given the option to delete only, or delete and return the book. Deleting the book only will free up space on your device, while deleting and returning the book will also free up space for another title in your Library to Go account.

Each device is different but most do offer you the option to return items early. To find out if your device has this feature, try to delete the item and see if you are asked whether you want to return the item as well. If you are not given the option, then look in the settings section for each borrowed item.

DOWNLOADING AN e-AUDIOBOOK TO YOUR COMPUTER

The process for finding and checking out titles is the same for eAudiobooks and eBooks. After checking out an eAudiobook click Open in the File Download window. Overdrive Media Console will open automatically. eAudiobooks are divided into parts to facilitate faster download times. You will need to tell Overdrive Media Console which parts to download by checking the boxes beside the parts you want. The default option is to download all parts. Once you have checked the parts you want, you can click the 'OK' button to download.

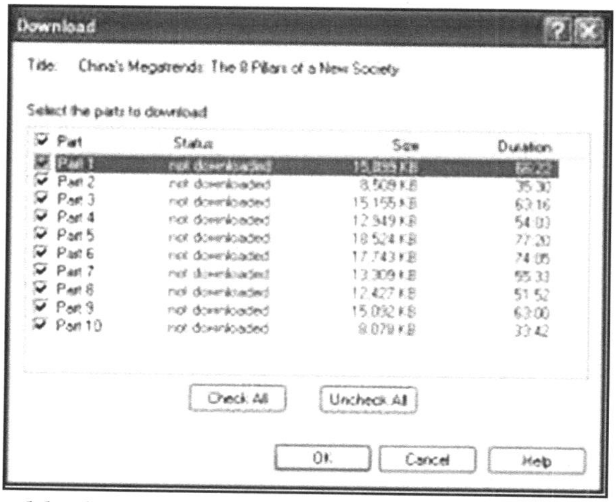

It could take a while to download depending on the speed of your Internet connection and how many parts you choose to download at once After the eAudiobook has downloaded, it will appear in Overdrive Media Console.

From here, you can click the 'Play' button in the top-left corner to listen to the eAudiobook on your computer. The 'Download' button lets you download any parts of the eAudiobook that you missed.

TRANSFERRING AN e-AUDIOBOOK TO A MOBILE DEVICE

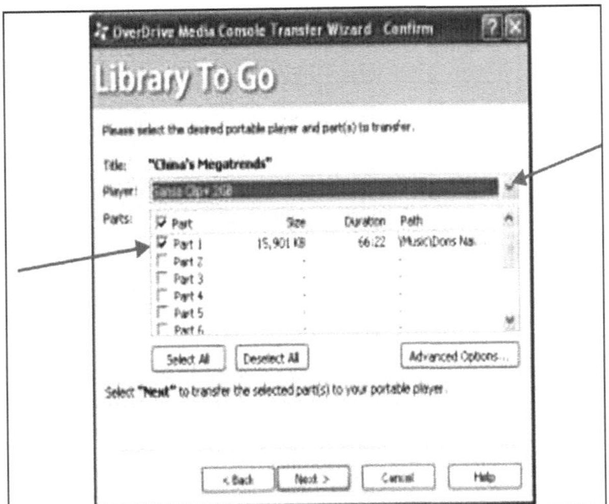

- Connect the device to your PC.
- Open Overdrive Media Console.
- Click the title of the eAudiobook you wish to transfer and click the 'Transfer' button in the topleft corner of the screen.
- Select your player and which parts of the eAudiobook you wish to transfer and click 'Next' to begin the transfer.
- Click 'Finish' and remove your player from the PC.

Special Considerations if Transferring to an iPod

- Some titles are not compatible with Apple devices st have iTunes v9.1 installed on your PC to transfer to an iPod.
- The iTunes setting 'Manually manage music...' must be enabled for Apple devices. Adjust this setting as follows.
  - Connect the device to your computer.
  - Open iTunes.
  - In iTunes, locate the device in the left vertical navigation panel and click the device.
  - If it is not already checked, place a checkmark next to the option 'Manually manage music...'and
  - Click the 'Apply' button.

Please note that at this time transferring WMA audiobooks to an Apple device running iOS 5 is not recommended due to compatibility issues between OverDrive Media Console and Apple iTunes. If you do attempt to transfer WMA files to an Apple device then please be sure to back up your files before starting the process. If you are still experiencing difficulty transferring an eAudiobook to your Apple device, please consult the Help section on the Library to Go web site for other possible solutions.

e-READERS

e-BOOK FORMATS

eBooks come in a variety of formats. Some publishers and sellers also place DRM protection on the books so they cannot be copied, viewed on multiple devices, or restricted to specific readers.

There is no consistent licensing as each licence is an agreement between author, publisher and seller:

- ePUB is an open source format and continues to develop. ePUB books can contain video and active links which make the books dynamic. ePUB is the most versatile of all eBook formats. Textbooks developers are looking to this format as it will allow for content and media rich books, moving away from what can be done with traditional text and print media. ePub can be read by most popular devices except Amazon's Kindle. Amazon currently offers an e-mail service that lets you convert ePUB documents and books into the AZW format for a fee, though formaang and interactivity may be lost.

- MOBI also known as MobiPocket is owned by Amazon and is similar to the AZW format for Kindle. The MOBI format can be read by most of the popular readers except the Nook. MOBI was once the most popular format but is losing ground to ePUB.
- PDF is a format that is commonly used to publish documents and images. PDFs are essentially images of pages and therefore do not allow text to flow between pages or to fit the screen size. PDFs are best read on larger computer screens and not mobile devices. PDFs can be viewed in most readers except the first edition Kindle.
- Plain Text formaang allows for a very small file size, allowing large books such as the Bible to be distributed in this format. Plain text is read by major readers except Nook.
- HTML is the markup language for web pages and most eBooks that use HTML can be read in a web browser. Some other eBook formats include HTML in their packaging of books.
- Kindle/ AZW is a version of MOBI and is exclusive to Amazon Kindle. It can be read on a variety of mobile devices with the Kindle App. It cannot be read on other readers such as the Nook or Sony reader.
- eReader was originally developed for Palm. This format supports hyperlinks and images. The Nook can read pdb files while the Kindle cannot.

WHERE TO FIND e-BOOKS

Before you go out and make a purchase for a dedicated reader it might be worth your while to explore what books are available in eBook format. Take some time to read a few books on the devices you already have access to such as your computer or smart phone if you have one. eBooks are not quite the same as print. Some eBooks contain images and some do not. Some free versions were entered by volunteers and may contain a typo or two.

Let's explore a few places to find eBooks:

- Google eBooks puts the power of the Google search engine to work scouring the web for eBooks. Some books are hosted by Google, others from major publishers and distributors. If you are not tied to a particular reader Google books is a good place to start to find the books in a variety of formats. You can find many free books from the public domain, as well as books for purchase.
- Project Gutenberg has a large collection of books in the public domain. Currently there are over 33,000 free eBooks available. The eBooks on Project Gutenberg are found in 3 main formats plain text, ePUB, and MOBI.
- eBooks.com has a wide range of eBooks for purchase including many academic titles for colleges. eBooks.com sells books in PDF, for computer based reading; ePUB, Mobi and MicrosoV reader for mobile devices. eBooks has an eReader app for iPod/iPad/ iPhone devices. eBooks from eBooks.com can also be read on a computer
- Amazon Kindle eBooks Books sold at Amazon for the Kindle are primarily in the AZW format, though some may be in MOBI depending on agreements with the publisher. AZW format is proprietary to Amazon and includes DRM protection. Amazon also offers some free ebooks that are in the public domain. Amazon offers the Kindle app for iPod/iPad/iPhone and other mobile devices.
- Barnes and Noble eBook store sells NookBooks formaXed for the Nook. They currently have over 2 million eBooks available. NookBooks are in the ePUB

format, eReader and some PDF, though most books have DRM protection on them. Barnes and Noble offers an app called the Barnes and Noble e-Reader for iPod/iPad/iPhone and other mobile devices.

- Borders has adopted the ePUB, PDF and Mobile format for its books; most have DRM protections. Like other book sellers, they also have free books in the public domain. Unlike Amazon and Barnes and Noble, Borders does not sell its own reader but recommends seven different readers on its web site. These are described in the last section on eReaders. Borders also offers a free eReader app for many mobile devices.

The Apple iBookstore currently sells books for reading only on Apple mobile devices, through the iTunes interface. Rumours persist that Apple will release its iBooks app for the Mac and PC in the future but there are always rumours surrounding Apple. Apple prefers the tactile sensation of 'turning pages' with the touch screen on its mobile devices that current desktop and laptops do not have. Apple iBooks are in the ePUB format and allow for interactivity such as viewing embedded video and active web links. Apple also sells fully illustrated books and magazines because of the colour planorm provided by its devices.

e-READERS

Reading eBooks can be done on a variety of devices with a range of apps and programmes. As suggested, begin with a look at reading on computers and multifunctional devices and end with a look at some of the major dedicated readers.

e-READING SOFTWARE FOR COMPUTERS

If you own a computer you can read almost anything though you may need more than one programme to do so. Reading on your computer is not as comfy as reading a book curled up on the couch or siang in your back yard, but you do have access to a vast library of books. Each of the major eBook sellers provides a version of their reader for your computer.

If you use a Windows based PC you can choose from Kindle for PC, Adobe Digital Editions, Nook for PC, or Borders eReader for PC. If you are a Mac user you have a similar selection of choices Kindle for Mac, Adobe Digital Editions, Nook for Mac, or Borders eReader for Mac.

EREADING ON MULTIFUNCTIONAL MOBILE DEVICES: iPODS, iPADS, AND MOBILE PHONES

Multifunctional mobile devices are just small computers, some with an added phone. These include iPods, iPads, iPhones, Android Phones, Blackberries and an increasing number of small tablets. Most of these mobile devices have LCD screens which make reading in bright light a bit of a challenge; most are colour and many have touch screens and support the interactivity of the ePUB format. Velocity Micro offers Android based tablets, Borders recommends two, these are described later on.

The device that offers the richest media content support for eBooks is currently the iPad. If you already have a number of gadgets in your bag you may wish for a multifunctional device so you have fewer devices to deal with. Similar to the computer, the devices can have a variety of e-reader apps installed so they can handle a large variety of book formats and work with all the major eBook distributors. Kindle Reading Apps, Nook Apps and Borders eReader Apps are available for mobile devices including apps for iPods/iPads/ iPhone, Android and Blackberry phones. Adobe Digital Editions which reads PDF and ePUB can be used on a variety of mobile devices.

DEDICATED e-READERS

When it comes to dedicated eReaders the ones that get the most coverage are the Amazon Kindle and the Barnes and Noble Nook. These two major book sellers have developed their own eReaders. Borders has taken a more open approach and does not market to a particular eReader allowing the reader greater choice. As suggested, begin with a brief summary of the Kindle and Nook readers currently available and then look at the 7 that Borders recommends. Amazon currently offers the Kindle 3 and Kindle DX. The two models each come in two flavours—wifi or wifi and 3G. 3G is provided free allowing you to purchase books and download them whereever you are.

The more recent release of the Kindles uses pearl e-ink which allows for crisper images and text, and reading in bright light. The screens are not touch screens, navigation is carried out via a keyboard and side buXons. The kindle 3 has a 6 inch screen and the DX 9.7 inch screen. Kindle supports; AZW, PDF, MOBI, TEXT formats. It does not support ePub, but a programme called Calibre can convert epub to MOBI. Amazon currently offers an e-mail service for a fee to convert files. The Barnes and Noble Nook now comes in two models the original in black and white and the new Nook Colour. Both have two flavour; wifi or wifi and 3G.

As with the Kindle the 3G is free. Both devices use e-ink and can be read in bright light. Nook Colour has a touch screen and designed for those who love reading magazines. The traditional black and white e-ink did not do justice to the visual images found in many magazines. Nook colour also has extras including some web browsing, e-mail access and games. It is clearly aimed at the iPad, though the Nook colour is not yet a true multifunctional device. The Nooks support the following formats: EPUB, PDB, PDF, MP3, JPG, GIF, PNG, PMB. It does not read Mobi, AMZ, LRX/LEZ, or Text

There are other eReaders on the market that are not tied to a specific vendor. Borders offers a comparison chart for a variety of readers it recommends.

Below is a brief summary of each:

- Aluratek Libre Pro supports books in the ePub, PDF, TXT, RTF, FB2, MOBI, PRC formats. It can play mp3 files and uses an LCD screen that is black and white.
- Kobo Wireless eReader support eReader, ePUB and PDF formats. It uses e-ink and has a 6 inch screen.
- Sony offers 3 models of eReader; the Pocket edition, Touch edition and the Daily Edition. The Sony models all have touch screen navigation and use e-

ink. The pocket edition is not wireless and requires a computer to sync books to. They support ePub, PDF, TXT, RTF, and BBeB formats. Sony also has its own eBook store.

Finally rounding out our look at eReaders the Cruz reader and Tablet from Velocity Micro. The Cruz Reader is not a standalone eReader, it more a multifunctional device. It is a colour eReader with 7" screen that also browses the web, plays mp3 files, watch movies, play games and has some productivity apps. The Cruz Tablet is a true multifunctional Android colour tablet. There are two versions of this device—one with Borders eReader and the other with Amazon's Kindle soVware.

There is a great deal of variety in this very fluid technology. It is apparent that eBooks are here and are gaining more and more ground. eBook readers continue to improve as time goes on. Just as with computers, change is inevitable. Reading is a very personal experience therefore each person should make the choice that works for them. It is clearly not a one size fits all experience. Do your research and make the choice that works for you.

5

Electronic Database

INTRODUCTION TO DATABASE SYSTEMS

Data management and especially the management of geodata is not bound to a specific technology. It would be possible to use analogous map archives or file based record systems. However, the term Geoinformationsystem implies some demands that exceed the storage and retrieval of data. These additional needs can be satisfied sensibly with database systems only.

This lesson is focussed on database concepts and architectures. After an introduction and the definition of some of the most important terms in the unit Definition of Terms as suggested, devote our selfs to the specific characteristics of the database approach.

The closer examination of various applications of databases in the unit Example Applications allows to become acquainted with the use of databases in different fields and contexts and to extend the knowledge about the characteristics of databases. A comparison of the database approach with file based solutions is made in the unit Advantages and Disadvantages.

DEFINITION OF TERMS

Before we start with the use and architecture of data management solutions we discuss the terminology of this field to get to know the basic terms like information, data, database systems. A lot of these basic terms are used daily but most often not in the right context.

Data *vs.* Information

Data (Especially Computer Data)

The presentation of facts, information or concepts which are created in a computer readable form or are translated into such a form.

Information

Information is a useable answer to a concrete question. Something is information if a specific question is answered and that answer increases the understanding of the questioner and enables him to come closer to a specific objective.

Information has the following aspects:

- Structured and syntactic
- Semantic
- Pragmatic

Relationship between Data and Information

The terms data and information are often used interchangeably and in the wrong context.

Therefore a list of distinguishing features is presented below:

- Semantic aspects of data are often coded. This codes need to be defined and interpreted after conventions previously agreed upon;
- Generally, information needs to be reconstructed or derived from data;
- Normally, data do not contain aspects relevant to applications.

Trying to read a letter in a foreign language we are able to recognise the structure and the syntactic aspects of it like the paragraphs, sentences, words, etc., but we cannot make out the meaning of the writing.

However, writing in our own language too cannot be called information in every case. At least we might be able to understand the content but if this content is irrelevant or not interesting to us then the important aspect of the usefulness is missing.

The Components of an Information System

Conceptually an information systems has got a layered structure. Move your mouse over the terms of the following interaction and get to know what parts make up an information system.

The data managements components of an information system are:

- *Data and Database:* An amount of data which are viewed by the operator as somehow going together plus additional data which is used by the DBMS to work correctly are called a database.
- *Database Management System:* A database management system (DBMS) is a software product for the persistent, consistent and application indepent storage and management of data. But also for the flexible and easy use of big and concurrently used databases.
- *Database System:* A database system (DBS) consists of a DBMS and one or more databases. Database management systems and database systems are in the focus of this module.
- *Information System:* A information system extends the database with a couple of software tools for querying, presenting, transforming and analysing the data. According to the first part of this unit where the difference between data and information was discussed, the tools of an information system enrich the data with semantic and pragmatic aspects. For sure you have already heard the term geoinformation system and maybe also read the one or other definition of it. The following paragraph defines the term geoinformation system and compares this definition with the one of an information system as discussed earlier in this unit.
- *Geoinformation System:* "A geoinformation system allows to capture, store, analyse and present all data that describe a part of the earths surface and all on

this part located technical and administrative equipment but also geoscientific, economic and ecologic features. (Translation)". This definition contains the most important aspects of the definition of an information system but focusses on data with spatial reference.

CHARACTERISTICS OF THE DATABASE APPROACH

In the unit Example Applications the use of databases in different fields is presented and according to these examples the most important features of the database approach revised. A comparison between the file-based approach and the database approach can be found in the unit Advantages and Disadvantages.

Concurrent Use

A database system allows several users to access the database concurrently. Answering different questions from different users with the same data is a central aspect of an information system. Such concurrent use of data increases the economy of a system. Data capturing and data storage is not redundant, the system can be operated from a central control and the data can be updated more efficient. Additionally, better use of the most often very expensive data can be made.

When using data concurrently the problem of how the system should behave if changes done are in competition needs to be solved. Additionally, there is a bigger security risk, for example, in the realms of data protection. In technical jargon changes to a database are called transactions.

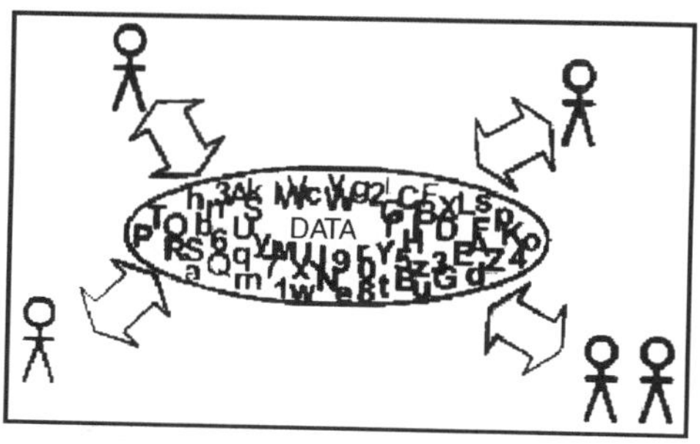

An example for concurrent use is the travel database of a bigger travel agency. The employees of different branches can access the database concurrently and book journeys for their clients. Each travel agent sees on his interface if there are still seats available for a specific journey or if it is already fully booked.

Structured and Described Data

A fundamental feature of the database approach is that the database systems does not only contain the data but also the complete definition and description of these data. These descriptions are basically details about the extent, the structure, the type and the format of all data and, additionally, the relationship between the data. This kind of stored data is called metadata. Metadata is used from the DBMS software but also from applications like GIS and from users of databases. As DBMS software is not written for one specific database application the metadata of a database is used to get information about the extent, the structure, etc., of it.

Structured Data

Data is called structured if it can be subdivided systematically and linked. Following a simple example how data can be described in a database. Below there is a database table. Because of the structure of this table, it is known that a entry in the first column must be a prename and an entry in the third column must be a postcode.

Prename [String]	Name [String]	Postcode [Number]	City [String]
Klaus	Meier	5369	Buhlwil
Sabine	Klett	4812	Moodorf
...	...	...	...

Separation of Data and Applications

As described in the feature structured data the structure of a database is described through metadata which is also stored in the database. An application software does not need any knowledge about the physical data storage like encoding, format, storage place, etc. It only communicates with the management system of a database (DBMS) via a standardised interface with the help of a standardised language like SQL. The access to the data and the metadata is entirely done by the DBMS. In this way all the applications can be totally seperated from the data. Therefore database internal reorganisations or improvement of efficiency do not have any influence on the application software.

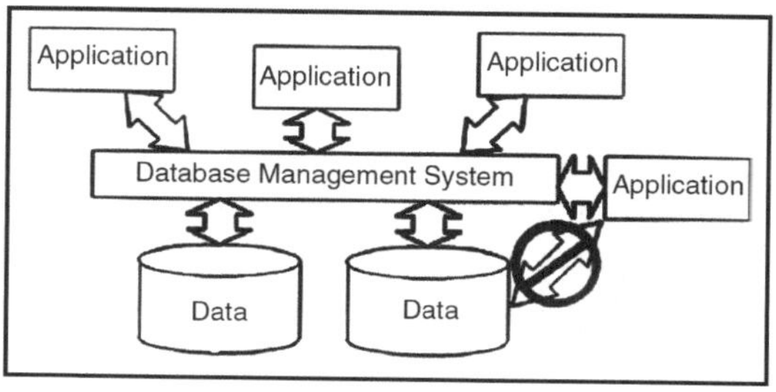

Data Integrity

Data integrity is a byword for the quality and the reliability of the data of a database system. In a broader sense data integrity includes also the protection of the database from unauthorised access and unauthorised changes. Data reflect facts of the real world. Logically, it is demanded that this reflection is done correctly. A DBMS should support the task to bring only correct and consistent data into the database. Additionally, correct transactions ensure that the consistency is maintained during the operation of the system. An example for inconsistency would be if contradictory statements were saved in the same database.

Two Database Tables with Contradictory Database

Wohnstrassen		Strassemplanung		
Strassen Name	**Fahrverbot**	**Strassen Name**	**Art**	**Einschrankungen**
Lind enstrasse	Nein	Haupt strasse	Kanton strasse	Keine
Rose nstrasse	Ja	Garte nstrasse	Quartier strasse	Keine
Garten strasse	19.00-7.00	Ja gerweg	Quartierweg	Fussweg
...		...		

Transactions

A transaction is a bundle of actions which are done within a database to bring it from one consistent state to a new consistent state. In between the data are inevitable inconsistent. A transaction is atomic what means that it cannot be divided up any further. Within a transaction all or none of the actions need to be carried out. Doing only a part of the actions would lead to an inconsistent database state. One example of a transaction is the transfer of an amount of money from one bank account to another. The debit of the money from one account and the credit of it to another account makes together a consistent transaction. This transaction is also atomic.

The debit or credit alone would both lead to an inconsistent state. After finishing the transaction the changes to both accounts become persistent and the one who gave the money has now less money on his account while the receiver has now a higher balance. Try it using the buttons at the bottom to the left which allow to navigate through the steps of this example.

Data Persistence

Data persistence means that in a DBMS all data is maintained as long as it is not deleted explicitely. The life span of data needs to be determined directly or indirectly be the user and must not be dependent on system features. Additionally data once stored in a database must not be lost. Changes of a database which are done by a transaction are persistent. When a transaction is finished even a system crash cannot put the data in danger.

Data Views

Typically, a database has several users and each of them, depending on access rights and desire, needs an individual view of the data. Such a data view can consist of a subset of the stored data or of from the stored data derived data. A university manages the data about students. Beside matriculation number, name, address, etc., other information like in which course the student is registered, if he needs to do a resit, and so on is managed as well. This extensive database is used by several people all with different needs and rights. The database administrator has a view on the whole database while other users in this example have only a restricted view on the database. The administration, for example, does not need information about names and matriculation numbers in case they want to create an anonymous statistic about the resits. In the student lists there should not be any sensitive data about the resits or similiar. However, the lecturer of a class needs the detailed information about the students in this class including resits and so on.

EXAMPLE APPLICATIONS

Current information technology solutions distinguish itselfs by having many distributed user which want to concurrently use constantly updated data. Therefore, database systems are used in different fields and there is rarely an information technology solution that gets by without. Following a couple of examples for the use of database systems are discussed. For each example the application is shortly described first and then the for this application specific database features are commented on. The respective features with their descriptions can be found in the unit Characteristics of the Database Approach which is linked from the keywords.

Management of Bank Accounts

The management of bank accounts are a demanding task which has used database systems as aid since, some time. Today, probably nobody could think about operating in the very complex world of finances without the help of database systems.

The most important characteristics of such database systems:

- *Transaction:* The successful and correct course of transactions is very important when managing bank accounts. It cannot be true that a credit is made to the wrong account or that a debit is made more than once.
- *Data Integrity:* Data integrity is very important. It needs to be clearly defined what the requirements and rules of consistency are and how these can be followed.
- *Data Persistence:* For an owner of a bank account it is reassuring to know that the persistence of the data is guaranteed. Data are not deleted arbitrarily or are lost mysteriously.

Timetable Information System

The online timetable of the SBB is an example of a web based information system founded on a database system from the bounds of public transport. Its main task is to inform the users with current and correct information about the best connections and the train operation of the SBB at any time.

The most important characteristics of such a database system:

- *Concurrent Use:* The database system of the SBB timetable can be used by different users and applications concurrently. While the information are used internally within the SBB information about the timetables and other specific information can also be used from the public via the Internet.
- *Data Integrity:* The users of the SBB timetables need current and correct information at any time. These makes great demands on the data integrity. Therefore, timetable or platform changes or any other changes need to be updated constantly in the database system.

Such a database system can get more than one call per second in record times.

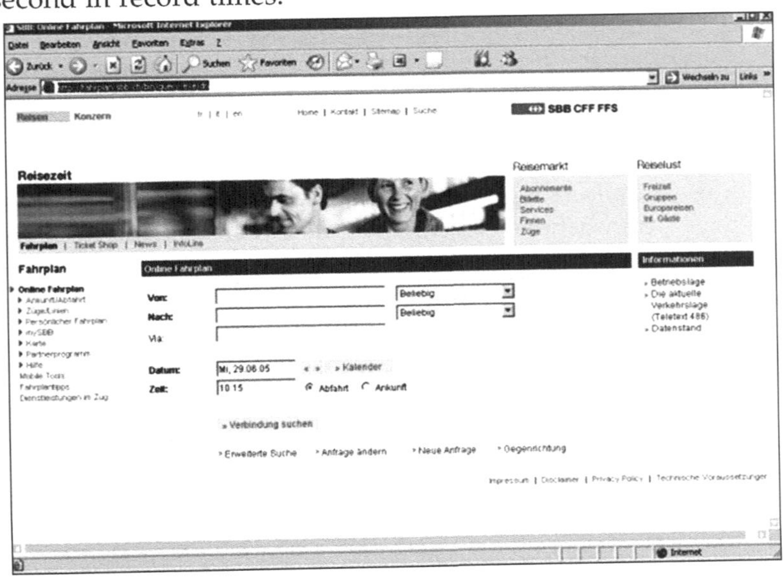

Library Catalogue

The library catalogue NEBIS is the catalogue of a network of libraries and information desks in Switzerland. With the help of NEBIS it is possible to search for specific books or publications in libraries all over Switzerland.

The most important characteristics of such a database system:

- *Structured and Described Data:* It is more than helpful to have a clearly defined structure when recording and updating several thousands of books, magazins and publications. Additionally, the description of the data allows to search selectively for specific objects. Further, a clear structure is also free of redundancy. This saves works as already a very small redundancy would lead to a multiple of work.
- *Data Views:* Depending on how detailled and specialised a search should be done a user needs more or less information from the database. Thus, for a coarse search title and author might already be sufficient. However, when looking for a specific edition of a book some more information is needed. With this in view the user can choose between different data views. Additionally, there are views for the manager of the catalogue which are not accessible be the public user.

Central Geodata Warehouse

Lately, it is getting more common in city and canton governments to manage and update spatial data of all parts of the government in one central data pool called geodata warehouse. This makes huge savings as the data is now stored redundance free and needs to be updated only once. Until now the some data needed to be stored and updated in different departements of the government. This made it enormously difficult to have current data at all places. Additionally, when doing bigger projects the data can now simply be taken out of the geodata pool and does not need to be gathered in tedious and lengthy work.

The most important characteristics of such database systems:

- *Concurrent Use:* A central geodata warehouse is a nice example of concurrent use of a database system. On the one hand different users get their data from it—the employees of the different departements. On the other hand different application software are used to access the geodata warehouse. Therefore, it is possible that the forestry departement uses GIS software A for access to the data while the surveyor departement uses GIS software B.
- *Separation of Data and Applications:* Different user with different applications get access to the data. This is only possible, if the data is separated from the applications. Would the data be connected to the application it would be much work to process the data in way that other applications could read and use it. This independence is especially import in cases where the DBMS software needs replacement. With the separation of data and applications this is possible without having to re-write all of the application software. Example: A Microsoft Word file is quite difficult to open with the Microsoft Excel software even though both applications are made by the same company.
- *Data Persistence:* The capture of geodata and other data is most often a lot of work and very expensive. Therefore, data persistence is a very important characteristic of a geodata warehouse. This way, it is possible to ensure that data is not lost and needs then be replaced costly.
- *Data Integrity:* Governmental data often give information about legal conditions like, for example, the cadaster. Therefore, these data need to be thoroughly correct and reliable. That is achieved through the definition and following of specific consistency requirements and rules.

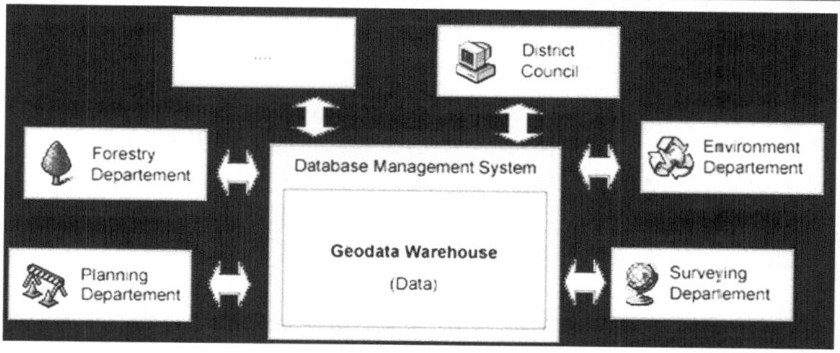

Fig. 5.1 Schematic Representation of a Geodata Warehouse and the Possible Access to it from Different Offices

ADVANTAGES AND DISADVANTAGES

Management and storage of data has changed a great deal over the years—from the file-card box, via the first digital version, to the modern database systems. The first part of this unit deals with file-based systems in comparison to data-base systems. Afterwards, the advantages and disadvantages of database systems are discussed.

Comparison DBS *vs.* File-based

Knowing about the characteristics of a database system as suggested, have a look at file-based systems. With a file-based approach each user defines and creates with a specific software the files he needs for a specific application. In comparison to the database system approach this results in some limitations. Move the mouse over the bold terms to the left and the limitations of the file-based approach in comparison to the data-base approach are explained in writing and graphic.

Using a file-based system it is possible that, for example, the administration of a school maintains information about the registration and fee payment of the students. Meanwhile the lecturers manage data about the students and their grades. Even though both user groups are interested in student data they both might have different files and different software to update and change these. Such redundancy in the definition and storage of data wastes storage space. Additionally, the work needed to update data in more than one system is multiplied by the number of systems. In case, a change of basic student data like the address might need an update in the system of the lecturer and in the system of the administration as well.

Advantages of a DBMS

Basically, all in the unit Characteristics of the Database Approach listed features can be listed as advantages here too:

- Concurrent Use
- Structured and Described Data
- Separation of Data and Applications
- Data Integrity
- Transactions
- Data Persistence
- Data Views

Additionally, there are some advantages which were not yet explicitely mentioned. Use the blue buttons to navigate.

Disadvantages of a DBMS

Beside the numerous advantages of a database system the disadvantages should not be kept secret.

DATABASE SYSTEMS
CONCEPTS AND ARCHITECTURES

Knowing about the advantages of database supported data management and the huge possibilities of applying database systems this lesson will explain the basic concepts and typical architectures of database systems. Firstly, it is discussed how a conceptual scheme can be transfered into a database environment and which typical database models can be used for this task.

Afterwards, the generic database architecture is explained which should allow understanding the important aspects of the co-operation between the different schemes and the interfaces for the communication with a database management system.

DATABASE MODELS, SCHEMES AND INSTANCES

With the help of databases facts and processes from the real world should be described and stored in digital form. The abstraction from the real world to the digital format is done with the help of models, so called database models. In this unit the most often used database models are presented. Following, database schemes are introduced as a formal description of a concrete database and their database instances or their database state.

Database Models

Database systems can be based on different data models or database models respectively. A data model is a collection of concepts and rules for the description of the structure of the database. Structure of the database means the data types, the constraints and the relationships for the description or storage of data respectively.

Network Model and Hierarchical Model

The network model and the hierarchical model are the predecessors of the relational model. They build upon individual data sets and are able to express hierarchical or network like structures of the real world.

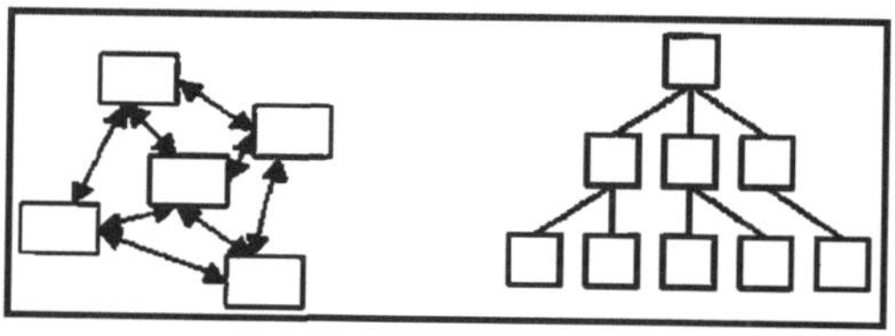

Fig. 5.2 Network Model and Hierachical Model

Relational Model

The relational model is the best know and in todays DBMS most often implemented database model. It defines a database as a collection of tables which contain all data. This module deals predominantly with the relational database model and the database systems based on it.

Table. 5.1 Relational Database Model

P-ID	Name	Prename	City	City-ID	Area	Type	...
1	Muller	Hans	Oberdort	5689	45869	Town	...
2	Meier	Jakob	Hinterwil	4758	23864	Village	...
3	Keiser	Joset	Unterdort	2145	86541	City	...
...	...	...	...	...	...	...	...

Object-oriented Model

Object-oriented models define a database as a collection of objects with features and methods. A detailed discussion of object-oriented databases follows in a advanced module.

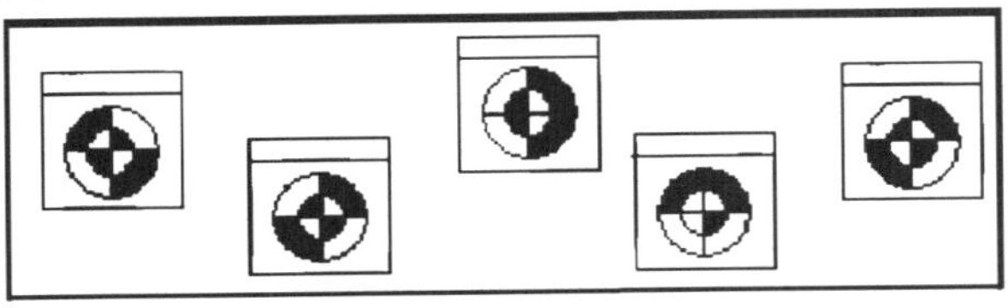

Fig. 5.3 Schematic Representation of an Object-oriented Database Model

Object-relational Model

Object-oriented models are very powerful but also quite complex. With the relatively new object-relational database model is the wide spread and simple relational database model extended by some basic object-oriented concepts. These allows to work with the widely know relational database model but also have some advantages of the object-oriented model without its complexity.

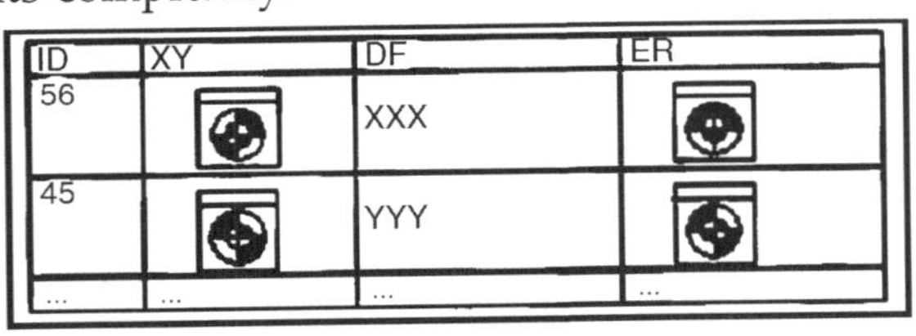

Fig. 5.4 Schematic Represenation of the Object-relational Database Model

Database Schemes and Database Instances

Independent from the database model it is important to differentiate between the description of the database and the database itself. The description of the database is called database scheme or also metadata. The database scheme is defined during the database design process and changes very rarely afterwards. The actual content of the database, the data, changes often over the years. A database state at a specific time defined through the currently existing content and relationship and their attributes is called database instance. The following illustration shows that a database scheme could be looked at like a template or building plan for one or several database instances.

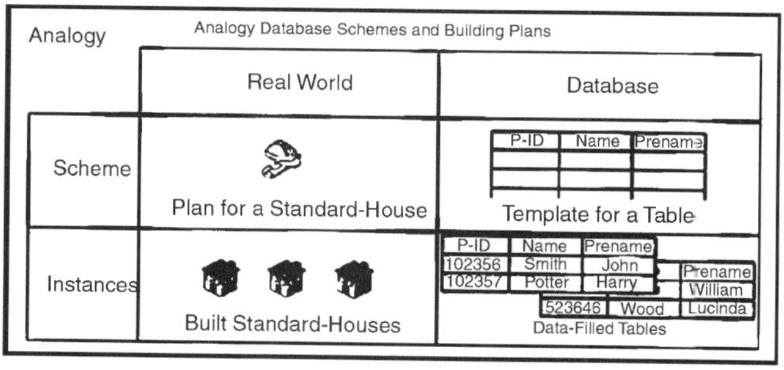

Fig. 5.5 Analogy Data-base Schemes and Building Plans

When designing a database it is differentiated between two levels of abstraction and their respective data schemes, the conceptional and the logical data scheme.

Conceptional Data Scheme

A conceptual data scheme is a system independent data description. That means that it is independent from the database or computer systems used.

Logical Data Scheme

A logical data scheme describes the data in a data definition language DDL of a specific database management system. The conceptual data scheme orients itself exclusively by the database application and therefore by the real world. It does not consider any data technical infrastructure like DBMS or computer systems which are eventually employed. Entity relationship diagrams and relations are tools for the development of a conceptual scheme. When designing a database the conceptual data scheme is derived from the logical data scheme. This derivation results in a logical data scheme for one specific application and one specific DBMS. A DB-Developmentsystem converts then the logical scheme directly into instructions for the DBMS.

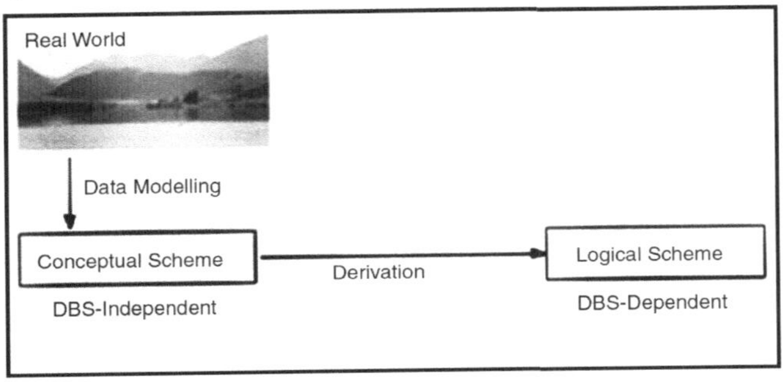

Fig. 5.6 Schematic Representation of the Different Schemes

Comparison of Spatial Models and Database Models

Knowing about data modelling the concepts and numerical models for the representation of spatial phenomena should be familiar. The following comparison should make the differentiation between spatial models and database models a bit easier.

Spatial Models

Spatial models allow to model or represent respectively spatial phenomena of the real world like facts and processes. This happens firstly on a conceptual level what means that, in general, the actual implementation of these models is not considered. Spatial models are often graphic oriented models like maps or plans and can be represented digitally or analogously.

Examples fo:

- The vector model as special case of the object model.
- The raster model as special case of the tesseral spatial model.

Database Models

Database models are from the category of informatic models and are therefore exact models or implementation models respectively. Database models can be used quite often and are not restricted to spatial types of problems.

Examples for database models:

- The relational database model
- The object-relational database model

In the intermediate module data management the representation of spatial data models in database models and the representation of spatial data in geodatabase system will be discussed.

DBMS—ARCHITECTURE AND DATA INDEPENDENCE

Database management systems are complex softwares which were often developed and optimised over years. From the view of the user, however, most of them have a quite similar basic architecture. The discussion of this basic architecture shall help to understand the connection with data modelling and the introductionally to this module postulated 'data independence' of the database approach.

Three-Schemes Architecture

Knowing about the conceptual and the derived logical scheme.

External Scheme

An external data scheme describes the information about the user view of specific users and the specific methods and constraints connected with this information.

Internal Scheme

The internal data scheme describes the content of the data and the needed service functionality which is used for the operation of the DBMS. Therefore, the internal scheme describes the data from a view very close to the computer or system in general. It completes the logical scheme with data technical aspects like storage methods or help functions for more efficiency.

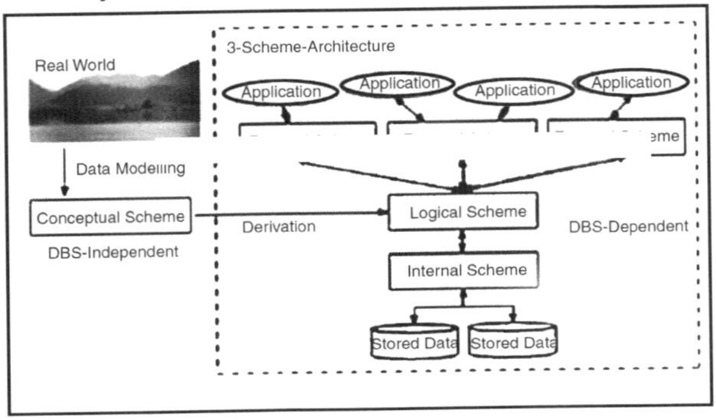

Fig. 5.7 Three-Schemes Architecture

The right hand side of the representation is also called the three-schemes architecture: internal, logical and external scheme. While the internal scheme describes the physical grouping of the data and the use of the storage space, the logical scheme describes the basic construction of the data structure. The external scheme of a specific application, generally, only highlights that part of the logical scheme which is relevant for its application.

Therefore, a database has exactly one internal and one logical scheme but may have several external schemes for several applications using this database. The aim of the three-schemes architecture is the separation of the user applications from the physical database, the stored data. Physically the data is only existent on the internal level while other forms of representation are calculated or derived respectively if need is. The DBMS has the task to realise this representation between each of these levels.

Data Independence

With knowledge about the three-schemes architecture the term data independence can be explained as followed: Each higher level of the data architecture is immune to changes of the next lower level of the architecture:

- *Physical Independence:* Therefore, the logical scheme may stay unchanged even though the storage space or type of some data is changed for reasons of optimisation or reorganisation.
- *Logical Independence:* Also the external scheme may stay unchanged for most changes of the logical scheme. This is especially desirable as in this case the application software does not need to be modified or newly translated.

DATABASE LANGUAGES AND DATABASE INTERFACES

Until now, we have got to know about data models, data descriptions and the components of a database system. In this unit is explained how 'a data models gets into a database system' and 'how the information gets to the users'.

More correctly formulated the following questions will be answered:

- How does an application interact with a database management system?
- How does a user look at a database system?
- How can a user query a database system and view the results in his/her application?

Database Languages

DDL

For describing data and data structures a suitable description tool, a Data Definition Language (DDL), is needed. With this help a data scheme can be defined and also changed later.

Typical DDL operations:

- Creation of tables and definition of attributes
- Change of tables by adding or deleting attributes
- Deletion of whole table including content

DML

Additionally a language for the descriptions of the operations with data like store, search, read, change, etc., the so-called data manipulation, is needed. Such operations can be done with a data manipulation language (DML). Within such languages keywords like insert, modify, update, delete, select, etc., are common.

Typical DML operations:

- Add data (INSERT)
- Change data (UPDATE)
- Delete data (DELETE)
- Query data (SELECT)

Often this two languages for the definition and manipulation of databases are combined in one comprehensive language.

Database Interfaces

Working Principle of a Database Interface

The application poses with the help of SQL, a query language, a query to the database system. There, the corresponding answer (result set) is prepared and also with the help of SQL given back to the application. That communication can take place interactively or embedded into another language.

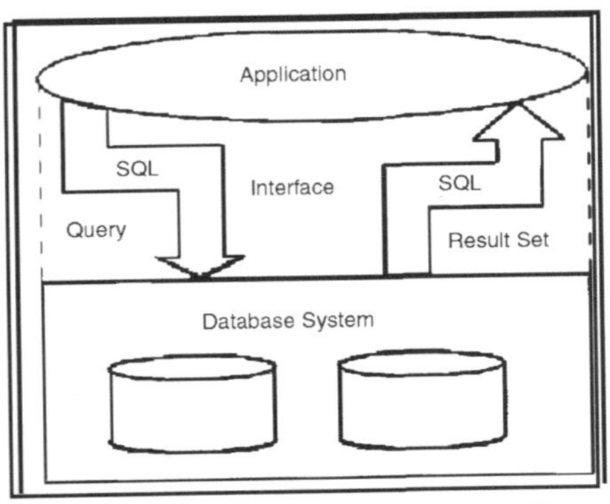

Fig. 5.8 Working Principle of a Database Interface

Type and Use of the Database Interface

Following, two important uses of a database interface like SQL are listed:

- *Interactive:* SQL can be used interactively from a terminal.
- *Embedded:* SQL can be embedded into another language which might be used to create a database application.

User Interfaces

A user interface is the view of a database interface that is seen by the user. User interfaces are often graphically or at least partly graphically constructed and offer tools which make the interaction with the database easier.

Form-based Interfaces

This interface consist of forms which are adapted to the user. He/She can fill in all of the fields and make new entries to the database or only some of the fields to query the other ones. But some operations might be restricted by the application. Form-based user interfaces are wide spread and are a very important mean of interacting with a DBMS. They are easy to use and have the advantage that the user does not need special knowledge about database languages like SQL.

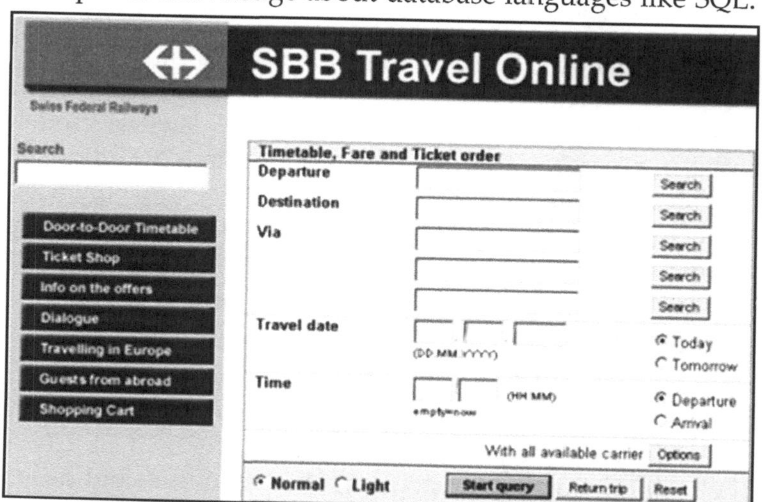

Fig. 5.9 Example of a Form-based User Interface

Text-based Interfaces

To be able to administrate the database or for other professional users there are possibilites to communicate with the DBMS directly in the query language via a input/output window. Text-based interfaces are very powerful tools and allow an comprehensive interaction with a DBMS. However, the use of those is based on active knowledge of the respective database language.

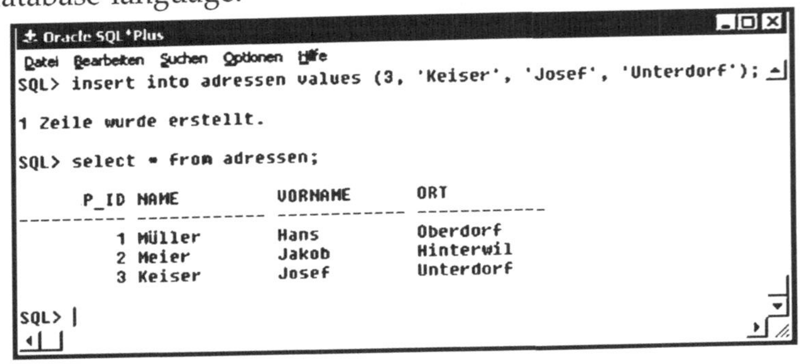

Fig. 5.10 Example of a Text-base User Interface

THE RELATIONAL DATABASE MODEL

The relational database model is used in most of today's commercial databases. It is used since, the early 80ies and was developed 1970 by E. F. Codd. The relational database model is based on a mathematical concept where relations are interpreted as tables. The focus of this stage lies in the conversion of a conceptual into a logical data scheme using an entity-relationship-schema. You will find more information about schemas in the stage about Database models, schemas and instances.

CONCEPT OF THE RELATIONAL MODEL

In contrast to the entity-relationship-model (ERM) which is a conceptual model, the relational model is a logical data model. It can be seen as lying one step or layer below the ERM. The relational model is not about abstract objects but defines how data should be represented in a specific database management system. The goal of a logical data model is to arrange the data in such a form that it is consistent, non-redundant and supports operations for data manipulation.

Data Organisation in a Relational Data Model

A logical data schema is in most cases based on a conceptual data scheme which, with the use of certain guidelines and rules, is transformed into a relational scheme. The main organisation unit in a relational data model is the relation. A relation can be represented as a table but the definition of the relation is not necessarily equal to the definition of the table and *vica versa*.

Why use the relational model?

- *Simplicity:* Data in a relational model is represented through values that are structured with only one construct: the 'relation'.
- *Classification:* The relational model is based on mathematical fundamentals: the set theory.

Definition

- *Domain:* A domain D is a set of atomic values that defines the value range of attributes.
- *Tupel:* A tuple t is a list with n values t = <d1, d2..., dn> where each value di is either an element of the domain Di or NULL. A tuple is a record in a relation.
- *Attribute:* A column of a table represents an attribute. It can also be described as a that a domain D has in a relation scheme R.
- *Relation Scheme:* A relation scheme R (A1, A2..., An) is made up of a relation name R and a list of attributes {A1, A2..., An}.
- *Relation:* A relation r is one instance of the relation scheme R(A1, A2..., An) containing a set of n-tuples r ={t1, t2..., tn}.
- *Relational Database Scheme:* A relational database scheme is a set of relation schemes S = {R1..., Rn} together with a set of integrity conditions. A relational database is a relational database scheme together with a database instance.

TRANSFORMING AN ERM TO A RELATIONAL DATABASE SCHEME

In this unit as suggested, learn the rules and methods to represent entity relationship models in relational database schemes. Each of the following mapping rules describes one of the components of the entity relationship model. To reduce an ERM into a relational scheme all 8 rules have to be worked out. Each rule has to be applied on every entity set or relationship set. Usually the correct processing sequence is: 1, 7, 8, 2, 3, 4, 5, and then 6. For every rule a definition and an example is given.

ERM Concepts

Entity Relationship Diagram

To understand the following mapping rules, you must be familiar with the concepts of the Entity Relationship Model (ERM). Using this flash example, you can refresh your memory about ERM.

Could any of the concepts be new, please consult the following book:

- Fundamentals of Database Systems, Elmasri, Ramez; Navathe, Shamakant B.

You should be familiar with the following terms: strong entity, weak entity, relationship, identifying relationship, attribute, derived attribute, multivalued attribute, composite attribute, identifier or primary key and discriminator.

Rule 1

In this first step, all strong entity sets are transformed into the relational database schema. For subclasses use rule 8.

- *Rule 1:* For each strong entity set G define a relational scheme R with the entity properties as attributes A. For multivalued attributes use rule 7. Define the primary key.
- *Rule 2:* In this step the weak entity sets are transformed into the relational database scheme. For each weak entity set S with owner G create a relational scheme R with the entity properties as

attributes A. For multivalued attributes use rule 7. Use the primary key of G as foreign key in R. Choose a discriminator that, together with the foreign key, will act as primary key for R. Note that only the combination of the foreign key together with the discriminator can act as primary key for R.

- *Rule 3:* In this step the binary relationships of the following type (1,1)(1,1), (0,1)(1,1) or (0,1)(0,1) are transformed into the relational database scheme. Search for all binary relationships B (1,1)(1,1), (0,1)(1,1) or (0,1)(0,1). Find the relational scheme S and T that are connected through relationship B. Choose one of them and insert the primary of the other relational scheme as a foreign key. Also add the properties of B as attributes into this relational scheme.
- *Rule 4:* In this step all binary relationships one to many/many to one (1,n)(1,1), (0,n) (1,1), (1,n)(0,1) or (0,n)(0,1) are transformed into the relational database scheme. Search for all regular binary relationships B of type (1,n)(1,1), (0,n)(1,1), (1,n)(0,1) and (0,n)(0,1) and for their relational schemes S and T of the corresponding entity sets. Choose the relational scheme on the '(1,1)'/'(0,1)'-side and insert there the primary key of T as a foreign key. Also add the properties of B as attributes into this relational scheme.
- *Rule 5:* In this step all binary relationships many to many (0,n)(0,n), (1,n) (0,n) or (1,n)(1,n) are transformed into the relational database scheme. Search for all regular binary relationships B of type many to many and the according relational schemes S and T. For each B create a new relational scheme R. The primary keys of S and T are used as foreign keys in R. Together they form the primary key of this new relational scheme R. Also add the properties of B as attributes into this relational scheme R.
- *Rule 6:* In this step all relationships of order n are transformed into the relational database scheme. This happens according to rule 5. For all n-ary relationship

types (n>2) use rule 5: Create a new relational scheme R and use the primary keys of all connected relational schemes as foreign keys. Together they form the primary key for this new relational scheme R.

- *Rule 7:* If in rule 1 multi-valued attributes are encountered, they are transformed into separate relational schemes according to this rule. Define for each multivalued attribute A a new relational scheme R′ which also contains this attribute A and the primary key of the according relational scheme R. Together they form the primary key for R′.
- *Rule 8:* If in rule 1 you find subclasses then transform them according to this rule. Define a relational scheme R for the superclass C with the attributes A(R)=(K, A1, A2.., An), where K is the primary key. For each subclass create a new relational scheme Ri with their attributes and the primary key K of superclass C as an additional attribute. The primary key of Si is also K.

Using the Eight Rules

The following flash animation allows you to practice the eight rules that you have now learned.

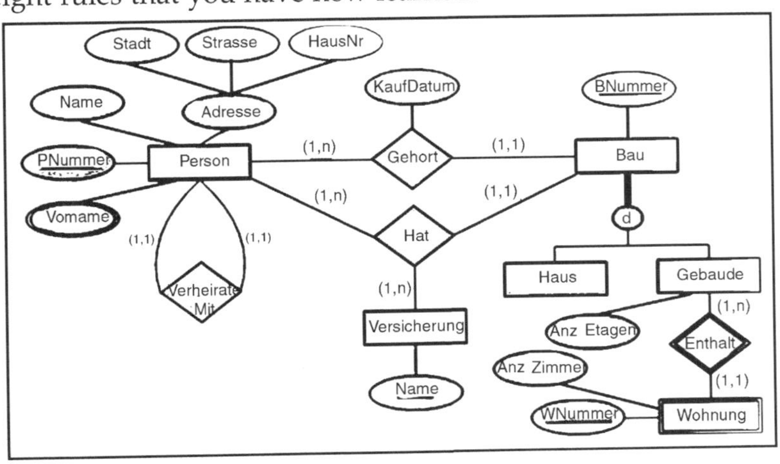

Fig. 5.11 Flash Exercise

Reducing an ERM to a Relational Scheme

Create a relational database scheme using the following conceptional data scheme (ERM-Entity Relationship Model) using the rules you here learned in this unit. Primary keys should be marked as underlined and foreign keys italic. Publish your solution as a Word-or PDF-document on the discussion board. Check out the solutions of the other students and comment them. Any problems with this exercise can also be published on the discussion board. The solutions and questions will be checked by a tutor and general feedback published.

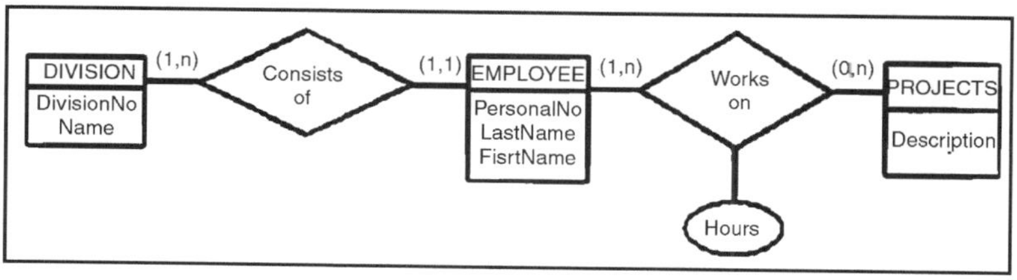

Fig. 5.12 A Conceptional Model (ERM)

DATA INTEGRITY

Integrity or consistency stands for the quality and reliability of data of a database system. A database is consistent if the data reflects the referenced objects correctly. It is inconsistent if there exist ambiguous or contradictory tuples, relations or tables in the database.

Key Integrity

Relations are defined as a unique set of tuples where no two tuples have the same combination of values for all their attributes. To be distinct, they must have some primary key that allows to reference each tuple.

Key constraints deal with this issue:

- *Candidate Key:* Each attribute or minimal combination of attributes that uniquely identifies any tuple in a relation is called a candidate key. Minimal means that removing an attribute leaves the key without the ability to uniquely identify any tuple and therefore not being a candidate key anymore.

- *Primary Key:* The primary key is one chosen key candidate that acts as the identification key for a relation. Usually this is a short attribute like a ID-number (identification key) or username. Attributes of the primary are commonly underlined.

EntityIntegrity

The entity integrity is a result of the key integrity: No primary key is allowed to be the NULL(=no value). If NULL-values would be allowed for primary keys, than two tuples could have NULL as key value and therefore could not be distinguishably anymore. The key integrity would not be respected. In SQL special routines (unique, not null) are used for key and entity integrity.

Referential Integrity

In a relationship model, in contradiction to an entity relationship model ERM, there is no way to model relationships between tuples explicitly. Therefore relationships are modelled implicitly using a primary-and foreign-key concept.

Foreign Key

An attribute in a relational scheme R1 is a foreign key if it is in relationship with a primary key from R2 and if:

- The domain (value range) of the foreign key in R1 is the same as the domain of the primary key in R2.
- The set of values of the foreign key in R1 is a subset of all primary key values in R2.

Foreign keys usually are marked dotted underlined. A relationship between two schemes is established by using the domain of the primary key in one scheme as the domain of a foreign key in a second scheme (with the according attributes). Referential integrity constraints ensure that any foreign key value is always pointing on a primary key of an existing tuple. References to non-existing primary keys are not allowed. In such a case the foreign key value must be set to NULL. The relational scheme containing the foreign key is called the referencing scheme, the scheme with the primary key is called the referenced scheme.A foreign key can also point to its own scheme. In the early days of computer databases, only workstations were able to check for referential integrity. Today most PC-based database systems are able to check for referential integrity.

Employee

ID	LastName	Division
1	Mueller	A1
2	Meier	A3
3	Tobler	A3

Division

Div No	Professor
A1	Informatiec
A2	Marketing
A3	Finance

Fig. 5.13 Example Referential Integrity

In the table Division we have Div_No as a primary key. In the second table Employee this key is used as a foreign key to associate each member to one department. For each department number in the table Employee there exists a department in the table Division. These tables are integer. If we would insert a tuple '4, Weber, A5' into table Employee then a database system should refuse this operation because in table Division there exists no value A5 and therefore there is no integrity.

Integrity Endangering Operations

There are three types of operation that could potentially endanger referential integrity:

- Inserting of a new tuple;
- Deleting an existing tuple; and
- Updating attribute values of existing tuples.

Of course with all these operations there has to be a check on all integrity rules. Selecting values (browsing in the database) does not change any values and is therefore no integrity endangering operation.

Inserting of a New Tuple

With this operation all three integrity rules are concerned. The following problems can occur:

- *Key Integrity:* The for this insertion used primary key value is already used in another tuple.
- *Entity Integrity:* The primary key of the new tuple is NULL.
- *Referential Integrity:* A foreign key without an associated primary key is used.

These operations must either be rejected by the database system or transformed into consistent operations according to defined rules.

Deleting an Existing Tuple

With this operation only referential integrity is concerned. If a foreign key points on a primary key that has been deleted, then the foreign key becomes invalid. The database system should react on a delete operation with one of the following solutions: Abort the operation, cascading delete (also the referenced tuple is deleted!) or set the value of the foreign key to NULL.

Updating Attribute Values of Existing Tuples

With this operation all three integrity rules are concerned. An update operation can be seen as first a delete of an existing tuple followed by a insert of a new tuple with updated values. Therefore all the rules must be applied. Problems arise only with the updating of primary or foreign keys. All other attributes can be updated without any restriction.

NORMALISATION

Normalisation is a process which we analyse and alter a database relation in order to get more concise and organized data structures. Normalised data is stable and has a natural structure.

We call a relation normalised if:

- It does not contain any redundancy
- It does not cause maintenance problems
- It is an accurate representation of the data

Relations that aren't normalised contain non-atomic attributes and therefore can contain redundant information. Detailed planning of the ERM can help creating normalised relations. The following steps will explain how existing relations can be normalised step by step.

Dependencies

In order to be able to normalise a relation according to the three normal forms, we must first understand the concept of dependency between attributes within a relation.

Functional Dependency

If A and B are attributes of relation R, B is functionally dependenton A (denoted A—> B), if each value of A in R is associated with exactly one value of B in R.

Example:

ID	Name
S1	Meier
S2	Weber

The attribute Name is functionally dependent of attribute ID (ID—> Name).

Identification key

If every attribute B of R is functionally dependent of A, than attribute A is a primary key.

Beispiel:

ID	Name	Surname
S1	Meier	Hans
S2	Weber	Ueli

Note: Attribute ID is the identification key

Full Functional Dependency

We talk about full functional dependency if attribute B is functional dependent on A, if A is a composite primary key and B is not already functional dependent on parts of A.

Besipiel:

ID	Name	IDProfessor	Grade
S1	Meier	P2	5
S2	Weber	P1	6

The attribute Grade is fully functional dependent on the attributes IDStudent and IDProfessor.

Transitive Dependency

If A determines B and B determines C then C is determined by (dependent on) A. We write A—> B and B—> C but not B—> A.

Example:

ID	Name	Konto_Nr	Bank_Code_No	Bank
L1	Meier	1234-5	836	UBS
L2	Weber	5432-1	835	CS

There is a transitive dependency between Bank_Code_No and Bank because Bank_Code_No is not the primary key of the relation.

STRUCTURED QUERY LANGUAGE (SQL)

SQL (Structured Query Language) is a query language for relational databases. The roots of SQL go back to SQUARE, a more mathematical oriented language and SEQUEL, a predecessor of SQL from the seventies. There exist different standards (ISO and ANSI) of SQL, but the most common one is SQL-92. The latest standard SQL-99 (or SQL3) even includes XML.

As suggested, give a simple overview of the most important SQL functions. SQL (Structured Query Language) is one of the main reasons for the commercial success of relational databases. The ANSI (American National Standards

Institute) and the ISO (International Standards Organisation) developed in 1986 the first SQL-version with the name SQL-86 or SQL1. In 1992 a second and more extended standard with the name of SQL-92 or SQL2 was established. The latest standard includes XML, dates from 1999 and is therefore called SQL-99 or SQL3. With the use of SQL in most commercial database systems the migration from one system to another has become easier for the user. In the ideal case, the user need not consider which system is used because query formation in SQL remains the same.

SQL CONCEPTS

SQL is a descriptive, entity-oriented query language for data manipulation with its roots in relational algebra. Today SQL is used either as a stand-alone programming language or within other languages like C, C++, Java, ADA, COBOL, FORTRAN, PL/1, PASCAL etc.

SQL actually consists of three sub languages:

- *DDL-Data Definition Language:* Used for creating databases and tables and for maintaining the structure.
- *DML-Data Manipulation Language:* Used for accessing and extracting data from a database (add, update, delete etc.
- *DCL-Data Control Language:* Used to control access to the database and therefore essential for the security system.

In most implementations of SQL functions from other programming languages (if-clauses, iterations etc.) have been added. Some SQL-versions, such as Oracle's PL/SQL, can therefore be seen as independent programming languages.

DATA DEFINITION (DDL)

In SQL the terms table, row and column are synonyms for relation, tuple and attribute. To create a new relation scheme in the database we start with the create table-command. Together with the creation we must provide the relations attributes and their domains (*e.g.* number, char or date). Additional we can define other constraints, checks and keys etc. The keyword NOT NULL tells the system that this attribute cannot be empty. Primary keys are declared using a special 'table constraint'-clause.

Table. 5.2 Code-Beispiel: Create Table

```
Create table Subscription (
   Name char (30) not null,
   CustID number (5) not null,
   SubType char (15) defult 'monthly' cheek (SubType
   in ('monthly' 'weekly')),
   SubStart date,
       constraint pk_sub primary key (Name, CustID),
       constraint fk_name foreign key (Name)
       references Magazine (Name),
       constraint fk_custid foreign key (CustID)
       references Customer (CustID));
```

This example shows how a new table is created in SQL. In the intermediate lesson we take a closer look at all the SQL statements. For the moment you don't have to understand these statements in detail.

DATA MANIPULATION (DML)

There are two sorts of data manipulation commands in SQL. The first type are only used for database queries and do not alter the tables. The second type are used for adding, updating or deleting values in a database.

DATA CONTROL (DCL)

Data control commands in SQL control access privileges and security issues of a database system or parts of it. These commands are closely related to the DBMS (Database Management System) and can therefore vary in different SQL implementations.

Some typical commands are:

- GRANT—give user access privileges to a database
- DENY—deny user access

- REVOKE withdraws access privileges given with the GRANT or taken with the DENY command.

Since, these commands depend on the actual database management system (DBMS), as suggested, not cover DCL in this module.

BASIC DATABASE QUERIES

SELECT-FROM-WHERE clause

In languages like SQL data from a certain domain (FROM) that match some conditions (WHERE) are selected and presented (SELECT). The result can be seen as a new relation.

The syntax of a basic SQL query is:

- SELECT <select-list>.
- FROM <from-list>.
- WHERE <condition>.

In this syntax the...

- <select-list> contains the names of the attributes (columns) values to be returned.
- <from-list> is the list of the relations (tables) used for the query.
- <condition> is an expression that identifies the tuples that we are looking for.

We saw the basic statements that are needed for making queries with SQL. Of course there are extensions which allow more specific or more flexible queries.

These extensions include:

- Multiple conditions (in boolean AND/OR combination).
- Complex conditions (subqueries, joins etc.).
- Pattern matching and arithmetical operators.
- Non-relational functions (sort, group, aggregate).
- Set operators (union, intersect, minus).

Multiple Conditions

In SQL it is possible to have multiple conditions and combine them with boolean operators (AND, OR). For negating a condition the NOT operator is used.

Complex Conditions

Nested Queries

Conditions are usually made of an attribute, a value and an operator that forms the condition (*e.g.* Name='John'). But the values themselves don't have to be constants, they can be the result of another sub-query. We then talk about nested queries. Using the IN-operator nested queries can be as deep as necessary.

Comparison Operators

SQL supports different comparison operators like ==,<,>,<>,<=,>=,between etc. If an operator is used to compare an attribute with a constant, we talk about restriction. If the operator is used to compare two attributes, then we talk about a join. With joins, data from different relations can be compared and combined. Of course only attributes with the same domain (value range) can be compared.

CREATING AN ELECTRONIC DATABASES SELECTION EXPERT SYSTEM

CHALLENGES AND ISSUES

When users need to find relevant information in today's computer-based information retrieval environment, they are first faced with the task of identifying the appropriate resource database(s) to search. This process has been complicated with the rapid development of information technology and the proliferation of digital information resources. At UIUC we've gone from having only a handful of single-workstation CD-ROM databases accessible to end-users in 1990 to having over 100 online journal article databases (accessible campus-wide) and over 200 CD-ROM databases available to end-users in 2000.

More than half of the growth in available resources has taken place during the last 3 years. The situation is exacerbated by constant change. Software migration, updates, product changes, vendor mergers, changes in database producer-vendor agreements, changes in database availability or cost, have all contributed to constantly changing search interfaces, database coverage, database features, and the selection of databases available at any time.

It's difficult for Library faculty and staff to keep up; it's unrealistic to expect users to keep up with such constant change. At UIUC, the highly distributed nature of the Library system (more than 40 separate public-service points distributed in more than 20 campus buildings) further complicates the problem. Most CD-ROM databases are available for searching at only one location, some at multiple libraries, and only a few are available at all library locations. This makes it all the more difficult for end users to know of the existence of all the electronic resources available system wide. Nonetheless, demand for and use of these resources is high.

In terms of number of searches performed, the combined end-user use of journal article index databases available campus-wide has exceeded total use of the online public access catalog by UIUC Library patrons for the past several years. User surveys done at UIUC confirm that these resources are highly valued. They also confirm that users are struggling to find the best resources to use for specific information needs. The result is that these resources aren't always being utilised to best advantage.

CURRENT PRACTICE

Library user observations suggest that patrons who used certain databases before have a tendency to select just those familiar databases, ignoring others which could be more appropriate for their topics. New and remote users may feel confused when professional assistance is not readily available. Informal observations by library staff indicate that many users waste hours searching irrelevant databases.

Even professional librarians with previous experience in selecting from among available electronic resources are having difficulty maintaining their expertise. This further encourages heavy use of general-interest databases, and the overlooking of other resources that might be more appropriate and relevant to the topics of interest. Many valuable specialised databases appear to be underutilised.

This conclusion has been borne out by recent transaction log analyses done at UIUC. Libraries are making concerted efforts to help point users to the best resources, but the most common practices are becoming less effective and more difficult to maintain as the diversity and sophistication of available resources continues to increase rapidly. Most libraries now provide on their web site at least some organisation of available resources.

The current UIUC Gateway provides four views of campus-wide online journal article index resources: listed alphabetically by Title; grouped by vendor; categorised under eight subject headings; and segregated according to whether they include links to article full-text. Many subject specialist librarians also generate selective lists of resources particularly useful to their area of specialisation. Users also can get help from finding aids available in print and/or over the Web and from online tutorials provided by some of units. The end result however is that users generally must pick from static lists, relying only on resource titles to make their selection of which resource to search.

THE UIUC SMART DATABASE SELECTOR PROJECT

In 1998 preliminary research was done examining alternative methods of helping users better identify the information resources most likely to assist them in their search and reviewing work being done elsewhere in this area. With funding from the UIUC Research Board and the UIUC Library's Research and Publication Committee, a project was undertaken in 1999 to create a prototype of a Web-based expert system tool that could assist users in identifying the most appropriate online or CD-ROM database to meet a particular information need.

The project objectives:

- To identify and better understand computer-assisted techniques for guiding users to the databases most suitable for their particular information needs;

- To pioneer innovative methods to improve user services given the proliferation of electronic databases and digital information within individual institutions; and
- To improve the ease of access to information by taking advantage of the Web and related protocols and technologies.

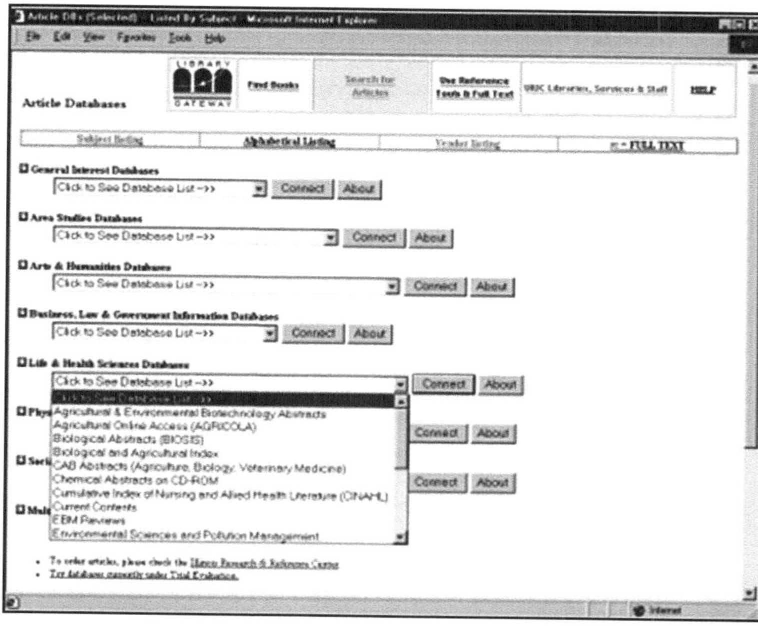

Fig. 5.14 Article Index Database Pick List Organised by Subject

A prototype system designed to assist users in selecting from among the article databases, directories, statistical and government document electronic resources presently available at UIUC has been created and is being reviewed by members of the Library faculty. Limited end-user testing and focus group evaluations also are in progress.

Using this prototype tool, users are able to select resources by any of 3 methods:

- Searching for relevant resources using free-text keywords and phrases;

- Browsing available databases by subject categories; or
- Choosing desired database by characteristics only (*e.g.*, material types indexed, chronological coverage, etc.).

Figure shows query entry screen for this tool. Several filters can be used to narrow keyword and browse selections.

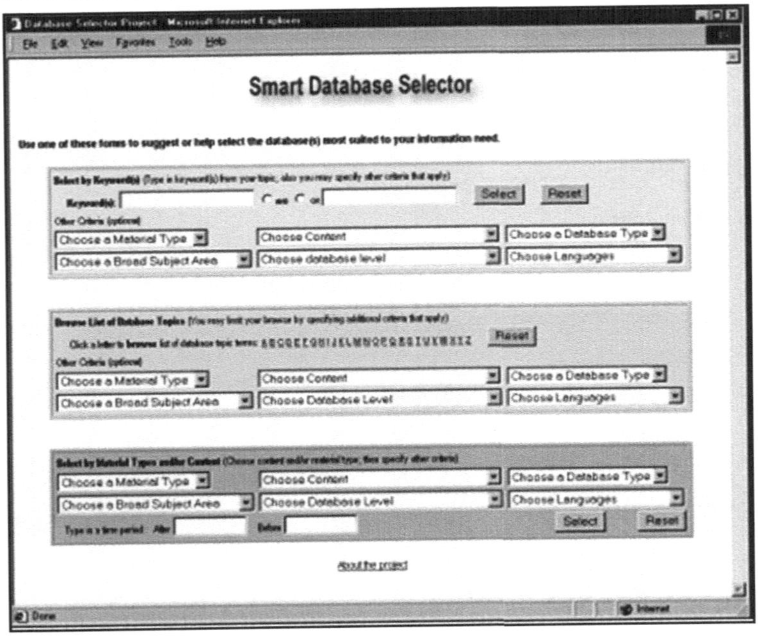

Fig. 5.15 User Interface of Expert System Database Selection Tool

The approach we've taken varies from earlier and ongoing library projects elsewhere—*e.g.*, EasyNet, DialIndex/DialogWeb, UCSD's 'Database Advisor'—in that it does not involve simultaneous, real-time searching of multiple resources, which enables inclusion of a diverse collection of Online and stand-alone electronic databases, such as CD-ROM databases and licence restricted access databases. It also differs from generic Web search engines—where the emphasis lately has been on query formulation, interface design, and results display—in that more extensive filtering is possible and automatic indexing of resources is augmented with manually assigned characteristics. The approach we've taken is to create a selection database containing rich and extensive characterisations of the available resources.

User queries and characterisation filters are then applied against that selection database to come up with a ranked list of resources of possible interest. The process is intended to mimic the process a librarian uses when selecting a database to search for a particular information need. Resource characterisations were developed using database documentation, standard reference sources, information supplied by librarians most knowledgeable about the subject area of each resource, and whenever available, the controlled vocabularies of the resources themselves. A standard form was created and terminology defined to assist in the gathering and assigning of resource characteristics.

Controlled vocabulary information was obtained using 2 techniques:

- Direct processing of the complete controlled vocabulary as supplied by the database producer; or
- By large-scale random sampling of recent database records.

The latter approach had the advantages of being more highly automated and of returning a selection of controlled vocabulary terms biased towards the most heavily used terms. At this time, one advantage of the approach taken is that all the data used to assist in resource selection resides on local systems.

The process is not dependent on primary data sources being always available and therefore tends to scale better in the current environment (the prototype selection database contains information for about 150 resources with controlled vocabulary data for more than half that number). The biggest drawback of this approach is that the thorough characterisation of the resources takes considerable manual labour, both initially when a resource is first added to the selection database and then (to a lesser extent) on an ongoing basis to maintain resource entries.

RESOURCE SELECTION ALGORITHM

The process of actually identifying relevant resources based on the characterisation information stored in the selection database was designed to mimic the way sophisticated end-users and librarians accomplish this task. The search patterns of users seeking information were analysed and the strategies which reference librarians use to respond to users' information requests were studied. A database selection algorithm, which attempts to replicate the professional librarians' database selection strategy and from the discussions and inputs of several UIUC librarians consulted.

Resource Selection Algorithm:

- Topic/subject category term +/ broad subject +/ format +/ content +/ level +/ database type => database.

This Formula States: Topic keywords or specific subject terms combined with broad subject area, format of information sought, type of content sought, level of information need, and/or database type will determine the databases relevant to the topic.

The following process demonstrates how a librarian's decision-making model is translated to an algorithm for database selection:

- *Topic Keywords:* A user who needs to search electronic databases should have a topic or specific subject to research. He/she can often express that topic in appropriate natural language. For example, a user would express his or her topic: "The position of women and the attitudes towards women in Hispanic American community.' Nouns and noun phrases (*e.g.*, 'women' and 'Hispanic American community') can then be extracted and used to help identify appropriate information resources that should be consulted.
- *Subject Category Terms:* If the user has difficulty expressing a topic in natural language terms, a browse list of detailed subject terms assigned to resources by knowledgeable librarians is an appropriate alternative.

- *Broad Subject:* When a librarian is approached for assistance, the librarian usually first tries to determine the broad subject area of interest to the user. For example, the topic 'cloning' can have many aspects–technical/medical (how to clone), social effects of cloning, legal aspects of cloning, etc.
- *Format:* The librarian then might determine what format(s) the patron is interested in–*e.g.*, newspaper articles, magazine articles, journal articles, conference proceedings, government documents, patents, dissertations, trade publication, etc.
- *Contents:* The librarian might also try to find out what type of materials are of most interest to the patron–*e.g.*, biographical information, current events, historical information, statistical information, etc.
- *Level:* Often the librarian also will try to characterise the research level of the patron's interest. Is the patron wanting to do a brief paper for Freshman rhetoric, a senior class design project, initial research for a thesis, research for a possible article publication or conference presentation, etc.
- *Database Type:* Based on the information obtained from the reference interview and knowledge of what is available in the library, the librarian may also make an assessment as to which type of databases is most suitable, *e.g.*, bibliographic, full-text, directory, or statistical.
- *Database:* Combining all or some subset of the filters and search criteria described in the proceeding steps, the librarian then will be able to point the patron to the resources most likely to help meet the information need.

BUILDING THE PROTOTYPE SYSTEM

Having defined the approach to be used, gathered the characterisation data required, and developed a model of the selection decision process, what remained was to construct a prototype version of the system. An obvious requirement was that the system needed to be Web-based. A simple, 3-tier Web application architecture was defined and is depicted in figure. Hardware used was a dual-Pentium II server. Microsoft Internet Information Server and SQL Server were selected for the application backend. Where feasible complete controlled vocabularies were obtained in ASCII format from the database producers. Any pre-processing of these files was done using customised VBScript modules.

The files were then uploaded into SQL tables. In some cases where digital versions of controlled vocabularies were not readily available, we were able to capture controlled vocabulary terms directly from database records. Typically 10 to 20 per cent of the records for the most recent complete calendar year available were sampled, and controlled vocabulary terms were harvested. This process was accomplished using a VBScript module that generated the appropriate Z39.50 protocol queries, processed the results returned, and then loaded the terms captured into SQL tables. For a few of the resources that lack formal controlled vocabularies (*e.g.*, Current Contents) a similar process was used to sample other fields (*e.g.*, author-assigned keywords).

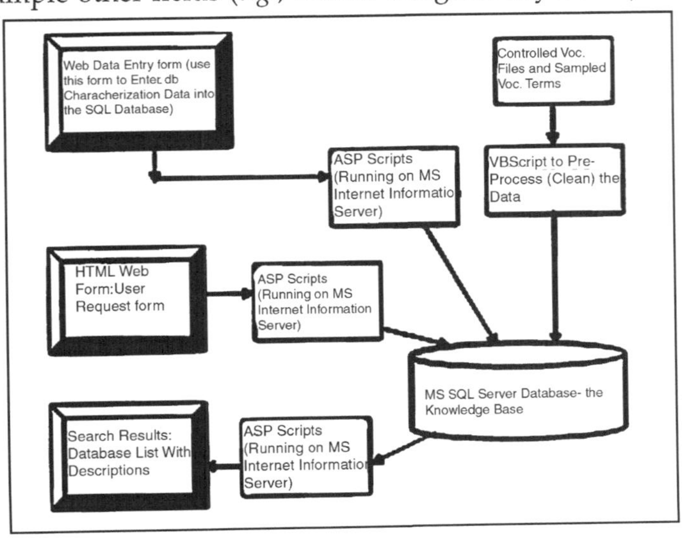

Fig. 5.16 The Architecture (Components) of the Prototype System

Web data entry form (use this form to enter db characterisation data into the SQL database) ASP scripts (running on MS Internet Information Server) HTML Web Form: User request form ASP scripts (running on MS Internet Information Server) Search results: Database list with descriptions ASP scripts (running on MS Internet Information Server) Controlled voc. files and sampled voc. Terms VBScript to preprocess (clean) the Data MS SQL Server database—the knowledge base.

The selector database was designed as a multi-table, relational database. A master record was generated for each resource and was stored in the primary table. Characterisation data used for basic filtering were stored in discrete tables with linking or pivot tables used to link such characteristics to each master record. Assigned subject category terms and controlled vocabulary terms were stored in separate tables, and Microsoft SQL 7 full-text catalogs of the fields in these tables were made. These full-text catalogs are essentially indexes automatically created by the database application by analysing the terms in the tables. Noun phrases are extracted from the terms and indexed. Stopwords are discarded. The indexes are optimised for efficient keyword and phrase searching. This approach obviated the need to manually build our own special keyword indexes or rotated term indexes from the controlled vocabulary and subject category data. The current controlled vocabulary full-text catalog was built after analysis of 2.4 million different terms consisting of 690,000 unique words. Search performance using this built-in feature of Microsoft SQL 7 in this way has been quite good. The SQL query structure used is moderately complex.

A crude ranking of databases satisfying the query criteria is done using the frequency of term matches as the figure of merit. This tends to under rank databases for which there are no controlled vocabulary entries. Further investigation of how to minimise any bias against databases for which controlled vocabulary can't be obtained remains to be done.

REMAINING ISSUES

The work done in designing and creating this prototype tool indicates that the approach has promise. There remains a great deal of evaluation work to be done to better quantify that promise, and there remain a number of issues to resolve before the prototype could be upgraded to a more production-ready utility.

In terms of evaluation, it's still not clear how useful librarian-assigned terms and classification schemes, even in combination with database controlled vocabulary, really are in resolving end-user queries. Whether this approach might offer better or comparable recall and precision to schemes that simultaneously search multiple databases remains to be seen. By soliciting user feedback and monitoring how users make use of the prototype tool, we hope to shed further light on this issue. There also remain major cost and production implementation issues. Based on our experience the initial investment to properly characterise resources is high. However, this task could be eased and better distributed by having the library's subject specialists more involved in the database characterisation process.

It's not yet clear whether the cost to maintain this information is also high. That will depend on how rapidly major and fundamental changes are made to individual databases. Re-sampling of database controlled vocabulary could be largely automated to keep up with changes in controlled vocabulary and the use of that controlled vocabulary. Frequent changes in database scope, format, etc., would be more costly to keep up with, but currently such changes are less common.

Finally, there would need to be some measure of cooperation on the part of database producers. Producers have legitimate intellectual property claims with regard to controlled vocabulary and also may have concerns about how their databases are otherwise characterised in systems such as the one investigated. Reluctance to provide information about their databases, or severe constraints on how such information may be used would inhibit development of this kind of system. Better consistency in the information provided by the various database producers about the resources they make available would facilitate development of this kind of system.

THE IP PROTECTION OF ELECTRONIC DATABASES

Electronic databases are collections of recorded data or information in an electronic or digital form. Databases form the core of information technology. Tremendous resources are often invested to assemble large quantities of information into databases. Still, the resulting products are vulnerable to piracy. Technological innovation has rendered databases vulnerable to unauthorised access, reproduction, adaptation and publication. The possibilities for the creation of recompiled and derived products are beyond the imagination, let alone the knowledge, of the original owner. It has been noted that, from an economic point of view, all electronic databases have two characteristics in common—'they are costly to produce, but they are easy to reproduce or copy'.

COPYRIGHT PROTECTION OF DATABASES

Traditional principles of copyright law require a measure of originality in the selection or arrangement of data in a compilation, before it will attract copyright protection. Article 2(5) of the Berne Convention for the Protection of Literary and Artistic Works grants copyright protection to collections of literary or artistic works (such as encyclopaedias and anthologies) which, because of the selection and arrangement of their contents, constitute intellectual creations.

This protection arises without prejudice to the copyright in each of the works forming part of such collections. Bare facts cannot be protected by copyright, but compilations of facts are within the subject matter of copyright protection if these compilations constitute original works of authorship. Copyright protection has frequently been extended to compilations of non-copyright material because of the labour and skill involved in selecting and arranging the material.

For example, protection has been granted to compilations such as a street directory; a list of stock-exchange prices; an alphabetical list of railway stations in a railway guide; a trade catalogue; a racing information service; chronological fixture lists of football clubs; a directory of telefax users; and a catalogue and price list. Traditional copyright principles require a measure of originality or creativity in the selection or arrangement of data in a compilation, or other indications of creative authorship, for the compilation to attract copyright. The requirement of originality for copyright protection of compilations is interpreted differently in various legal systems.

The United Kingdom and Commonwealth courts have favoured the 'sweat-of-the-brow' approach to database protection. If an author has expended labour and skill in creating the work, it will enjoy copyright protection, notwithstanding the bland nature of the work. Under traditional German copyright principles, most factual databases do not qualify for copyright protection unless their 'selection, accumulation and organisation' has been the subject of expertise beyond that of the average programmer. In terms of French copyright law, which requires original works to reveal something of the author's own personality, and Dutch Copyright law, most compilations will not enjoy copyright protection

THE LEGAL PROTECTION OF DATABASES IN THE EU

The European Union adopted a novel approach in the Council Directive on the Legal Protection of Databases after nearly eight years of deliberation. The Directive provides a two-tier form of protection. It strives to create a harmonised level of copyright protection for 'original' databases. A novel 'sui generis' right to protect investments in databases was also introduced. Both rights differ in terms of requirements for protection, duration of rights, scope of protection, the exceptions or limitations that apply and the determination of the right holders (both natural and legal).

The Database Directive extends copyright protection to databases that constitute 'the author's own intellectual creation'—databases which evidence some measure of 'originality' or 'creativity' on the part of the author. Article 5 states that compilations of data or other material, in any form, which by reason of the selection or arrangement of their contents constitute intellectual creations, are protected as such.

Article 5 adopts the approach of the American Supreme Court's decision in Feist Publications Inc *vs.* Rural Telephone Services Co in which it was held that only the selection or arrangement of a compilation of facts, and not the facts themselves, can be protected under copyright. The Database Directive rejected the traditional approach of the United Kingdom and Ireland and raised the threshold for copyright protection.

The approach chosen in the Directive was to harmonise the threshold of 'originality'. Those 'non-original' databases that did not meet the threshold would be protected by a newly created right. A high standard for originality, akin to that of droit d'auteur countries were adopted. This new standard of originality had the effect of protecting fewer databases by copyright (which was now limited to so-called 'original' databases). Those databases that fell below the originality bar, but which were created through substantial investment attained a 'sui generis' form of protection. This database right prevents the extraction and reutilisation of the whole or a substantial part of the contents of a non-original database. While 'original' databases require an element of 'intellectual creation', 'non-original' databases are protected as long as there has been "qualitatively or quantitatively a substantial investment in either the obtaining, verification or presentation of the contents' of a database.

The 'sui generis' right is a Community creation with no precedent in any international convention and no other jurisdiction has adopted the sui generis right. The distinction between 'original' and 'non-original' databases is alos unique to the European Union. In essence, the Directive sought to create a legal framework that would establish the ground rules for the protection of a wide variety of databases in the information age.

It did so by giving a high level of copyright protection to certain databases ('original' databases) and a new form of 'sui generis' protection to those databases which were not 'original' in the sense of the author's own intellectual creation ('non-original' databases). The effect of the Database Directive has recently been evaluated. All 25 Member States have transposed the Directive into national law. National jurisprudence evidences the adoption of a wide notion of the term 'database', embracing listings of telephone subscribers; compilations of case law and legislation; web sites containing lists of classified advertisements; catalogues of various information and lists of headings of newspaper articles under its ambit. The European Court of Justice (ECJ) has also embraced a broad interpretation of the definition of 'database' in the Directive.

CASE LAW IN THE EU

Substantial Investment

The sui generis provisions of the Database Directive protect the contents of any non-copyrightable database that is the product of substantial investment in obtaining, verifying, or presenting the database's contents. There are no specific standards for determining the substantiality of an investment. The test is quantitative as well as qualitative in nature. The investment may concern the obtaining, verification, or presentation of the content. Not every compilation of information will be considered a 'database' for the purpose of the sui generis right.

To qualify for protection, a database must be 'a collection of independent works, data or other materials arranged in a systematic or methodical way and individually accessible by electronic or other means'. The precise meaning of the term 'substantial investment' as contained in Article 7 of the Directive has become the focal point of the textual ambiguities of the 'sui generis' right. On the one hand, the cost of collecting and maintaining up-to-date information concerning several thousands of real estate properties was held to be a 'substantial investment' by a district court of The Hague.

On the other hand, the district court of Rotterdam regarded newspaper headlines as a mere 'spin-off' of newspaper publishing and the court therefore held that it did not reflect a 'substantial investment'. 'Spin-off' databases are databases that are by-products of a main or principal activity.

Where the database is a single source database it is normally regarded as a spin-off database. In certain Member States, notably the Netherlands, the 'spin-off' theory forms a bar against 'sui generis' protection for 'spin-off' databases. 'Deep-linking' through search engines are another source of divergent case-law.

A deep link is a special for of linking which enables the user to access content on an internal page of a web site, bypassing the home page of the web site. In some cases, the heading, the Internet address (URL) and a brief summary of a press article have been held not to constitute a substantial part of a database and the hyper linking of headings of press articles has been held not to infringe the owner's 'sui generis' right. However, in most cases the systematic bypassing of the homepage of the database maker (including banner advertisements) was found to be an infringement of the database maker's 'sui generis' right. A Danish court in Danish Newspaper Organisation *vs.* Newsbooster held so-called 'deep linking' is a breach of copyright. The case was brought by the Danish Newspaper Organisation (DNO) against the Newsbooster service, which linked to articles on 28 of the plaintiff's news web sites without going through their home pages.

The court held that the newspaper articles were copyrightable works. The court held as follows: 'The text collections of headlines and articles, which make up some Internet media, are thus found to constitute databases enjoying copyright protection pursuant to section 71 of the Danish Copyright Act. Under section 71(1) of the Act, the makers of the databases, *i.e.* the Principals, have the exclusive right protected by the said provision." On liability for linking, the court held that by means of its search engine, Newsbooster offers its users regular relevant headlines with deep links to articles on Newsbooster's web site or in Newsbooster's electronic newsletters.

These links need to be supplemented and updated on a regular basis and consequently, Newsbooster' s search engine needs to crawl the web sites of the Internet media frequently for the purpose of registering headlines and establishing deep links in accordance with the search criteria defined by the users. As a result, Newsbooster repeatedly and systematically reproduces and publishes the Principals' headlines and articles. Newsbooster has a commercial interest in this business and this activity is in conflict with section 71(2) of the Danish Copyright Act.

The court ruled that Newsbooster is prohibited from offering a search service with deep links from the web sites newsbooster.dk and newsbooster.com directly to the plaintiffs' news articles; reproducing and publishing headlines from the Internet versions of newspaper articles; distributing electronic newsletters with deep links directly to the newspaper articles; and reproducing and distributing headlines from the newspapers. A similar ruling was made in Copiepresse *vs.* Google Inc. Four cases concerning single-source databases of sports information in the areas of football and horseracing have been referred to the ECJ. The cases were referred from national courts in Greece, Finland, Sweden and the United Kingdom. The ECJ gave its judgements in these cases on 9 November 2004.

With respect to the extensive lists of runners and riders drawn up by the British Horseracing Board (the 'BHB') in its function as the governing body for the British horseracing industry, the ECJ simply stated that:

- "The resources used to draw up a list of horses in a race and to carry out checks in that connection do not constitute investment in the obtaining and verification of the contents of the database in which that list appears".

Obtaining or Creating Data for Database

The ECJ thus distinguishes between the resources used in the 'creation' of materials that make up the contents of a database and the obtaining of such data in order to assemble the contents of a database. Only the latter activity is protected under the 'sui generis' right. This leaves little protection for bodies like the BHB, which 'create' the data that makes up the contents of their database. Arguably, other industries like the publishers of directories, listings or maps, remain protected as long as they do not 'create' their own data but obtain these data from others. The ECJ distinction between 'creation' and obtaining of data means that sports bodies such as the BHB cannot claim that they obtained the data within the meaning of the Directive.

Therefore, such bodies cannot license their own data to third parties. While going against the Commission's original intention of protecting 'non-original' databases in a wide sense, the judgements have the merit of pointing to the serious difficulties raised by attempting to harmonise national laws by recourse to untested and ambiguous legal concepts ('qualitatively or quantitatively substantial investments in either the obtaining, verification or presentation of contents"). The ECJ's judgement would probably apply to the databases created by broadcasting organisations for the purposes of scheduling programmes: they would not be able to assert a 'sui generis' right in the contents of such databases. In addition, the European Court ruled that on-line betting activities on football matches and horse races carried out by betting companies such as Svenska Spel or William Hill was not infringing in nature.

The Court noted that such use did not affect the whole or a substantial part of the contents of the plaintiffs' databases, and they therefore did not prejudice the substantial investment of the latter in the creation of their databases. In British Horse Racing Board *vs.* William Hill the British Court dismissed the BHB's arguments aimed at showing that its database was protectable by the 'sui generis' right under Article 7(1) of the Directive. The court held that the scope of the 'sui generis" protection does not include the 'creation' of the underlying data. A soccer fixture list would usually not be protected under the 'sui generis' right.

THE POSITION OBTAINING IN SOUTH AFRICA

In terms of section 1(1) of the Copyright Act the definition of a literary work includes tables and compilations, including tables and compilations of data stored or embodied in a computer or a medium used in conjunction with a computer. This clearly includes electronic databases. The South African legislature has thus opted for the protection of electronic databases as a form of compilation, which is a species of literary work. Dean submits that under South African law an electronic database, like any other work, should be 'original'. No higher standard or level of creativity is required.

In US law, a minimal degree of creativity or so-called 'creative spark' is required to satisfy the originality requirement. In South Africa, on the other hand, creativity is not required to make a work original–the so-called 'sweat of the brow' is sufficient. The requirement of originality is satisfied solely by the fact that the contents of a particular compilation must have been independently collected through the author's own skills or labour, and not copied from another. In Haupt t/a Softcopy *vs.* Brewers Marketing Intelligence (Pty) Lt d (supra) Streicher JA confirmed that, as our present Copyright Act originated from UK law, creativity is not a requirement for copyright in SA law.

The court then confirmed the test for originality in SA copyright law to be as follows: 'Save where specifically provided otherwise, a work is considered to be original if it has not been copied from an existing source and if its production required a substantial (or not trivial) degree of skill, judgement or labour." The 'sweat of the brow' doctrine is still firmly entrenched in South African copyright law. Electronic databases were protected by copyright prior to the 1997 Amendment Act, as the material embodiment requirement could be met by digital embodiment. The South African database owner is in an advantageous position: the originality requirement is set so low that both original and non-original databases qualify for protection.

The Database Directive has not been an outstanding success and the repeal of the sui generis database right has even been proposed. International instruments are not likely to follow. Stone and Kernick note that a comprehensive database, which contains the entire universe of relevant data, may be commercially useful, but is not copyrightable, as 'selection' requires the exercise of creative judgement in culling facts, and not using the relevant universe. In essence, this amounts to the protection of means to access information. Policy considerations underlying the regulation of access to information and access to knowledge should be heeded.

It can never been seriously proposed that information itself should be protected (except by the law regarding trade secrets). Information technology has become an indispensable development tool, and a crucial means of information and knowledge exchange. Electronic databases are the tools that provide information about information; they are regarded as the new building blocks of knowledge. Their importance cannot be too heavily underscored as they form the core of information technology and all information systems. The copyright protection of such comprehensive databases remains problematic.

This may be especially problematic for digital databases such as those accessed through the Internet, since, their very appeal is their all inclusiveness. Copyright law has emerged as one of the most forceful means of regulating the flow of ideas and knowledge-based products. 'Sui generis' protection comes close to protecting data as property. There is a long-standing principle that copyright should not be extended to cover basic information or 'raw' data.

However, as evidenced by the ECJ's differentiation between the 'creation' of data and its obtaining demonstrate, the 'sui generis' right comes precariously close to protecting basic information. South Africa, as developing country, should devise its own strategies to cope with the proliferation of protectionism within the context of the widening digital divide.

EVALUATION OF THE VALUE OF THE DATABASE RIGHT

Introduced to stimulate the production of databases in Europe, the 'sui generis' protection has had no proven impact on the production of databases. Nevertheless, as the figures discussed demonstrate, there has been a considerable growth in database production in the US, whereas, in the EU, the introduction of 'sui generis' protection appears to have had the opposite effect. With respect to 'non-original' databases, the assumption that more and more layers of IP protection means more innovation and growth appears not to hold up.

6

Operation and Development

SORTING SEARCH RESULTS OF LITERATURE DIGITAL LIBRARIES

An OLDL (Online Literature Digital Library) is a library in which collections, *i.e.*, publications from one or more domains of study, are stored in digital formats and accessible by users through the Internet.

Examples of well-known OLDLs are:

- IEEE Xplore
- CiteSeer
- Google Scholar
- PubMed

Digital libraries are rapidly growing in popularity. For instance, ScienceDirect, the world's leading scientific, technical and medical information resource celebrated its billionth article download in November'06 since, launched in 1999. Besides usage, digital libraries are also rapidly growing in terms of size and diversity of topics.

For instance:

- In Computer Science, ACM Digital Library has close to one million full-text publications collected over 50 years, to search and download.
- In Electrical Engineering and Computer Science, IEEE Xplore, another OLDL, provides users with on-line access to more than 1,700 selected conferences proceedings.

These high growth rates introduced several challenges facing the information access capability of OLDLs. Next we list few challenges that probably guides future research related to LDLs.

CHALLENGE 1: LARGE SIZES AND TOPIC DIVERSITY OF SEARCH OUTPUT RESULTS

Search outputs of OLDLs tend to suffer from the 'topic diffusion' problem, where commonly, keyword-based searches produce a large number of publications over a large number of topics, where not all topics are of interest to the user. One way to solve this problem is to assign scores to search results. Assigning scores to publications helps OLDLs to present the most important relevant publications to the user first, Citation-based publication score measures are commonly used for ranking publications. At the present time, OLDLs lack effective and accurate publication ranking.

CHALLENGE 2: LACK OF EFFECTIVE SCORING FUNCTIONS FOR PUBLICATIONS

At the present time, OLDLs lack effective and accurate publication rankings. Providing accurate publication scores can help users in reducing the time spent in searching OLDLs, and thus enhances the scalability of OLDL usage as users can quickly identify important relevant publications to their topic of interest.

CHALLENGE 3: LACK OF EFFECTIVE SCORING FUNCTIONS FOR SEARCH OUTPUTS

In the field of literature digital libraries, citation analysis is employed to order digital library search outputs. Examples of citation-based measures are citation-count and PageRank. However, as noticed by, citation-based measures compute popularity of publications based on the 'current' state of a citation graph that continuously changes and evolves.

Thus PageRank is effective in capturing the popularity of publications based on the current citation-graph inhand. We show that PageRank may assign inaccurate popularity scores for both old and recent publications. And thus PageRank cannot be used to rank OLDL search outputs. We therefore need effective techniques to order search results based on their importance and relevance to users' interests.

EVALUATING PUBLICATION SCORING FUNCTIONS IN DIGITAL LIBRARIES

This section deals with the issues of defining score functions for publications in digital libraries, and evaluating how good they are.

Presently, digital libraries do not assign scores to publications, even though they are potentially useful for:

- Providing comparative assessment, or 'importance', of papers; and
- Anking papers returned in search outputs.

Using social networks or bibliometrics, one can define a number of publication score functions. Existing citation-based publication score functions are all based on the notion of prestige in social networks and bibliometry. The well-known PageRank algorithm determines the importance of a publication by the number and importances of publications with links to it. The Hyperlink Induced Topic Search (HITS) algorithm is similar to the PageRank algorithm in that HITS involves computing two scores for each publication; hub and authority scores. Authorities represent high-prestige publications, whereas hubs are publications that have links to authorities.

Other citation-based score functions can be derived as follows:

- Use normalised citation count as the basis for a score function.
- Revise the score of a paper using the score of its publication venue.
- Add weights to citations, *e.g.*, citations by an 'important' author's work are more significant.
- Revise the score of a paper using temporal distributions of citations; *e.g.*, citations in the last 10 years are more significant than earlier citations.
- Revise a paper score using the score of its citation venue; that is, capture the notion of a hub or an authority, *e.g.*, survey journal represents a hub, whereas a research paper represents an authority.
- Revise a paper score by the score of its author.

Citation-based Publication Score Functions

PageRank

Importance of papers that cite a particular paper determines its importance. PageRank and HITS were designed based on this assumption. PageRank scores is computed recursively using the formula

$$P_{i+1} = (1-d)M^T P_i + E$$

Where *Pi* and *Pi+1* are the current and next iteration PageRank vectors respectively. *M* is a matrix derived from the citation matrix *C* by normalising all row-sums in *C* to *1*. *C*, in turn, is the adjacency matrix of the graph *G* formed as follows; the papers represent the graph nodes, and the citation relationships between these papers represent the edges. *C* is of size *NxN*, where *N* is the total number of papers in the system. Finally, *d* and *(1-d)* are the future citation probability. Given that an author *A* who is writing a new paper and already cited paper *u* which in turn cites paper *v*, and let *w* be a paper in AnthP selected randomly. The parameter *d* represents the probability that A will cite *w*, and *(1-d)* is the probability that *A* will cite *v*. To guarantee the algorithm convergence, it is assumed to have a hidden link between each pair of the graph nodes. This link is represented by the user-defined parameter *E*. A variation of *E* is simply *E1=d*. Another variation of E that is used in is,

$$E_2 = d / N[1_N]P_i.$$

Hubs and Authorities

Authority score of paper *P* is computed by summing up the hub scores of the papers citing *P*. Hub score of *P* is computed by summing up the authority scores of the papers that *P* cites. Computation is recursive until results converge after a number of iterations. One difference between HITS and PageRank is that the first one works on papers in the result set of a query, while the latter considers all the papers independent of the query.

Citation Count

A paper, normally, does not cite another paper unless the cited paper is relevant. And, large number of citations to a paper gives an indication that the paper is important. Based on this fact, one can use citation count as a measure for paper importance. For a given paper *P*, let CitationCount (*P*) be the number of times paper *P* is cited by other papers. Using the number of citations, paper *P* is as important as those papers that have the same number of citations and more important than those papers that have fewer citations. As suggested, refer to this paper ranking measure as PCitation_Count.

Evaluating Publication Score Functions

Figure shows the three score functions, namely, PageRank (PPgRank), Authorities scores of HITS (PAuth) and, the Citation-count (PCitCnt). As it is clear from the figure the three functions are highly skewed, and do not separate scores well over the interval. This figure is based on the AnthP digital collection from the field of data management. In the author observed the skewness and inseparability of these functions independently in computer science and life sciences publications as well. And, it is shown that distributions of citation-based score functions are also highly skewed and decay very fast. Studies show that the cause is topic diffusion since, scores are computed with respect to the full publication set.

In the authors compared and evaluated several publication score functions, including PageRank and Authorities scores, both adopted from the www search domain, and citation-count scores from the bibliometrics domain. The authors observed the separability problem with all of these functions which is that none of these scoring functions assigns scores that distribute well over a given scale, *e.g.* Instead, distributions of existing publication score functions are highly skewed, and decay very fast resulting in a much less useful comparative publication assessment capability for users.

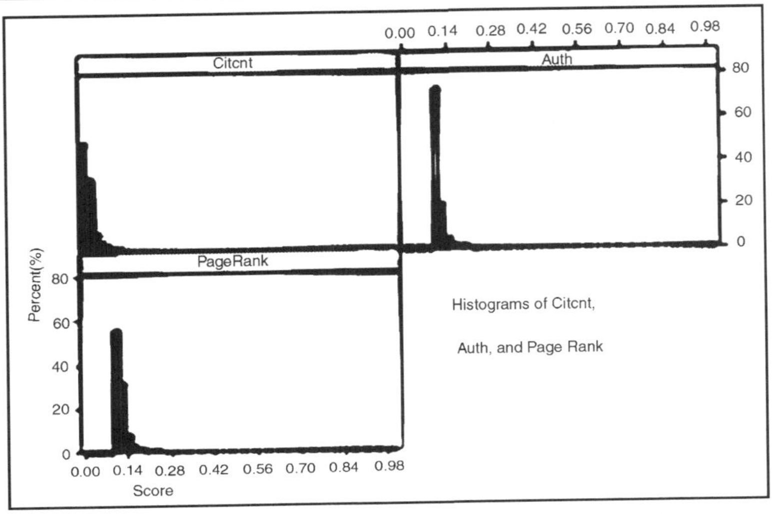

Fig. 6.1 Skewness of Score Distribution of the Three Main Citation-based Publication Score Functions

This lack of separability is caused by the 'rich gets richer' phenomena, *i.e.*, a very small number of publications with relatively high numbers of in-citations have even higher chances of receiving new citations. Yet, these scoring functions are still not very accurate, probably caused by topic diffusion in search outputs. In the following section, and by using the research-pyramid model proposed in, the authors in normalise scores of publications within their own research pyramids, which allows for a fair comparative assessment of publications as publications are compared to their peers in their own research pyramids.

IMPROVED PUBLICATION SCORES VIA RESEARCH PYRAMIDS

Providing accurate publication scores for search results and ranking publications returned as search results accurately can help users in reducing the time spent in searching OLDLs. And, better publication rankings are also useful for comparative assessments of publication venues and scientists as well. At the present time, OLDLs lack effective and accurate publication rankings. For instance, ACM Digital Library returns rankings of publication search results that are unexplained and not useful to users.

Moreover, search outputs of OLDLs tend to suffer from the 'topic diffusion' problem, where commonly, keyword-based searches produce a large number of publications over a large number of topics, thereby producing scores that are non-specific to topics. The research evolution model proposed in suggests that citation relationships between research publications produce multiple, small pyramid-like structures, where each pyramid represents publications related to a highly specific research topic. A research pyramid is defined as a set of publications that represent a highly specific research topic, and usually has a pyramid-like structure in terms of its citation graph.

Publications within an individual research pyramid are:

- Motivated by earlier publications in the topic area is motivated in part by citations; and
- Use techniques proposed in publications from other research pyramids in part uses some of the techniques presented in citations.

Other 'reasons' for citations may also be observed. In this section, our goals are to:

- Provide a solution to the OLDL search output ranking problem due to the topic diffusion problem, by grouping search outputs at the most-specific topic level and without identifying the topics themselves;
- Eliminate the low separability problem of score functions; and
- Improve the accuracy of three score functions, namely, PageRank, Authorities and Citation Count score functions.

The research pyramid (RP) model is used to improve the separability and accuracy of publication scores, and is based on normalising publication scores within a limited scope, namely, within individual research pyramids. These improvements come from the fact that publications are now compared to their peers within their peer groups, namely, their own research pyramid publications that are on the same topic. In two approaches to identify research pyramids are presented and evaualted.

The first, called LB-IdentifyRP, uses Link-Based Research Pyramid identification, which captures research pyramids by identifying pyramid-like structures from the citation graph of the publication set. The second approach, called PB-IdentifyRP, uses Proximity-Based Research Pyramid identification, utilises a graph-based proximity measure, namely SimRank to compute similarities between publications, and then restructures the k-most-similar publications into a research pyramid.

Properties of Research Pyramid Model

In the authors have observed three properties of research publications in three separate data sets, namely, ACM Anthology which is a collection of 15,000 publications and computer sciences and life sciences publication sets, each with 70,000 publications. These properties are utilised in the identification of research pyramids.

Property 1 (Maximum Citation Age)

In OLDLs, most publications receive most of their incitations within a fixed number of years after their publication dates. We refer to this value as the Maximum Citation Age, and denote it by CAgeMax. It has been observed in that, in the AnthP, CSSet and the LSSet datasets, most publications receive 90 per cent of their in-citations in 10 years, *i.e.*, CAgeMax=10.

Figure presents the citation age distributions in AnthP. We give a tighter bound for citation age within which topical similarity within an RP is maintained between citing and cited publications. In rare cases, publications may cite works older than CAgeMax.

It is found that a great proportion of these citations are for historical reasons, which we interpret as: old cited works:

- Have coarse similarity to citing papers; and
- Do not belong in the RP of the citing publication.

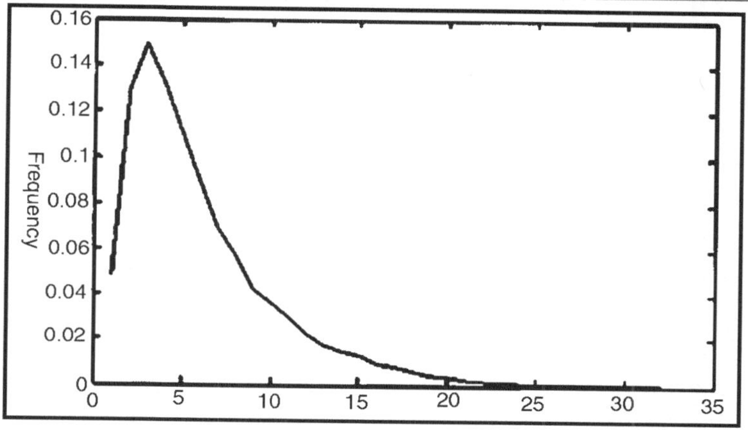

Fig. 6.2 Citation Age Distribution Curve of AnthP

Property 2 (Topic Specificity Over Time)

Scientific research publications quickly become very topic-specific over time, usually referable via a highly specific topic.

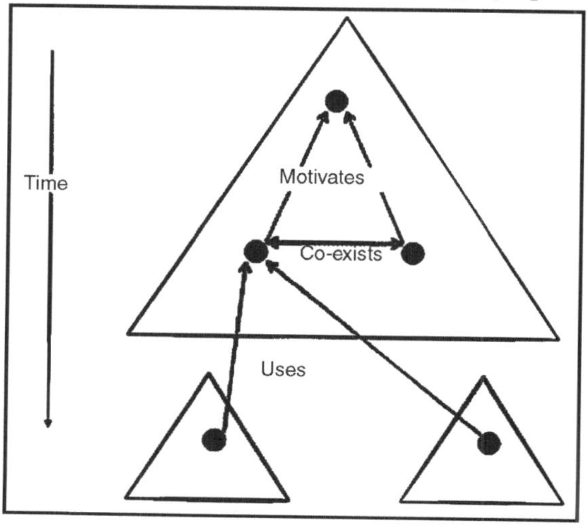

Fig. 6.3 The RP-based Model

As illustrated in figure, an old research pyramid that covers a certain research topic leads to instantiations of new research topics, and thus to creations of new RPs, that use techniques proposed in the publications of parent RP(s). Again, such old citations carry topical similarity between the citing and cited publication at a coarse granularity level. Possible citation exchanges between different RPs also occur and are of type 'uses', *i.e.*, the citing paper uses techniques proposed by the cited paper.

Example

Codd's paper E. F. Codd, 'A Relational Model of Data for Large Shared Data Banks', Commun. ACM 13(6): 377-387 is about the topic relational model, and cited around 580 times. A new and more specific topic of 2000's say, rank-aware join algorithms, is coarsely related to the more general topic relational model in that, a publication P in the RP of rank-aware join algorithms and citing Codd's paper 'uses' the techniques proposed in the RP of the relational model.

Property 3 (Topic Similarity Decay Over Citation Path)

After very small citation path distances, topical similarity between papers decays significantly. From figure, after a citation path of length 3, the topical similarity, as measured by SimRank, significantly decays. We refer to this value by LMax-TopicDecay. This observation led the authors in to build RPs of height at most 3 in the experimental results section.

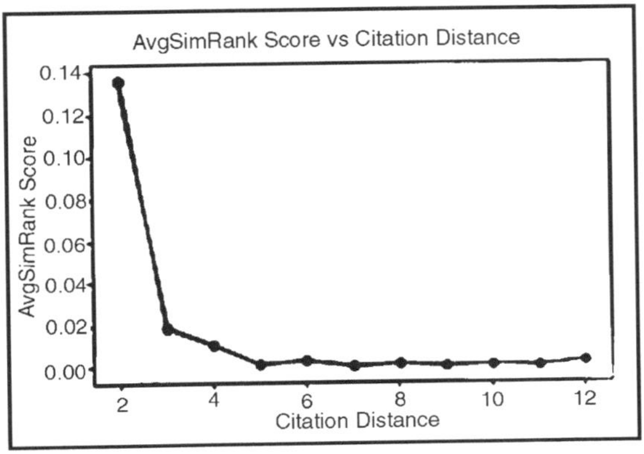

Fig. 6.4 SimRank Scoer Change with Citation Distance

Property 4 (Topic Similarity Decay Over Citation Age)

After a certain citation age, topical similarity between the citing and the cited papers significantly decays. From figure, in the AnthP set, after a citation age of about 5 years, the topic similarity between the citing and cited papers decays significantly. We refer to this value by CAgeMax-TopicDecay. This observation led the authors in to build RPs in the experimental results section such that the maximum citation age within an RP is 5 years. The two characteristics that identify a research pyramid RP are.

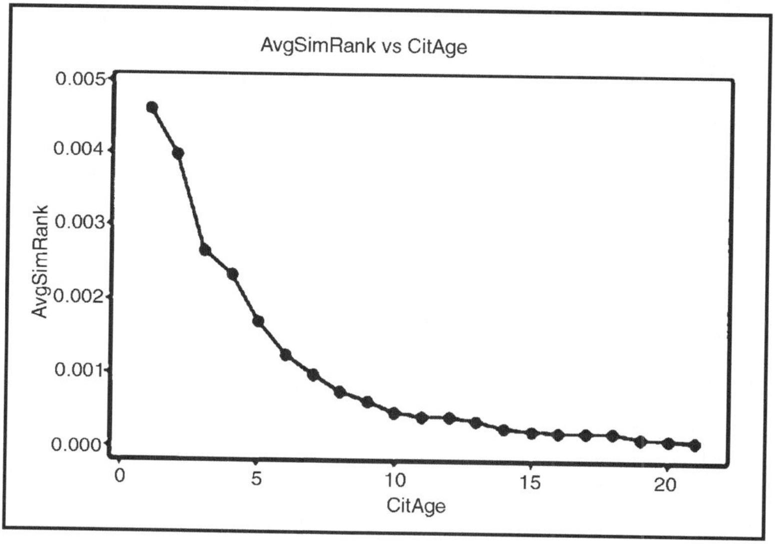

Fig. 6.5 SimRank Score Change with Citation Age

RP-Property 1 (High Topic Specificity)

An RP, usually organisable into a pyramid, is a set of publications that represent a highly specific research topic. We maintain high topic specificity of RPs by applying properties 3 and 4, and keeping the height of research pyramids low. Note that we make no attempts to identify the topic associated with an RP, as our approach does not need the topics explicitly. But, in interactive environments, providing topics to users is useful.

RP-Property 2 (Research Pyramid Construction)

RPs are arranged into pyramid structures either directly by using citation graphs (*i.e.*, the link-based approach) or indirectly using the publication times and close proximity of papers.

Research Pyramid Identification Procedures

Based on the properties of publications and characteristics of RPs, next we propose two offline research pyramid identification procedures, namely, the link-based (LB) and the proximity-based (PB) RP identification procedures. Both procedures start by choosing a candidate root node for an RP, called the cornerstone paper. The paper that is located at the root of a research pyramid receives more citations than others as other publications within the research pyramid are 'motivated' by it, and directly or indirectly cite it. Thus, our approach is to identify papers with high in-citations as cornerstone papers (*i.e.*, the roots) of RPs to be constructed. The link-based procedure locates research pyramids by identifying pyramid-like structures in the citation graph of the publication set.

In summary, within an individual RP, publications are topically related and motivated by each other and we use the four properties to identify citations within RPs—as summarised next. In AnthP, the average number of citations to a paper, denoted by CI, is 2.066. Note that, in our experiments, we consider only the AnthP citations that are completely within AnthP; any citation from a paper within AnthP to a paper that is not in AnthP is removed. Using Property 3 and RP-Property 1, we limit RP heights to 3. Thus, the expected number of papers within a research pyramid RPP with paper P as the root and with height 3 is |RPP| = 1 + CI + CI2 + CI3 H' 15. Of course, the actual identified RP sizes vary.

Some RPs may deal with active research topics, and, in such cases, the number of in-citations of publications are noticeably higher than CI, leading to noticeably higher RP sizes as well. Figure presents the link-based LB-IdentifyRP procedure. The proximity-based PBIdentifyRP is similar, except that the function call to LB-FormRP is replaced by the function call PB-FormRP.

The procedure LB-IdentifyRP:

a. Selects a cornerstone paper P from the existing publication set as an RP root, by simply picking the current most-cited publication;

b. Calls LB-FormRP to locate the RP set RPP of P; and

c. Eliminates RPP from the current publication set CurrAnthP, and repeats (a)-(c) again, until no more publications are left in CurrAnthP.

Note that our approach in this chapter is to create distinct and non-overlapping research pyramids. An alternative approach, not reported here due to space limitations, is to allow overlapping research pyramids as follows: Do not to eliminate any papers from the original publication set; instead, simply colour each selected publication, and continue until all publications are coloured, meaning that, when the algorithm ends, each paper belongs to at least one RP set, and possibly more.

The two main functions of the link-based LB-IdentifyRP procedure are ChooseRoot and LB-FormRP. ChooseRoot chooses publications that are cornerstone papers, or roots of research pyramids. The function LB-FormRP forms the RPP of a root publication P by adding direct citers of P into RPP, and indirect citers of P at a level up to the LMax; in experiments, we choose LMax as 3, by following the property 3. The function Citers(P, l, CAgeMax-Topic-Decay) returns the set of publications that cite P at a level l (which is at most LMax) where the citation age of the citing paper with respect to P is less than the maximum citation age CAgeMax-Topic-Decay. In more detail,

- Paper-id pidP of root P along with its level 0 is inserted into RPP and the queue Q, which holds paper-ids for future expansions and their distances to the root paper P.
- Two-tuple <Pi, A > in Q is dequeued, and expanded by locating direct or indirect citers of Pi so long as

their levels with respect to P is at most LMax-TopicDecay and their citation age with respect to P is less than the maximum citation age CAgeMax-TopicDecay. All expanded publications and their level info with respect to P are inserted into the queue Q.

- The above two steps are repeated until Q is empty; then RPP is returned.

```
proc LB-IdentifyRP(AnthP, RP-Sets)
{
RP-Sets:= Ø;
CurrAnthP:= AnthP;
while (CurrentAnthP = Ø)
{Root:=ChooseRoot(CurrAnthP);
RPRoot:=LB-FormRP(Root,LMax-TopicDecay);
RP-Sets:=RP-Sets U RPRoot;
CurrAnthP:=CurrAnthP-RPRoot;
}
}
```

(a) Procedure LB-IdentifyRP

```
funct ChooseRoot(CurrAnthP)
return TopCitedTopicDecay(CurrAnthP);
```

(b) Function ChooseRoot

```
funct LB-FormRP(P, LMax)
{Set RPP:={P}; Queue Q;
Q.Enqueue({P},0);
while(Q is not empty)
{<Pi, A>:=Q.Dequeue;
if(A<LMax)then
{CiterSet=Citers(Pi, A, CAgeMax-TopicDecay);
Q.Enqueue(CiterSet,(A+1));
RPP = RPP +CiterSet;
}}}
Return RPP}
```

(c) Function LB-FormRP()

```
Funct PB-FormRP(P, LMax)
{Set RPP={P}; Queue Q;
Q.Enqueue(P,0);
```

```
while(Q is not empty)
{<Pi, A>:=Q.Dequeue;
if(A<LMax) then
{CiterSet(Pi):=Citers(Pi, A, CAgeMax-TopicDecay)
TopSimSet:=TopSim(Pi,|CiterSet(Pi)|, CAgeMax-
TopicDecay);
Q.Enqueue(TopSimSet, A +1);
RPP= RPP+TopSimSet;
}}
Return RPP}
(d) Function PB-FormRP()
```

Fig. 6.6 Functions of LB-and PB-IdentifyRP Algorithms

The function PB-FormRP of the proximity-based approach utilises a graphbased proximity measure, namely SimRank to compute similarities between publications.

It captures RPP of the root publication by locating publications that are most similar to P and yet:

- Are linked to P with a citation path length of at most LMax-TopicDecay; and
- Have a citation time distance less than CAgeMax-TopicDecay. SimRank iteratively computes similarity scores between nodes in a graph G following the rule that "two nodes are similar if they are linked with similar nodes".

In other words, the SimRank similarity between two nodes a and b, S is iteratively computed using the formula:

$$S(a,b)=\left[C/|I(a)|\ |I(b)\ |\right]*\sum_{i=1}^{|I(a)|}\ \sum_{j=1}^{|\ I(b)|} S\left(I_i(a),I_j(b)\right)$$

where I(a) and I(b) are sources of in-links of a and b, respectively. C is the decay factor between 0 and 1. We choose C=0.8. If |I(a)|or|I(b)|= 0 then S(a, b)=0 by definition, in the case where a=b, S(a, b)=1. The space complexity of the naive SimRank algorithm is O(N2) where N is the graph size. We prune as in by considering node pairs that are near each other in the range of radius r. We choose r=6, which is twice the value of the expected research pyramid height.

PB-FormRP receives as input the root P, the maximum level LMax from root, and utilises the maximum citation age CAgeMax-TopicDecay and returns the RP set RPP of publication P following the same main steps of LB-FormRP with one main difference: the way the twotuple <Pi, t > dequeued from Q is expanded, as follows:

- Top |Citers Pi,□ A,CAgeMax-TopicDecay| similar papers, based on SimRank, to Pi are identified. The number of citers of Pi is used to capture the density of the RP being identified, and thus to expand RP at Pi accordingly;
- The identified similar papers are added to RPP and also enqueued to Q for further expansion, this time with the level increased by 1. Similar to LB-FormRP a maximum level of LMax-TopicDecay is employed.

Advantage of PB-FormRP over LB-FormRP is that it successfully captures co-existing members of RP as well as those that are not reachable through any citation path from RP's root. We give an example.

Example

Figure shows two RPs; RP1 and RP2. RP1 contains two co-existing roots A and B. Such a case occurs when two researchers work on the same problem simultaneously. At some point of our RP identification process, A will probably be recognised as a root of a new RP, say RP3, as it has more in-citations than B. And, since, B is not reachable through any path from A, LB-FormRP will fail to identify B as a member of RP3. PB-FormRP will succeed to place both A and B into RP3 in this case as B is very similar to A.

A similar problem will be observed with paper C that is not reachable through any path from the root. Furthermore, LB-FormRP may incorrectly identify F, that probably 'uses' a technique proposed in A, as a member of RP3 when F is really a member of RP2 which co-exists with RP3. PB-FormRP successfully repels F from RP3 as F is not similar to A or any of RP3's members, based on SimRank. We observe here that PB-FormRP may capture pyramid-like structures, but not exactly pyramid structures.

SimRank computes similarity between two papers P1 and P2 by averaging the similarity of the citers of both. However, note that similar papers to a member of an RP will be the other members of the same RP since, members of an RP are usually cited by each other.

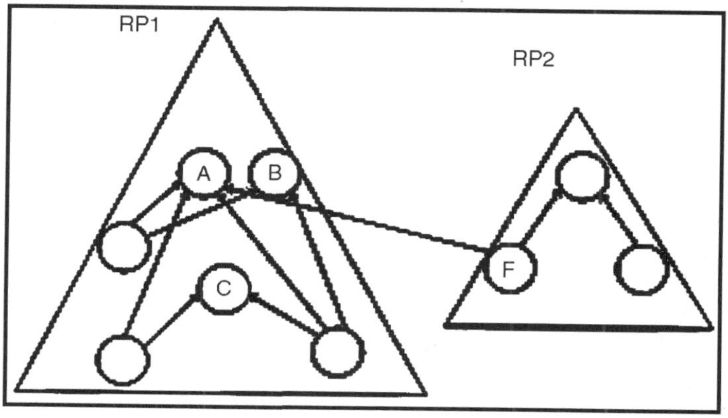

Fig. 6.7 Examples where PB-FormRP is more Successful than LB-FormRP

Improved Publication Scores Via the RP-Model

In the authors have applied the two RP-identification algorithms on the AnthP set. After that, they normalized publication scores within the research pyramids identified. The authors observed that, for RP-based scores, the observed skew values range in the RP-based scores. In comparison, the original scores showed highly skewed values that range between 8.12 and 13.04, which mean that they are sharply left-skewed. They also observed that, for RP-based scores.

In comparison, in the case of globally normalised scores, Kurtosis values range between (113.28) and (291.10). The enhancement of score distribution comes from the fact that publications are being compared to their peer groups, *i.e.*, publications that belong to the same scope, and thus have the same chances of receiving new citations.

The observations on PageRank (PPgRank, PPgRank-LB, PPgRank-PB) also apply to Authorities scores (PAuth, PAuth-LB, PAuth-PB).

Table. 6.1 The Means, InterQuartile Ranges (IQR), Skewness, and Kurtosis Values of the Publication Score Functions Applied on the AnthP set

	Mean	IQR	Skewness	Kurtosis
CitCnt	0.02527	0.01845	8.12	113.28
Auth	0.11352	0.01134	13.04	291.10
PageRank	0.12091	0.01733	8.84	134.65
LBCitCnt	0.55698	0.88462	-0.05	-1.81
LBAuth	0.81266	0.37723	-1.02	-0.26
LBPageRank	0.77649	0.46181	-0.80	-0.84
PBCitCnt	0.20802	0.21910	1.88	2.65
PBAuth	0.62386	0.32036	-0.07	-0.58
PBPageRank	0.55653	0.31615	0.30	-0.60

Here we report only PageRank-related results as we have observed that PAuth and PPgRank scores are highly correlated with a correlation coefficient of 0.98, and the correlation between PPgRank and PCitCnt is 0.74. The authors in have also performed multiple searches and manually evaluated the accuracy ranking publication via the RP-Model. They observed that research-pyramid-based scores resulted in 16 per cent-25 per cent more accurate search outputs than the PageRank-based quality scores. Accuracy was measured for the top-k publications in the result sets, where k is 10.

Section Summary and Conclusions

The Research-Pyramid model proposed in used to solve the separability and accuracy problems of publication score functions.

We showed that:

- Normalising publication scores within their research pyramids provides more accurate and less skewed scores, moreover;
- Ranking search results by these scores promises to give higher accuracy compared to ranking by globally normalised publication scores due to reduction of topic diffusion effect.

However, as noticed by citation-based measures compute popularity of publications based on the 'current' state of a citation graph that continuously changes and evolves. Thus PageRank is effective in capturing the popularity of publications based on the current citation-graph in-hand. We show that PageRank may assign inaccurate popularity scores for both old and recent publications.

And thus PageRank cannot be used to rank OLDL search outputs. We therefore need effective techniques to order search results based on their importance and relevance to users' interests.

ON POPULARITY QUALITY: *GROWTH AND DECAY PHASES OF PUBLICATION POPULARITIES*

In the field of literature digital libraries, citation analysis is employed to evaluate the impact of publications and scientific collections. It is also employed to order digital library search outputs. Examples of citation-based measures are citation-count and PageRank.

However, as noticed by citation-based measures compute popularity of publications based on the 'current' state of a citation graph that continuously changes and evolves. Next we present two scenarios where usage of such popularity scores becomes problematic.

Example

Table shows a sample search output from Google Scholar, a digital library search tool by Google, for keywords 'top-k query processing for semistructured data'. On the left-side of table, relevant documents are ordered based on text-based relevancy to query terms and the citation-based popularity of the document. On the right-side, documents are ordered based on their publication date.

The most relevant document to our query, the one entitled by 'TopX: efficient and versatile top-k query processing for semistructured data', is published in 2008, and appears at the top of the right-side search output list. Given that users usually check only a few pages of a returned list of documents, this publication may not even have a chance to develop popularity unless, in time, awareness of readers increases, *i.e.*, it becomes known to users.

Table. 6.2 Searching Google Scholar for 'Top-k Query Processing for Semi-structured Data.'

All Articles	Recent Articles
[PDF] Top-k query evaluation with probabilistic guarantees-all 6 versions »	TopX: efficient and versatile top-k query processing for semi-structured data
M Theobald, G Weikum, R Schenkel-... Conference on Very Large Data Bases (VLDB), Toronto, Canada, 2004-cse.iitb.ac.in... error relative to 'exactly top-k' queries, translatable into guarantees about queryresult precision... on algorithmsthat process index lists by...	M Theobald, H Bast, D Majumdar, R Schenkel, G ...-... VLDB Journal The International Journal on Very Large Data ..., 2008–Springer... As for our data model, we focus on a tree model for semi-structured data, thus following the W3C XML... TopX: top-k query processing for semi-structured data...
Cited by 85-Related Articles-View as HTML-Web Search IO-Top-k: index-optimised top-k query processing-all 5 versions »	Web Search- BL Direct IO-Top-k: index-access optimised top-k query access processing-all 5 versions »
H Bast, D Majumdar, R Schenkel, M Theobald, G ...-... of the 32nd international conference on Very large data ..., 2006-portal.acm.org... index-access steps in TA-style top-k query processing in the... In these cases, the query optimiser needs to find a... attributes that are relevant for top-k queries...	H Bast, D Majumdar, R Schenkel, M Theobald, G ...-... of the 32nd Very large international conference on data ..., 2006-portal.acm .org... index-access steps in TA-style top-k query processing in the... In these cases, the query optimiser needs to find a... attributes that are relevant for top-k queries...
Cited by 20-Related Articles-Web Search -BL Direct SPIDER: a multiuser information retrieval system for semi-structured and dynamic data-all 3 versions »	Cited by 20-Related Articles-Web Search-BL Direct [PDF] Top-k query evaluation with probabilistic guarantees-all 6 versions »

(Contd...)

P Schäuble -Proceedings of the 16th annual international ACM SIGIR ..., 1993 -portal.acm.org.. The retrieval of information from semi-structured data collections is supported by an appropriate re... Let q be the user's query and let k be the... The top k exact...	M Theobald, G Weikum, R Schenkel-... Conference on Very Large Data Bases (VLDB), Toronto, Canada, 2004-cse.iitb.ac.in... error relative to 'exactly top-k' queries, translatable into guarantees about queryresult precision... on algorithms that process index lists by...
Cited by 40 -Related Articles-Web Search	Cited by 85-Related Articles-View as HTML-Web Search

Example

The two plots in figure show in-citation counts of two relatively highly cited publications from CiteSeer.

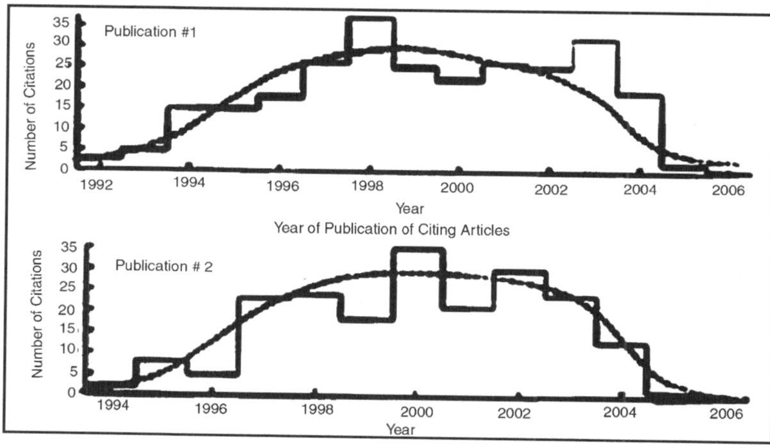

Fig. 6.8 Citation Count per Year for Two Publications that Appeared in 1992 and 1994 and Cited Around 300 Times each

Notice that the popularities of the two publications have dropped significantly after 2004. We observe that the probability that a publication receives new citations drops as it gets older. And, we also observe that PageRank scores of old publications reach a certain value, and do not change after that, even when they are not cited anymore. The reason is that citations do not age or disappear, and as we shall shortly explain, citation graphs around old publications minimally change.

We thus conclude that PageRank scores of old publications represent their peak popularity but not their current popularity. This means that, even though old publications may in time be of lower interest to present users, their PageRank scores do not change. Based on the examples, we argue that, although PageRank is effective in capturing the peak popularity of publications, PageRank may assign inaccurate popularity scores for both old and recent publications.

In a web-user model is introduced and a new popularity growth model of webpages is presented. Using the growth model, Cho *et. al.* derived a quality estimator to compute webpage quality as opposed to its peak-time popularity. We experimentally validate the popularity growth phase model of publications proposed.

Moreover, we observe the following differences between publication citation and web-link graphs that the popularity growth model does not take in consideration:

- Publication citations do not ever disappear like web links;
- Unlike web links, once two papers are published, no new citations between them are added;
- Also unlike web links, new citations to old papers are very unlikely to occur; and
- Indirect citations to a publication are of lesser effect on its PageRank score.

We observe that these differences result in popularity decay for old publications overtime, which we refer to as the publication popularity decay phase. These differences guide us in extending the popularity growth model to accurately capture popularity decay of publications in technology-driven fields of study where authors tend not to cite publications that get older, and publication quality becomes less relevant.

We demonstrate that our proposal successfully assigns accurate publication scores that are in turn useful for two tasks:

- *Ranking Search Results of user Queries in Literature Digital Libraries:* Accurate publication scores may help users retrieve new and yet promising publications; and new publications may contain undiscovered ideas at the frontiers of the topic of interest for users. Our extended quality estimator identifies high quality papers, presents them to the user, and thus gives new papers a better chance to accumulate awareness more quickly.
- *Modelling Popularity Life Cycle of Publications:* Coupled with the probabilistic model of researchers' citation behaviour popularity life cycle of publications in different publication venues can be modeled. Cho *et. al.* analytically verified that the quality estimator they propose can successfully be used for pages with changing quality. However, they did not investigate the popularity decay of pages probably because of the difficulties in capturing such web data and the complexity of web-link graph dynamics. Studies show that, for literature digital libraries, the popularity decay phase can be successfully modelled and integrated with the popularity growth phase.

Our two-phase publication popularity model, *i.e.,* the popularity growth and decay model, is in heavily different than the webpage popularity model. To illustrate the differences, figure shows two popularity growth and decay curves, one for a webpage and another for a publication.

Notice that the popularity of a webpage keeps increasing as the webpage becomes known and those who 'like' it place links to it in other pages. After the webpage reaches the peak, its popularity decays until it reaches a steady-state popularity value. In comparison, the decay of publication popularity has a much different curve. Studies show that researchers rarely cite old works, especially in fastmoving fields like computer and life sciences. Consequently, we show that, by properly modeling users' citation behaviour along with accurate publication quality estimators, we obtain realistic publication popularity growth and decay curves similar to the dashed curves of figure. Empirically, we observe that the majority of publication 'citation count per year' curves conform to this growth and decay model.

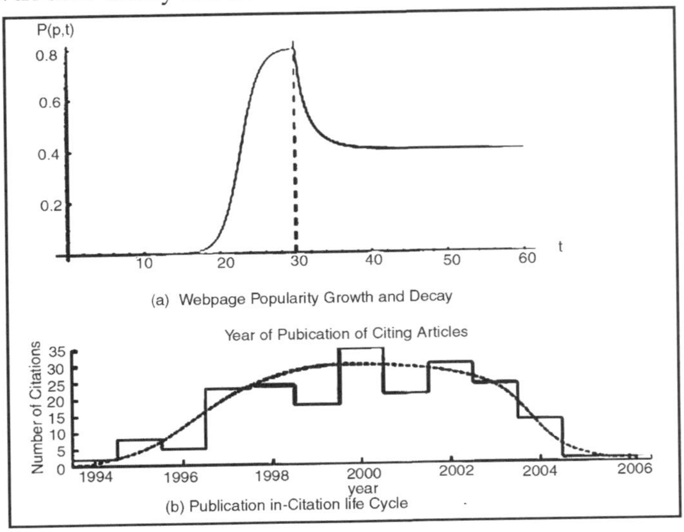

Popularity Drop of Webpages, as Opposed to Observed In-citation Life Cycle of Publications

Page Quality and Webpage Popularity Evolution Model

Cho via a simple user-web model, developed a formula for the popularity growth of webpages, and then used the formula to estimate page quality. Publication quality, based on the web-user model, is defined as the popularity of the publication given that all possibly interested authors are aware of it and those who like it have cited it.

After getting published, a paper goes through two main phases:

- A popularity growth phase where its popularity increases as more authors become aware of it and cite it. After some time, the publication's popularity reaches to a certain value. During the growth phase of the publication;

- Researchers develop awareness of the publication, *i.e.*, more authors get to know it; and,
- Research problems inspired by the paper get studied by authors. This means that the longer the growth phase of a paper, the better the quality of the paper; and
- The authors who like the paper cite it in their works.

- A saturation phase: after the transient growth phase, the publication's PageRank score settles at a certain value, and minimally changes.

Definition:

- The growth region of a publication is the time interval during which the publication popularity grows.
- The saturation region of a publication is the time interval that starts at the saturation point; and, afterwards, the publication usually does not receive new citations.
- The popularity function p (p, t) of publication p, is a function that computes the popularity of p at time t.
- Publication quality Q (p) is the intrinsic and (saturation-time popularity) quality of a publication.

We empirically calculate an estimation $\tilde{Q}(p)$ for the publication quality Q(p) of publication p as the PageRank score at the saturation region. Or, $\tilde{Q}(p) = PR(p, t_{sat})$ where $PR(p,t_{sat})$ is PageRank score of p at the saturation time point t_{sat}. The popularity growth function P(p,t), proposed in is derived as:

$$P(p,t) = Q(p)/(1 + C_{1.e} - \beta t).$$

Note that the function P(p,t) is monotonically increasing with time t. The constant Q(p) is the intrinsic quality of the publication p (that is estimated as p's PageRank score in the saturation region), constant C_1 is the rate of PageRank score growth in Cho's PageRank score growth model. For new publications, $P(p,0) \cong 0$. In time, the exponent component, $e^{-\beta t}$, approaches zero as t increases, and, consequently, P (p,t) converges to Q(p) the intrinsic quality score of the publication, over time.

Remark

The popularity of a publication p at time t is estimated as the p's PageRank score based on the citation graph at time t. Also, the quality of publication p is estimated as the PageRank score at saturation phase. The remark forms a bridge between the PageRank score change curve and Cho et. al.'s popularity growth model base their model on the fact that the quality of a page is time-invariant and does not change overtime.

Thus; Q (p) is assumed to be a constant estimated at any time as the sum of:

- The current popularity or PageRank score of p, and
- The relative popularity (PageRank) rate of change, *i.e.*,

$$\tilde{Q}(p) = PR(p,t) + \frac{1}{c} \cdot \frac{dP(p,t)}{dt} \cdot \frac{1}{PR(p,t)}$$

where $0 < c \leq 1$ is a constant which we choose to be 0.1. A high quality publication is one with a scientific value, and one can intuitively estimate the quality of a publication based on its impact on other authors. Quantitatively, the quality can be measured as the conditional probability that an author will like the publication (L_p) given that s/he has became aware of it (A_p). Mathematically, Q (p) = P (L_p | A_p).

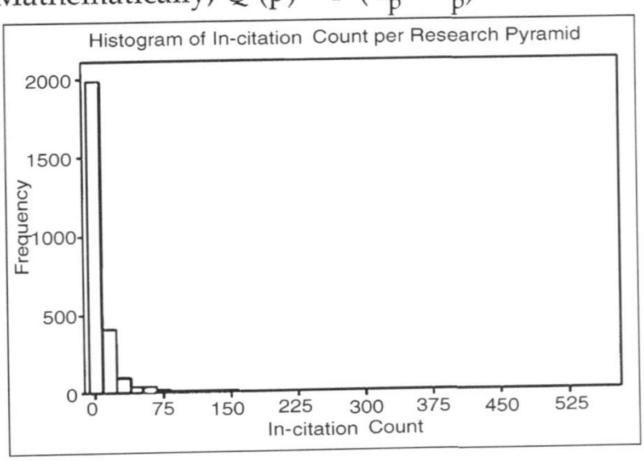

In-citation Per Research Pyramid (Inter-research Pyramid, *i,e.* Citations from Publications outside an RP to Ones inside it.)

We argue that we need to distinguish between two measures of quality for a publication:

- The first measure represents the scientific value of that publication. This value is time-invariant and is represented by Q (p).
- The second measure represents the value of the paper to the user at the time s/he is searching the digital library. This value, in contrast to Q (p), is time-dependent, especially in fast-moving fields of study. We refer to this quality measure as the Publication Quality with Aging Factor.

We show that publications go through the popularity growth phase during which publications gain awareness and thus popularity. We empirically show the popularity growth curves conform to the 'sigmoidal' evolution pattern derived.

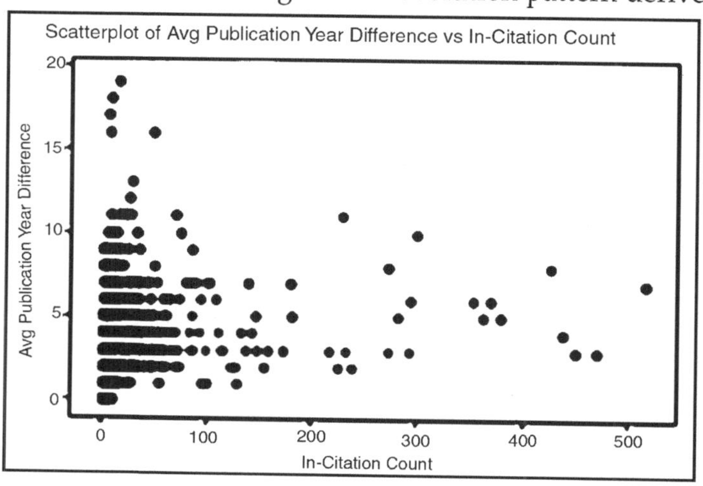

Inter-pyramid Citation count (x-axis) *vs.* the (average Difference in Publication Dates of Publications in a Research Pyramid).

Properties of Publication Citation Graphs and Research Pyramids

In this section we validate Cho et. al.'s popularity growth phase by:

- Using PageRank as a popularity indicator; and

- Utilising the research-pyramid model of research evolution to show that popularity scores of publications converge to a steady-state value that can be estimated by equation.

We first note one difference between a publication citation graph from a web citation graph: Publication citation graph evolution behaviour is to some extent more controlled than web graphs and can be anticipated.

A webpage that has been on the web for a relatively long time may still receive new links; old publications, however, are rarely cited. Consequently, publication citation graphs are highly unlikely to face structural changes around relatively old publications. This special characteristic of publication citation graphs allows for developing accurate mathematical models for changes to publication's PageRank scores, and thus better estimation of publication quality. In contrast, a web graph may face abrupt structural changes at any time in any part of the graph. Studies show that, every week, around 8 per cent web pages are replaced and that about 25 per cent new links are created.

Next we describe the research-pyramid (RP) model of publications that also suggests time-dependent growth patterns in publication citation graphs. The RP-Model is based on the observation that citations between research publications produce multiple, small pyramid-like structures, where each pyramid represents publications related to a highly specific research topic.

A research pyramid is defined as a set of publications that represent a highly specific research topic, and usually has a pyramid-like structure in terms of its citation graph. The RP-Model suggests that publication citation graphs evolve in a time-controlled manner through the stimulation of most-specific research topics from one another as follows. A publication that deals with a new specific research problem appears, and proposes the first solution for it. More publications appear after that publication, addressing the same problem and proposing enhanced or refined solutions to that problem.

In time, the research problem:

- Is either solved.
- Settles down with 'good-enough' solutions, or; and
- Subdivided into more specific research problems.

Publications within an individual research pyramid are:

- Motivated by earlier publications in the topic area, or
- Use techniques proposed in publications from other research pyramids.

We have observed that citations between different research pyramids conform to a highly left-skewed distribution which indicates that as research pyramids of a particular research topic is formed and new research pyramids are instantiated, the RPs already formed receive few external citations from other research pyramids.

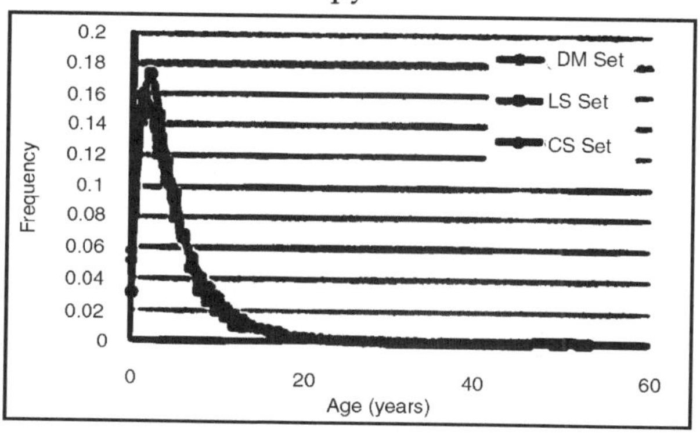

Empirical Citation-age Probability Distribution Curves (*i.e.*, Citation Age *vs*. Frequency of Citations with that age) of Publications in Three Datasets *(i)* Data Management *(ii)* Life Sciences and *(iii)* Computer Science.

Consequently, publication citation graphs are highly unlikely to face structural changes within an already constructed research pyramid because:

- Citations do not disappear like web links.
- Once two papers are published, no new links between them are added;
- New citations to old paper are less likely to occur, and

- Indirect citations to a publication are of lesser effect on its PageRank score.

Structural changes affect only the developing research pyramids. Thus, popularity of publications is expected to converge over time to a steady-state value, which is the essence of the popularity growth model.

The User Citation Behaviour Model

Figure shows that user interest in citing a particular paper significantly decays over time. The best probabilistic distribution that fits the citation-age PDFs of figure is the Weibull distribution.

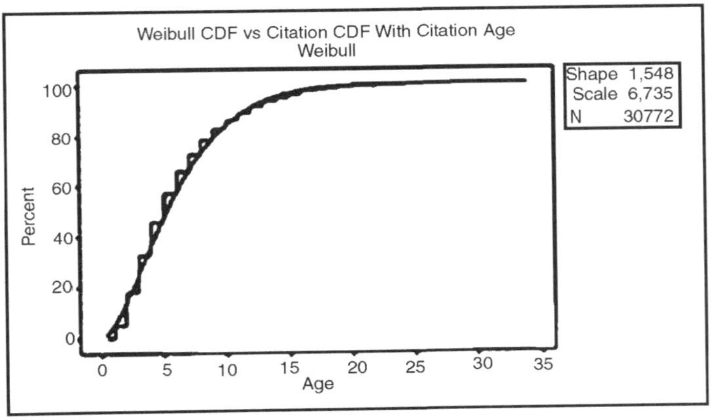

***(a)* Age vs Frequency of Citations of Publications.**

***(b)* Weibull Distribution CDF.**

Figure contains the cumulative distribution function (CDF) of the Weibull distribution, and the empirical CDF of the citation-age distribution for the data-management dataset. The two CDF curves show a high match. Using Minitab, 2008 software, we have observed that the citation age curve conforms to the Weibull distribution with the estimated parameters shape (g)=1.548 and Scale (a)=6.735. Thus, the probability P (u ® v) of the citation from u to v to occur, is computed as,

$$P(u \rightarrow v) = f_{weibull}(|age(u,v|;\gamma,\alpha)$$

where |age (u, v)| is the absolute time difference (in years) between the publication years of u and v. The probability density function of Weibull distribution is given by,

$$f_{weibull}(x;\gamma,\alpha) = \frac{\gamma}{\alpha}.(x/\alpha)^{\gamma-1} e - \left(\frac{x}{\alpha}\right)^{\gamma}$$

assuming that $f_{weibull}(x;\gamma,\alpha) = 0$ for $x < 0$ (which is true in our case as a publication will not receive any citation if it is not published). We use this formula in estimating the publication quality considering the aging factor.

Publication Quality with Aging Factor

Assume that a user issues a search query at time t. Viewing the user as a potential author of an upcoming publication, the user will probably follow the Weibull distribution in his/her citations. *i.e.*, the user cites a relevant publication v with probability equal to $f_{weibull}$ (t – t_{Year} (V)) where t_{Year} (v) is the publication year of v.

Thus, we argue that considering both the publication quality and the aging factor together leads to a better search output ranking.

One possible way to order user search query results is to consider three factors:

- Text-based relevancy of v and the query terms;
- The publication quality; and
- The probability that the user will cite the publication given the ages of relevant publications.

Thus, for a given search query term w, and output (publication) v, one possible form of combining the three factors is as follows,

$$final_{score(v)} = Sim(w,v) * \hat{P}(p,t)$$

where Sim (w,v) is the text-based similarity between w and v, and $\hat{P}(p,t)$ is the temporal popularity of the publication at time t which is computed as,

$$\hat{P}(p,t) = f_{weibull}(t - t_{Year}(v);\gamma,\alpha) * P(p,t)$$

EXPLORING DIGITAL LIBRARIES THROUGH VISUAL INTERFACES

Libraries are long standing institutions, providing an important service of making information widely available. So it is with Digital Libraries (DL), but this evolution into a computerised format does not come without its own unique challenges. The variety and quantity of information available in the digital space is truly astounding. However, as this growth continues, traditional methods for searching are becoming less effective to support the needs of users to find information quickly and easily.

The conventional library book search system provides several attributes associated with books as a response to the users' enquiry. This includes title, author, publication year, ISBN, page total, and similar information. While considering the increasing volume of data, the current text-based approach to result presentation is not an ideal solution for the modern digital environment. Particularly in the case of comparing a lengthy list of search results, this approach is ill-suited, as it is inefficient and non-intuitive. Assistance, such as ranked results, can aid in such problems but the user will still be relied on to investigate the top results individually.

Additionally, the current popular approach of presenting a summary of content may not accurately reflect what is of value to the user. The advancements and trends that allow for the rapid growth of DL also permit more elaborate interfaces with which to access them. Information Visualisation is one such avenue, which has proven to be an effective approach in acquiring information from a large compilation of data. By making use of users' perceptual cognition for navigating extensive digital workspaces, their ability to understand, and speed with which they review the information space is improved. Previous studies have proven the significance of visualisation in the users' information forage.

One common approach to assist users' search activities uses visualisation techniques combined with information filtering. The users' interaction defines the attributes of interest that easily filter out unrelated data. The following visualisation procedure transforms the remaining data into graphical illustrations. FilmFinder and HomeFinder are interactive visual interfaces which assist the user to narrow down the search scope and easily compare results using the visualisation. Another common approach focuses on presenting the underlying information through visualisation.

A novel text visualisation interface, TileBars, shows the distribution behaviour of a set of query terms. This presentation allows users to compare multiple documents compactly and concurrently. Other visualisation techniques in this category concentrate on showing a portion of the information at a great level of detail while maintaining the overall structure of the information. Information clustering is another method for supporting navigation of a large data collection. Related documents are clustered together, whose notable characteristics are visualised using a mixture of attributes. Visualisation methodologies have shown that the illustration of data has contributed to improving the user's ability to comprehend information quickly.

This, in turn, leads to increased speed and accuracy in finding desired information. We can apply these kinds of visual abstractions to enhance searches on different types of data domains. By presenting information in such a way, a large amount of content can be displayed in a format which is more intuitive. This has the benefit of allowing the user to analyse data more effectively, increasing the user's ability to comprehend results and make better content selections. Periscope, for example, is a visualisation system targeted at web search results.

It provides a series of different visualisations which users can utilise to analyse and explore the result set. A holistic interface can be used to organise documents into various categories, such as language and format, or web related attributes such as DNS domains. An analytical interface allows for up to seven attributes to be relayed at a time, through use of X, Y, Z axes, colour, size, shape, and animation. The search based on the underlying content will increase the accuracy in finding targeted information from the available resources. Think for a moment how one might search a physical book for a topic of interest.

The logical place to start would be the index. Indexes are valuable resources for referencing major terms which appear in a book. The categorical and hierarchical layout of terms in the index allows us to identify associated topics easily, along with their relationships without reading the underlying contents. The page numbers coupled with each entry makes it possible to estimate the amount information relating to a particular subject. The index will represent the overall layout of entire book contents. Due to a lack of readily available sources, this valuable information has been under utilised. The current trend of digitising books in recent years allows us to exploit content in searches, instead of just depending on superficial book attributes.

The visualisation techniques utilising this information will further enhances the user's search on the DL system. The main objective of this stage is on the utilisation of visualisation techniques for exploring the DL system. The following stage will survey and summarise various visualisation approaches which applied to DL. As suggested, introduce a visual interface which presents general book information through iconic representations. This stage also proposes a novel visualisation which utilises the book index for mimicking the content analysis.

It will allow for detailed comparison of index-based information between selected works. Two different visualisations for this detail view are implemented, each with different strengths. The procedure and analysis of results for a usability test follow, along with discussion and future possibilities, and final conclusions.

RELATED WORKS

The efficacy of visualisation in searching a large information space has been proven in many previous studies. DL are one promising area that should exploit visualisation techniques in searching on various forms of archived information, such as text, imagery, multimedia, citations, and even computer mediated communication. The 3D Vase Museum is one example applying visualisations for browsing photographs in a digital library collection. A Focus+Context type visualisation displays a set of Greek vases in the Perseus digital library in a simulated 3D virtual museum. By moving around the virtual space, users can appreciate vases with accompanying text data. Christel and Martin introduced visualisation techniques for browsing and navigating another type of multimedia, video documents. Meanwhile, Chen proposed a novel approach utilising a different side view of information in accessing the digital library.

It visualises semantic structures and co-citation networks extracted from a collection of documents. This method displayed the author co-citation networks in a 3D virtual space attempting to reveal the structure of a field of hyperlinks with co-citation patterns of authors. Borner and Chen explained that there are three common usage requirements for visual interfaces to the DL: *First*, to support the identification of the composition of retrieval result. *Second* is to understand the interrelation of retrieved documents to one another. *Lastly*, to refine a search, gain an overview of the coverage of a DL and to visualise user interaction data in relation to available documents.

The goal would be to evaluate and improve DL usage. Clarkson *et al.*, developed a visual interface emphasising on the hierarchy of the repository in presenting the DL search results. They used the hierarchical representation in digital repositories for developing an interface for enhancing query-based search engines. A treemap, a well-known technique, is used to organise results in a space-efficient hierarchical display.

The system, known as ResultMap, maps each document in the hierarchical tree structures to a treemap where items matched with given query are highlighted. ResultMap presents the full contents of a hierarchical dataset while providing a view of underlying levels. The experimental results from two controlled lab studies showed that participants expressed preferences to use ResultMap system and produced comparable performance to a text-only engine. When using physical books, people tend to view multiple at once.

This is to better compare and review information across multiple sources, and to have a better overall understanding of the domain. In their study, Good et al, identify this to be a major weakness in current DL displays. To address related issues, researchers have conducted studies applying visualisation techniques for book searches and presenting various forms of search results for easy comparison. Envision is a visual interface presenting book search results in a rigid matrix. The search results are presented as icons in a 2D grid where the visual attributes represent the characteristics of returned documents. Envision allows the user to organise the visualised output interactively based on their information needs.

The Graphical Interface for DL (GRIDL) and ActiveGraph adopted a similar approach in presenting search results. The GRIDL displays a hierarchical cluster of the relevant data to a query on two-dimensional display. This system provides an interactive grid layout, the axes of which are selectable from a variety of different attributes. Results were displayed within each cell as a collection of different size icons, colour coded by document type. ActiveGraph presented search results based on scatter plots. ActiveGraph also provides similar functionalities to specify shape, colour, and size of nodes representing various forms of digital resources. Because ActiveGraph system results in much more node clustering and overlap, a logarithmic transformation is provided, along with the ability to filter out unwanted items.

Many studies mainly focus on aiding the user in comparing the search results effectively by presenting book properties such as book title, author, publication, year, through various visual attributes, but they don't express in detail the amount of content related to user interest. Citiviz is a visual interface tool kit combining text mining and information visualisation. In order to present the insight of similarity among documents as well as traditional document attributes, this system used two visualisation techniques: an animated 2D scatter plot to represent document attributes and a dynamic hyperbolic tree to show hierarchical relationships among documents.

By allowing users to manipulate the manner in which data is displayed, these visualisations provided a better chance to find patterns within the data that may not typically be apparent. Lin proposed another approach through a graphical table of contents (GTOC) that tries to exploit a different perspective of underling information by utilising the table of contents of the book. GTOC showed the dimension of items in the table of contents based on Kohonen's self organising feature map algorithm. The paper introduces how documents can be organised and then visualised to allow the user easy access of underlying contents.

The GTOC prototype describes various interactive tools to assist the user exploring document contents and analysing relationships among terms in the table of contents. Both the attributes associated with documents and its underlying contents are valuable resources finding the relevant information of the users' interest. The increasing computing power and performance of graphics devices make it possible to exercise these information in presenting search results. The following section introduces a newly developed visualisation system that will assist the user's search while utilising the book index, which has been underutilised as a visualisation resource.

METHOD

The Visual Interface for Digital Library Search (VIDLS) system utilizes an Overview+Detail approach for presenting book search results. This is a visualisation technique that uses multiple images to display the entire data space, as well as show an up-close, detailed view of the data. Similar to traditional library searches, the overview will present outline of the book search results through graphical illustration. The user interactively selects a subset of visualised icons that will allow them to execute content level exploration. When a user provides search terms of interests, the Detail view presents a visualisation which relates, in depth, the information presented by the index. For our pilot study, we developed two possible visualisations for this view of the index, each with its own strengths. One emphasises space utilisation, whereas the other is designed to focus on clearly presenting term relationships.

Visualisation

The Overview allows the user to perform a general search on the data space, similar to traditional library tools. This visualisation utilises a tabular layout which offers a familiar spread-sheet style organisation of book search results. The attribute of each axis can be independently selected by the user, allowing for a more targeted display and increasing the users' comprehension of the data set. This functionality will assist the user in customising the search based on their own judgement of which attributes are more important. In the Overview, each book is represented as a circular node, located in the appropriate cell based on the axes.

To deliver the estimated amount of content, node size is determined by the normalised page count of the book compared to the rest. Books with a greater number of pages naturally map to the largest nodes. This will allow users to quickly identify the amount and distribution of content available.

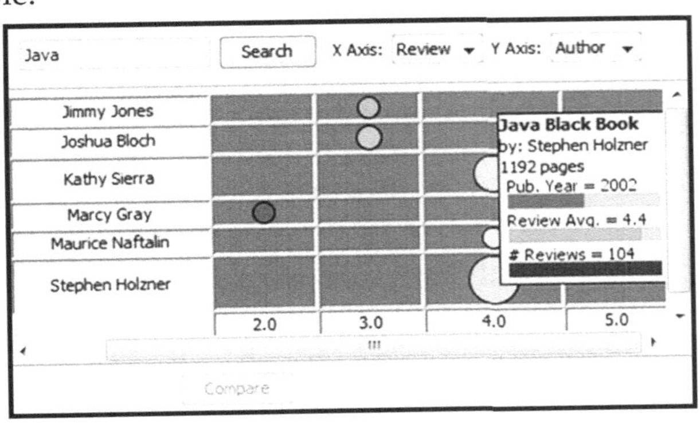

Fig. 6.9 Overview Interface Displaying Search Results with Tool-tip

The system presents other book attributes through a colour coding scheme. The green component is derived through collaborative filtering. This is a content-filtering technique based upon the opinion of users whom have already evaluated the item in question. This will be a valuable piece of information to know regarding the quality of the book. In the case of VIDLS, collaborative filtering would be done by collecting user reviews, much like you found find at a merchant web site. Higher intensity of the green component would indicate a more positive response from reviews.

The accuracy of the content-filtering is highly correlated with the number of evaluators and their preferences. As an example: the mean score of a book which has a low number of reviews could potentially be misleading and unreliable. To account for this, the Overview associates the blue component with the number of unique evaluations given to a book. The publication year is a valuable attribute to find the most up to date information.

This metric has been represented through the red component. With the utilisation of the RGB colour scheme, the larger more recent books with a solid review will be closer to white in intensity, while older, smaller, poorly reviewed works tend towards black. If the user needs to know more precise information for the components, or other detailed information of the work, the system provides this via a tooltip interface.

Detailed Visualisation

Once a user makes a set of selections from the Overview, the system will provide a detailed view of those items. This display is tasked with presenting visualised index data for each book, allowing the user to perform more refined queries, and compare and contrast each work in detail. Two visualisations were implemented on a data model to present the same information while emphasising different attributes: one a radial graph, and the other a sunburst-like display.

Data Model

The underlying model for the detailed visualisations relies on several important characteristics associated with a term in the index. These are: number of pages, number of occurrences, content density, and location relative to the parent term. Although this information is readily available in the index, it is unintuitive in a text format. Presenting these attributes via graphical illustration, the user should gain greater understanding of the content, and make more informed choices of which books to choose.

The number of pages associated with a term by the index is a potential indicator as to how much coverage a topic receives in a book. A work with a greater number of pages on a subject is intuitively going to have more potential value than one with less. Naturally, this attribute is represented by size in the visualisations. To assist the user in quickly making general comparison between each book, this attribute is further expanded to be a cumulative page total of the term along with its sub-terms. The number of occurrences and content density are related through a colour code.

This is intended to give the user a better understanding of the comparative value of each term being displayed. Term occurrence within the book is related by the green component. Although one work may have more information referenced in a single index entry for a topic, that does not necessarily make it the better choice. If another book contained references of a particular term in many different locations within the index, that may be an indication of a greater breadth or complexity of coverage on that topic.

The number of term occurrences are normalised across the display, with the instances of greatest coverage mapping to the highest green intensity, and the one with the fewest having no green intensity. Although two books may have the same total of pages for a particular topic, this should not be taken to mean they have equal value. Consider the situation in which one index allocates ten pages for a topic, but they are separate and not listed as a single range of pages.

Another index containing the same topic, but listed as a single range of ten pages, such as 152-161 may be more valuable to the user. The first may have fragmented references of the topic, but no detailed coverage, whereas the second may have a full section or stage dedicated to the subject. To relate this information to the user, the content density is mapped to the blue colour component. The value is given by calculating the ratio of page continuity to the total number of pages for a term. This is shown by *equation 1,* where *Cib* is the blue intensity for term *i*, $\sum_{j=o}^{n} P_j^c$ is the number of individual page ranges for *i, Ti* is the total number pages for the term *i,* and *Imax* is the brightest intensity of blue possible on the machine. This gives terms with more concentrated information a stronger representation in the visualisation.

$$C_{ib} = \left(1 - \left(\frac{\sum_{j=0}^{n} P_j^c}{T_i}\right)\right) * \mathrm{I}_{\max},$$

The last attribute represents the relationship between a sub-term and its parent. Similar to the previous attribute, a sub-term which is located close to its parent within the book could be an indication of cohesive coverage of the topic. A user may regard such a case with more value than one where the sub-term is more removed from the parent's location. The value of this attribute is calculated by *equation 2.*

$$D_j = ABS\left(\frac{NORM\left(\sum_{k=0}^{n} P_j^k - \overline{Root_i}\right)}{N}\right)$$

Dj is a normalised distance between the root node and associated sub-node *j*; P_j^k is the page number contains sub-term *j*; $Root_i$ is the mean page number having the root word *i*; and *NORM* and *ABS* are a normalisation and absolute function respectively.

Visualisations

The two visualisations share several aspects, in addition to the attributes described previously. Each displays the matching term of the search prominently in the center, with the sub-terms radiating outward. Since, each term is sized based on the cumulative page count of itself and sub-terms, the root node will give users a quick guidance as to which book has more content. Additionally, each graph has a context side-bar that indicates which term is currently moused-over, along with a histogram displaying its colour components. The similarities end here for the two visualisations.

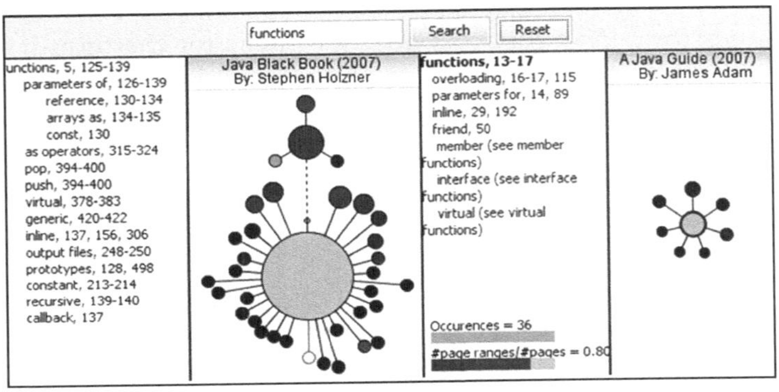

Fig. 6.10 Diagram shows Two Books being Compared in the Detail View. The Left Shows Expanded Sub-terms and an Overflow Node. The Right has Context Highlighting of Text List and Bar Display from User Interaction

The first visualisation approach employs a radial graph layout; with each term presented as a circular node branching off the parent. Sub-terms are sized in the same way as the root, with node size directly correlated to the total number of pages. The largest sub-terms start from the top towards the bottom of the visualisation. This is done to prevent over-crowding of the display. Terms with the fewest pages are considered less important, and are collapsed into a single node, indicated by a red outline, if not enough space is available. Another way in which space is conserved is by displaying only the first level of sub-terms.

A node with hidden sub-terms has a ridged outline. These along with the red 'overflow' node can be clicked show the hidden terms. In contrast, the second visualisation follows a sunburst-like design. Sub-terms are displayed in concentric sections around the center, extending from their parent term. Each sub-term 'slice' is sized as a percentage of its page allocation from the parent's. This has the benefit that all terms can be displayed compactly without hiding any. No additional user interaction would be required to explore the full term hierarchy. One potential downside of this design, compared to the previous one, is that terms are crowded together. This may cause difficulty in picking them out from their neighbours.

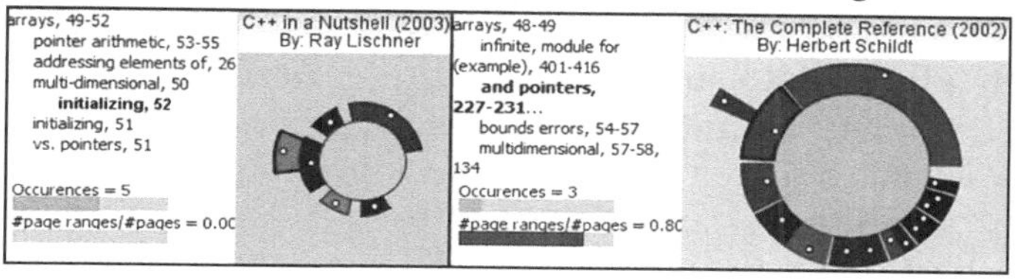

Fig. 6.11 Alternate Sunburst Detailed View

In the radial graph, the relation between a sub-term and its parent is indicated by the branch length. Terms which appear on pages near those of the parent naturally are drawn with shorter branches. Since, the sunburst approach has forgone branches to conserve space, a different analogue is required. Each slice instead contains a bubble, which will relate this information. As the closeness to parent is normalised, the term with the closest relationship has a bubble at the base of the slice, while the term with the most distant has a bubble on the outer edge of its slice. As was previously noted, the chief difference between the two visualisations is their concern for space conservation.

With its emphasis on the term relation branch, and distinct nodes, the radial graph may have more clarity, but at the cost of poorer space utilisation. This results in the need to hide terms considered less important. The other visualisation puts more value in making better use of space, and is able to display all terms efficiently. However, when many terms are displayed at once, the resultant crowding could make smaller slices difficult to see. The addition of the bubble overlay to each slice can add to this difficulty.

EXPERIMENT

To measure the effectiveness of VIDLS, a series of usability tests were performed to compare it to more traditional text-based interfaces. In this set of experiments the VIDLS system, using the radial graph detailed layout, was used in conjunction with a text-only interface for the same information. Each usability test consisted of a small group of three to five students, comfortable in the use of computers, whom had no prior experience with VIDLS.

Each group was given a brief orientation presentation, and then allowed to acclimate to the functionality of both applications for a few minutes. The tests then began, with each user asked to search for books and information with the text-only application and then with the visualisation based approach. Once the test concluded, participants then filled out a survey to measure their quantitative and qualitative feedback of VIDLS in comparison to the text-based format. The questionnaire has 14 questions which utilise a 5 point Likert scale; 5 indicating the highest level of satisfaction, and 1 the lowest.

Table shows the survey results that summarises the user's feedback to VIDLS over a text-based library search system. Participants overall found the VIDLS system to be satisfactory, with some comments highlighting that unfamiliarity with the visualisations led to preference of the text-based design. The Overview visualisation was well received, with 82 per cent of testers responding that it improved their ability to quickly identify desirable books.

This was supported through the exploratory aspects of the system, which participants indicated positively as giving meaningful result displays, and facilitating better understanding of the information.

The radial graph visualisation of index level information was also seen in a positive light, as 65 per cent found it to be a useful representation, and only 11 per cent preferring the familiar text-only listing of results. As with the Overview, testers considered the Detail View to also be useful in expressing the concentration of information, and improving selection among the results. Table shows a summary of survey results.

Table. 6.3 Post Experiment Survey Results

Question	Pos.	Neut.	Neg.
VIDLS overall was preferable to a text-based search	53%	35%	12%
The Overview improved identification of desirable books	82%	6%	12%
Use of the selectable axis facilitated a better understanding of a set of books.	71%	24%	5%
The Overview helped in selecting a subset of books.	65%	29%	6%
It was easy to discern book attributes based on node colour	53%	18%	29%
The Detailed view was preferable to a text approach	65%	24%	11%
It was easy to discern term attributes based on node colour	47%	24%	29%
The Detail view made relevant book selection easier	88%	12%	0%
The relation between a term and it's child was understandable	65%	35%	0%
The Detail view helped identify terms related to the search	94%	6%	0%

AUTOMATING THE MAINTENANCE OF GREENSTONE COLLECTIONS

Many applications generate multimedia documents, such as images and video, on a daily basis. For example, many municipalities have a photo-radar system to catch vehicles that violate traffic laws such as speeding or ignoring red lights. Many pictures of vehicle licence plates are created every day. If these images are organised into a digital library, the collection would need to be updated regularly to incorporate new images. Another example is a traveller who wants to update a digital library of trip photos with new pictures of her travels while travelling around the world. When documents and metadata are added to a digital library collection on a regular basis, such as hourly, daily or weekly, an automated and scheduled approach to collection maintenance is preferred over having to manually update the collection. In addition, an automated approach should be simple to use, therefore making time available for other important tasks. Digital library software such as Greenstone, DSpace and Fedora require that items be added manually to the collection.

In Fedora, data is retrieved at the time of viewing. However, a location needs to be manually configured. Further, although Fedora and DSpace do provide Application Programming Interfaces (APIs) to extend functionality, programming knowledge is required for using an API and for setting up tools based on it. We present a solution for automating and scheduling updates that occur on a regular basis. Our solution is implemented in the Greenstone digital library software system and comes in two parts. The first part of our approach is a command-line scheduling module. The Scheduler both automates the construction and modification of a collection, and schedules the construction to occur at specific intervals, such as hourly, daily or weekly.

In addition, the owner of a collection can update the collection manually, without affecting the scheduled collection builds. Further, the Scheduler interacts with the existing task scheduling mechanism on the host system, which keeps the Scheduler minimal, yet powerful. The second part of our approach involves incorporating the Scheduler into the Greenstone Librarian Interface (GLI). This will allow users who are more comfortable with managing collections through a graphical user interface to take advantage of the functionality of the Scheduler. In addition, this allows us to handle certain tasks associated with scheduling in a uniform and flexible manner.

GREENSTONE

Greenstone is a suite of software for creating digital library collections and making them available locally or via the Internet. A collection can contain documents of different formats, including images, PostScript and PDF files, audio, formatted and unformatted text, and many others. A collection built using Greenstone can be customised in many ways. For example, a collection owner can customise the types of documents that can appear in the collection, the appearance of the interface to the collection, and how the collection will be accessed by other users. In addition, Greenstone is extensible.

For example, functionality to support other data formats that are not provided with Greenstone can easily be added to a collection. There are two types of accessors in Greenstone. The first is an index that provides support for searching. The second is a classifier that provides support for browsing. A collection can be configured for browsing by any metadata that is specified by the collection owner or extracted by Greenstone. Furthermore, a collection can be configured for searching on the same metadata fields, as well as full text.

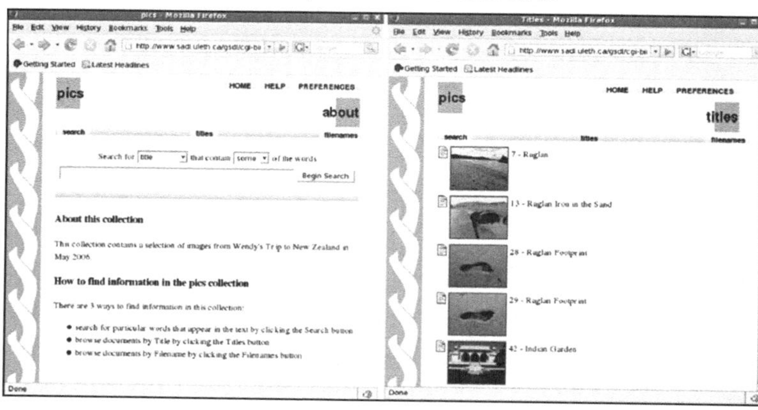

Fig. 6.12 Pics Collection in Greenstone *(a)* Front Page of Pics Collection *(b)* Viewing Pics Collection

Figures *(a)* and *(b)* depict a Greenstone collection called pics. The pics collection is configured to accept images only. Figure *(a)* shows the front page of the collection, which provides general information on the collection. In addition, the collection is configured for both browsing and searching by either Title or Filename. Figure *(b)* shows a display of some images from the pics collection. In this view, the collection is being browsed by Title. The user can click on any image to obtain a larger image for viewing.

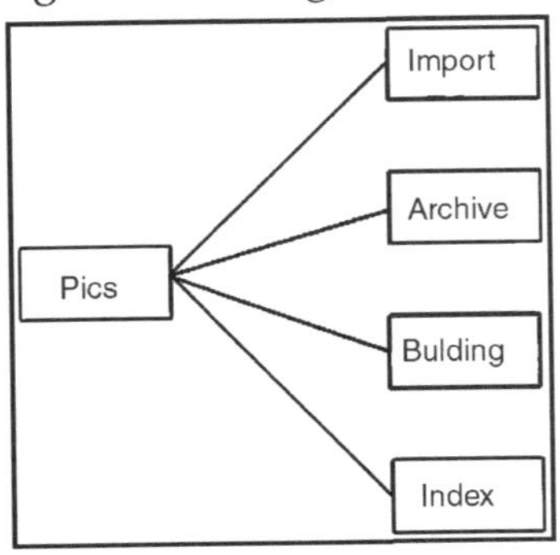

Fig. 6.13 Internal Representation of a Greenstone Collection

Figure depicts the internal representation of a Greenstone collection. Here, the four main directories of a collection—import, archives, building, and index—are displayed.

The purpose of each is described below:

- *Import:* The import directory contains all documents that are to be added to the collection. If desired, the documents can be organised in a hierarchical directory structure within the import directory.
- *Archives:* The archives directory stores all documents that have been processed from the import folder and added to the collection. All documents in the archives directory are represented in a canonical XML format.
- *Building:* The building directory is a working directory for creating all indices and classifiers that are specified for the collection.
- *Index:* The index directory contains the indices and classifiers after they are created.

A Greenstone collection is created or modified by the following four steps: document addition, document importation, accessor creation, and collection activation.

Each step is described in detail below:

- *Document Addition:* New documents that will be added to a collection are placed into the import directory for the collection.

- *Document Importation:* Each document in the import directory is processed for inclusion by creating a canonical XML representation for it. This is accomplished by specifying an import command. Different importing options can be specified by the user. For example, documents in the import directory can be added to an existing collection by using a–keepold option. Alternatively, all documents in the import directory—new and existing—can be used to create a new instance of the collection by using a-removeold option. All imported documents are placed in the archives directory.
- *Accessor Creation:* After the documents in the import directory are added to the collection, indices and classifiers are set up by processing the canonical XML representations of all documents. This is accomplished by specifying a build command. New indices and classifiers can be built by specifying a–removeold option. Alternatively, existing indices and classifiers can be modified by specifying a-keepold or-incremental option. The resulting indices and classifiers are located in the building directory.
- *Collection Activation:* Finally, the collection is activated by moving the indices and classifiers from the building directory to the index directory. The collection is now viewable online.

The command for each step can be executed in a terminal or command window, or via the Greenstone Librarian Interface.

GREENSTONE LIBRARIAN INTERFACE

The Greenstone Librarian Interface (GLI) is a graphical user interface that provides a user-friendly method to build and configure Greenstone collections. It incorporates the steps above. The only steps that are required by the user are to place documents to the import directory via the Gather panel, and to add the documents to the collection via the Create panel. In addition, the Librarian Interface allows a user to create new collections, select metadata sets, configure which document types to allow, and select import and build command options. Figure shows the Librarian Interface.

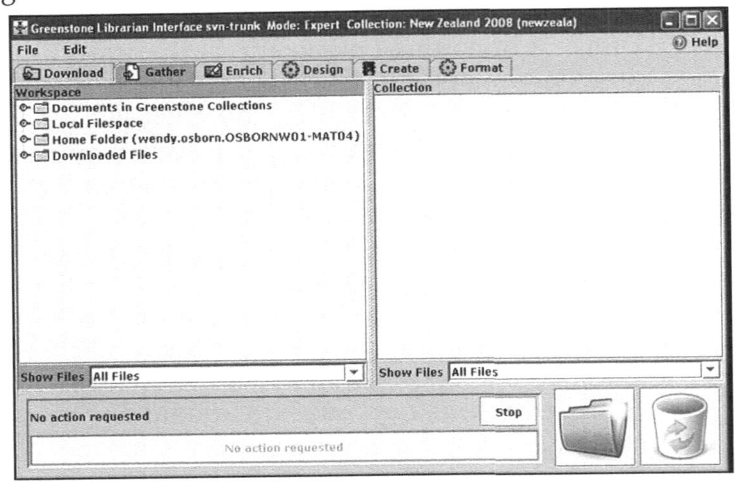

Fig. 6.14 The Greenstone Librarian Interface

CRON

Cron is a programme for users to schedule tasks that will run automatically at a specified time. A task can be one command, or a script containing several commands that are executed in sequence. Initially, Cron was implemented for Unix and Linux platforms, with most systems running Vixie Cron. Mac OS X also runs Vixie Cron. In addition, versions of Cron now exist for Windows platforms, such as Pycron. We summarise the general ideas behind all implementations of Cron that are applicable to our work. Cron runs continuously in the background of the operating system. Every minute, Cron reads several task configuration files. Each such file is called a crontab file.

A crontab file contains a record for every task that is scheduled for execution. Cron locates and runs all tasks that are scheduled at the current time. The format of a crontab record is, where min, hr, dom, moy, and dow are the minute, hour, day of month, month of year and day of week, respectively, user is the username that the command will run under, and task is the command or script that is executed at the specified time.

A task can be scheduled to run hourly, daily, weekly, monthly, or yearly:

- *Hourly:* An hourly scheduled task executes every hour at a specified minute.
- *Daily:* A task that is scheduled daily executes at a specific hour, which is required, and a specific minute. If no minute is specified, execution will occur every minute during the specified hour.
- *Weekly:* A weekly scheduled task runs on a specified day, which is required, and at a specified hour and minute. If no hour is specified, execution will occur every hour during the specified day.
- *Monthly:* A monthly scheduled task runs on a specified day.
- *Yearly:* A yearly scheduled task runs on a specified month.

Any unspecified values are replaced with an asterisk in the crontab record. Systems that use Vixie Cron support two types of crontab files-system crontab and user crontab. The system crontab files are primarily for system administration and maintenance tasks. Also, even if all tasks have a specified low-level username, root privileges are required for modifying a system crontab file.

User crontab files, on the other hand, can be set up by any user on the system to execute tasks under their own username. Assuming the user has permission to execute the task, no root permissions are required. In addition, Pycron only supports user crontab files. Therefore, the Scheduler will employ a user crontab file.

```
30 * * * */ collect/pics/gsdl.pl
59 23 * * * /usr/bin/cleanup.bash
00 6 * * 7 /home/someuser/alarm
00 0 1 1 * echo 'Happy New Year!'
```

Sample Crontan File

Figure displays a sample user crontab file. It contains 4 tasks that are scheduled for specific times. The first task,/ collect/pics/gsdl.pl, is scheduled to be run at 30 minutes past every hour.

The second task,/usr/bin/cleanup.bash, is scheduled for execution daily at 11:59pm. The third task, home/someuser/ alarm, is scheduled every Sunday at 6:00am. Finally, the fourth task, which echoes 'Happy New Year!', is schedule for execution every January first at 12:00 AM.

THE SCHEDULER

We first present our design for the Scheduler command-line module in Greenstone. The Scheduler is written in Perl and runs on Linux, Windows and Mac OS X. It also utilises the Cron scheduling service for scheduling collection re-building. We chose Perl because a Perl script can be executed across different platforms without the need to recompile. Similarly, we chose Cron because it is available for Linux and Mac OS X. Therefore, we can maintain the the crossplatform requirement of Greenstone.

The Scheduler requires the following parameters from the user as input:

- The collection to be rebuilt;
- The full import command that is required to import documents into the collection;
- The full build command required to construct the indices and classifiers for the collection; and
- A specification of either an hourly, daily, or weekly build.

For example, if the user wants the collection pics to be scheduled for construction on a daily basis, the parameters would look something like this:

- Schedule.pl pics 'import.pl–removeold pics'.
- 'Buildcol.pl–removeold pics' daily.

Where pics is the name of the collection, 'import.pl–removeold pics' is the Greenstone command for importing documents into the collection pics, 'buildcol.pl–removeold pics' is the Greenstone command for creating the required indices and classifiers for pics, and daily indicates that the collection will be scheduled for construction on a daily basis.

Using the arguments provided by the user, the Scheduler performs two main tasks:

- Create a script that automates the building of the collection; and
- Create a crontab record that schedules the execution of the build script at specified intervals.

Automation Script Generation

The Scheduler generates a build script for any import and build command, and for the Linux, Windows or Mac OS X platforms. The build script contains all instructions that are required for building the specified collection. The commands include those for setting the Greenstone environment variables required for the collection building process, the import command and the build command.

```
#!/usr/bin/perl
SENV{'GSDLHOME'}=' /gsdl';
SENV {'GSDLOS'}=' linux';
SENV {'GSDLLANG'}='EN';
SENV  {' PATH'}='/usr/local/gsdl/bin/script:/usr/
local/gsdl/bin/linux';
system('import.pl-removeold pics');
system('buildcol.pl-removeold pics');
system('\\rm-r/gsdl/collect/pics/index/*');
system('mv /gsdl/collect/pics/building/*
/gsdl/collect/pics/index/');
system('chmod-R 755 /gsdl/collect/pics/index/*');
```

Fig. 6.15 Sample Automation Script for Linux

Figure 6.15 shows a sample build script for Linux that contains the instructions for building the collection pics, as specified in the schedule.pl command above. The first four instructions set the environment variable that are required for the import.pl and buildcol.pl commands.

The next two instructions are the specified import and build commands. The remaining instructions handle cleanup in order to activate the collection.

```
#!/usr/bin/perl
SENV{'GSDLHOME'} ='C:\\gsdl';
SENV{'GSDLOS'}='windows';
SENV{'GSDLLANG'} ='en';
S E N V { ' P A T H ' } = C : / /
gsdl\\bin\\windows\\perl\\bin;C:\\gsdl\\bin\\windows;
C:\\gsdl\\bin\\script;C:\\Perl\\bin\\;
C:WINDOWS\\system32;C:\\WINDOWS;
system('import.pl pics');
system('buildcol. pl pics');
s y s t e m ( ' r d \ / s \ / Q
\'C:\\gsdl\\collect\\pics\\index\'');
system('md \'C:\\gsdl\\collect\\pies\\index\'');
system('xcopy                \/E              \/Y
\'C:\\gsdl\\collect\\pics\\building\\*\'
\'C:\\gsdl\\collect\\pics\\index\\\'');
```

Fig. 6.16 Sample Automation Script of Windows

Similarly, Figure shows a sample build script for Windows that is generated for the same schedule.

Crontab Generation

A crontab record is created to execute the automation script at a specified interval. The user has the option of specifying an hourly, daily or weekly build. An hourly build is scheduled for the beginning of the hour, a daily build is scheduled for midnight, and a weekly build is scheduled for Sunday morning at midnight. After creating the crontab record, it is added to the crontab file or replaces an existing crontab record.

```
0 0 0 * * * /gsd;/collect/pics/gsdl.pl
```

Fig. 6.17 Crontab Record for Linux

Figure 6.17 depicts the daily crontab record for the automation script in figure, while Figure 6.18 depicts the crontab record corresponding to the automation script in figure.

```
0 0 0 * * * C:\gsdl\collect\pisc\gsdl. pl
```

Fig. 6.18 Crontab Record for Windows

EVALUATION

The focus of our experiments is to evaluate the Scheduler for correct execution in specific situations.

For correct execution, we looked at the following:

- *Crontab:* Does the Scheduler generate a correct crontab record? A crontab record is correct if: 1) it is accepted by the crontab programme, and it causes Cron to execute the automation script at the proper time.
- *Automation Script:* In addition, does the scheduler generate the correct automation script to build a collection. An automation script is generated correctly if the collection it is created for is rebuilt correctly given the parameters that are specified when the script is created.

We conducted three experiments. The first is an hourly build of one collection. The second is an hourly build of two collections. The third is a daily build of one collection. All three experiments were performed on both Linux and Windows. These tests were not performed extensively on Mac OS X. However, the scheduler was executed many times on this platform to ensure that it does work.

Hourly Build of One Collection

The focus of this experiment is to ensure that the Scheduler produced a correct crontab record and automation script to re-build a collection of images every hour for 24 hours. To determine that each execution of the automation script was successful, we looked at the following. For Linux, Cron was configured to send an e-mail message containing the output of the automation script.

The e-mail message for each of the 24 builds contains an output for a successful Greenstone build. For Windows, Pycron maintains a log that contains two records for each automation script execution–one record indicating the start of execution, and one record indicating the end of execution and a return code. The terminating records for all 24 builds have a return code of zero, which indicates a successful execution of the automation script. In both cases, a visual inspection of the collection was also performed periodically to verify the success of the Scheduler.

Hourly Build of Two Collections

The focus of this experiment is to ensure that if multiple collections are scheduled to be rebuilt at the same time, they are successfully rebuilt. We scheduled the building of two collections on hourly intervals for 24 hours. A perusal of e-mail messages (for Linux) and the log (for Windows) verify that both collections were rebuilt successfully.

Daily Build of One Collection

The focus of this experiment is twofold. The first is to ensure correct daily execution of an automation script generated by the Scheduler. The second is to simulate a situation of a collection that has images added to it on a daily basis. We schedule one collection to be built daily for seven days. The collection starts with 10 images, and 10 images are added daily. In addition to the successful daily build, the collection did reflect the addition of the new images that arrived daily.

SCHEDULING IN THE LIBRARIAN INTERFACE

The Scheduler is a minimal, yet powerful tool for maintaining Greenstone collections. It hides the details concerning the collection building process, and also the details for scheduling a Cron task. However, the Scheduler has two main limitations.

The first is that the user is still required to know the syntax and command-line parameters for both the import and build commands in order to perform scheduling. The second is that, currently, notification of collection building success—or failure—is still dependent on the version of Cron (and indirectly, the operating system it is running on) that is used. The Librarian Interface provides a user-friendly tool for building collections, including configuring the import and build commands. Therefore, it is ideal to extend the Librarian Interface to allow the configuration of the Scheduler as well.

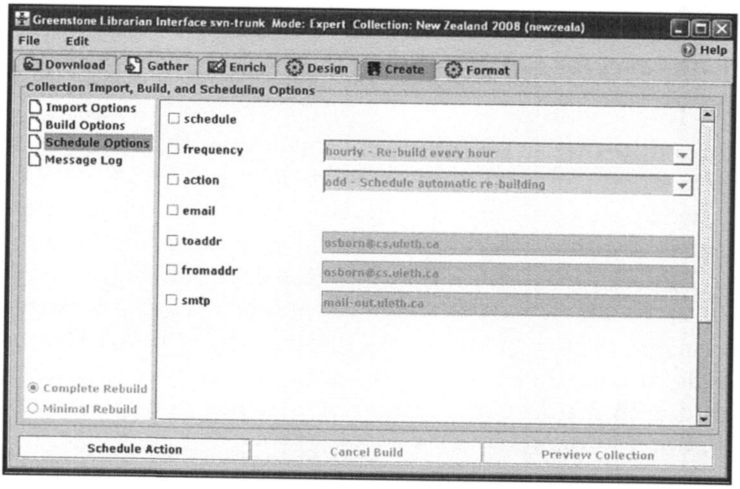

Fig. 6.19 The Schedule Options Panel

Figure 6.19 depicts the Librarian Interface extension to support the scheduling of collection builds. Currently, the Create panel is displaying most of the parameters (*i.e.*, Schedule Options) for the Scheduler. Notice that no explicit options exist for the import and build commands. This is because the import and build commands are created based on the arguments selected from the Import Options and Build Options panels. Therefore, the user no longer needs to know the exact syntax of the import and build commands.

User Modes

The Librarian Interface has four modes of use—Library Assistant, Librarian, Library Systems Specialist, and Expert—stepwise increasing the functionality available to the user. It was important to determine which modes would have access to the Scheduling Options, and for those modes that were granted access, how much access each would be granted. It was decided that Library Systems Specialists and Experts would be provided access to the Scheduling Options. In addition to determining which options to make available to each user mode, it is also necessary to determine how the Scheduler would interact with the existing import and build functionality in the Librarian Interface.

Mode Level for Options

The Scheduler was first modified so that the passing of command-line arguments conformed with that of other Greenstone commands, such as import and build. This also allowed us to easily specify which user mode could have access to each argument when it is added as a Schedule Option in the Librarian Interface. The Expert user mode is granted full access to all Schedule Options, while Librarian Systems Specialist is only granted limited access to options. This user mode can only specify whether or not to schedule a collection build with the default values—a frequency of hourly, and no sending of e-mail.

Scheduling and Building

Another important decision was how the Scheduler would interact with the collection building functionality of the Librarian Interface. The question asked was, should scheduling be done at the same time as collection building, or be a completely separate task? For Expert mode, the functionality for Scheduling is separate from that of collection building. This is because an expert user may want to configure and manually re-build their collection before scheduling an automatic re-build of it. For Library System Specialist mode, the Scheduling functionality is done at the same time as collection building. If the specialist chooses to schedule, a new scheduled build is created. If the specialist chooses not to schedule, any existing scheduled builds are deleted.

Cron Event Logs

It is important to maintain logs that keep track of the outcome of a scheduled collection build. Both Vixie Cron and Pycron maintain a log that keeps track of the attempted execution of all scheduled tasks. Neither scheduling service keeps track of the success or failure of a scheduled task, nor do they keep track of the output of a task. In addition, to view logs created by Vixie Cron, the user must have root access. Another desirable feature of maintaining logs is the ability to be able to only record output that is considered important, and to disregard all other task output.

For example, if the output from the input and build commands of Greenstone is required, but the output from moving indices and classifiers is not considered important, the log should reflect this. Therefore, the Scheduler is modified in two ways to handle the logging of building script output. The first is to create a custom log for each execution of the automation script. The automation script creates a unique filename every time it is executed by using a timestamp. The second is to specify in the automation script which actions will have its output redirected to the logfile. The actions whose output is to be ignored will have its output redirected to the 'bit bucket'.

E-mail Notification

It is also important than an e-mail notification service be provided, which will inform users of the outcome of their scheduled collection build.

We handle e-mail notification from the Scheduler and Librarian Interface for the following reasons:

- *User Notification:* Whether Cron notifies users about the outcome of a scheduled task depends on the its implementation. For Vixie Cron, the outcome of a task is e-mailed to the owner of the task. Pycron does not send e-mail notification.
- *Flexibility of Notification:* In Vixie Cron it is possible to suppress e-mail notification, either by setting an environment variable to null, or by redirecting all output to a file or the 'bit bucket'. However, this is normally an all-or-nothing event—either all output, or none, is sent by e-mail. Similar to logging, a desirable feature would be to send e-mail that contains only the most important parts of the building process, and ignores other parts of the building process.

- *Greenstone E-mail Support:* Greenstone comes with a Perl e-mail script, that is a wrapper for the Perl sendmail command. The e-mail script is platform-independent. Therefore, it is ideal to use it to provide a uniform way to send e-mail concerning the execution of a scheduled task. In addition, the script does not require the piping of build output directly to it, but instead can send the contents of a file.

Therefore, both the Librarian Interface and the Scheduler are modified so that e-mail notification is handled in a uniform and user-friendly manner across all operating systems. First, options have been added to the Scheduler that are required for the Perl e-mail script—specifically, a flag to specify that e-mail will be sent (–e-mail), the sender (–fromaddr), receiver (–toaddr) and the e-mail server that will be used to send the e-mail (–smtp). Also, the corresponding fields exist in the Schedule Options pane of the Librarian Interface. In order to assist users in using the e-mail features of scheduling, the Librarian Interface attempts to populate the fields-toaddr,-fromaddr, and-smtp in the Schedule Options pane by consulting the configurations for the Librarian Interface and Greenstone.

If suitable values are available from these sources, they are assigned to the appropriate fields. Second, the output from the building script must be captured and re-directed to the Perl e-mail script. The capturing of output already takes place, in the event log. This serves as the file that the e-mail script will send to the user. Also, since, it contains only the output that is considered important, this will be reflected in the e-mail message as well. Finally, the Scheduler is modified so that, if specified, the automation script will send an e-mail message containing the contents of the log to the specified recipient. An added bonus is that if e-mail is not specified, the log can still be consulted by the user if required.

Scheduled Building in Isolation

An important modification to the Scheduler is to ensure that a scheduled build is completed in its entirety without interference from another scheduled build. A build may take a significant amount of time depending on the size of the collection—from seconds for a small one to 33 hours for a collection containing 20 GB of raw text and 50 GB of metadata. To handle this, the automation script for the collection checks for a lock file, which indicates that a collection build is underway.

If the file exists, the collection owner is notified via e-mail and information is placed in the event log. Otherwise, a lock file is created before the scheduled build begins, and is removed when the build finishes. This ensures that multiples builds do not occur concurrently.

EXAMPLE: COLLECTING PICTURES WHILE TRAVELLING

We present a simple application of scheduling from the Librarian Interface. In this scenario, we have a traveller who wants to post pictures of their trip in a Greenstone collection for her friends to view. Instead of waiting until the end of the trip, the traveller wants to post her pictures from each day, incrementally adding to the collection on a daily basis. The traveller does not want to worry about obtaining the Librarian Interface to rebuild the collection while traveling. Instead, she simply wants to upload the pictures to the import directory of her collection, and have her collection rebuilt automatically and on a daily basis.

This can be accomplished by setting up a scheduled, automatic rebuild of the collection of travel photos from the Librarian Interface. First, before departing, the traveller runs the Librarian Interface and creates a new collection. Then, the user selects the Create tab to display the collection creation pane. From here, clicking on Schedule Options will display the available options for setting up a scheduled, automatic collection build of the collection of travel pictures.

Figure depicts the available scheduling options, which are displayed with default and derived values as appropriate. Here, the traveller selects schedule, which indicates that she wants to set up a scheduled, automatic build. Also, she selects a frequency of hourly and an action of add.

Fig. 6.20 (a) Schedule Options Panel

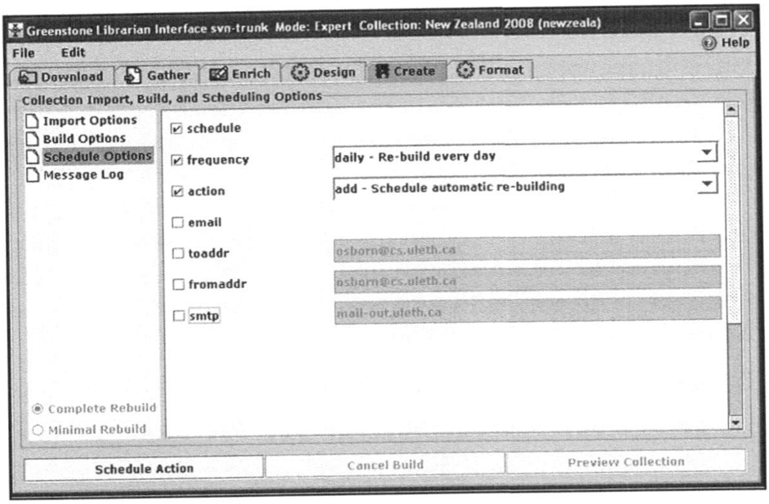

Fig. 6.20 (b) Build-First Day

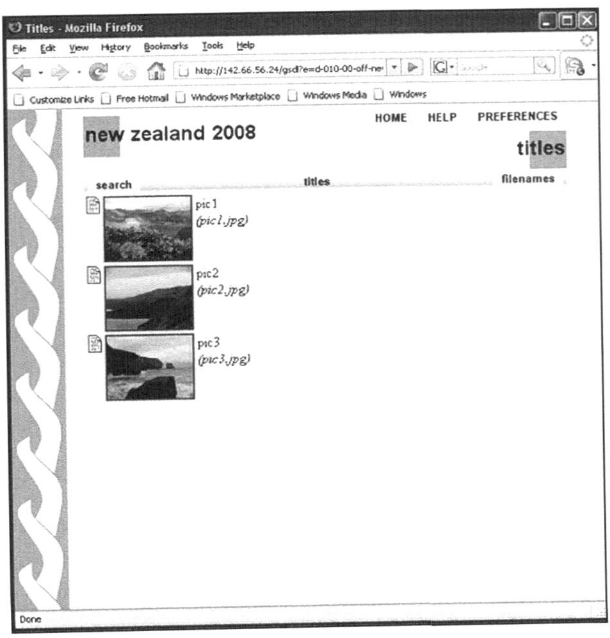

Fig. 6.20 (c) Build-Second Day

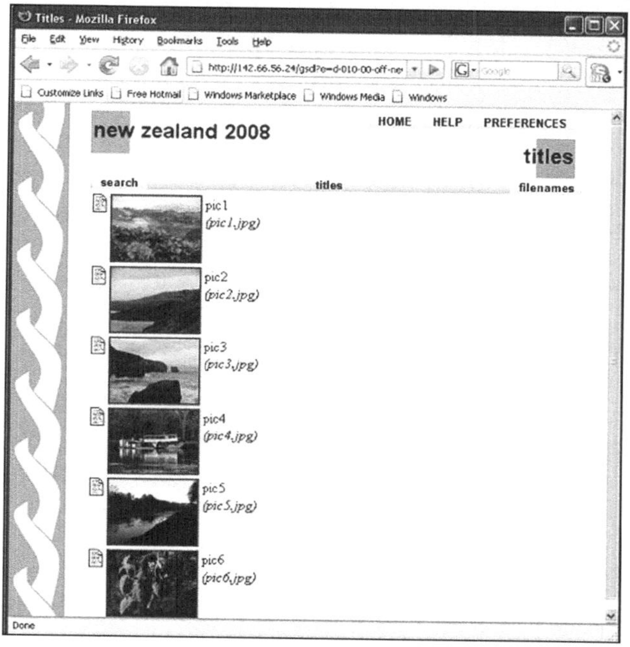

Fig. 6.20 Collection Build Scheduling

Next, the traveller clicks on Schedule Build. This will set up the building script for the collection of travel pics, as well as the crontab record that will indicate to Cron that the collection is to be rebuilt daily. The collection is now ready to be re-built while the traveller is away. At the end of the first day of travel, she uploads three pictures, which are added to the collection when the collection is re-built automatically overnight.

The updated collection is depicted in Figure. The next day, the traveller uploads three more pictures. When the collection is re-built overnight, these pictures are added to the existing collection. Figure depicts the updated collection with the new pictures. Although not shown here, the user can switch to the Import Options and Build Options and select any options that are required for collection importing and building. These options are incorporated into the automatic building script that is created for the collection. In addition, the user can manually build and configure their collection as many times as necessary to confirm the right sequence is being performed, before setting up a scheduled, automatic build.

SECURITY AND DIGITAL LIBRARIES

Security is an important issue in digital library design. Security weaknesses in digital libraries, coupled with attacks or other types of failures, can lead to confidential information being inappropriately accessed, or loss of integrity of the data stored. These in turn can have a damaging effect on the trust of publishers or other content providers, can cause embarrassment or even economic loss to digital library owners, and can even lead to pain and suffering or other serious problems if urgently needed information is unavailable. There are many security requirements to consider because of the variety of different actors working with a digital library. Each of these actors has different security needs.

Thus, a digital library content provider might be concerned with protecting intellectual property rights and the terms of use of content, while a digital library user might be concerned with reliable access to content stored in the digital library. Requirements based on these needs sometimes are in conflict, which can make the security architecture of a digital library even more complex. The design of the security architecture of a digital library must go beyond simply adding one or a few modules to a previously designed system. This is because there may be security holes in pre-existing modules, and because difficulties can arise when attempting to integrate the modules.

The security architecture of a digital library must be designed so that security concerns are handled holistically. A security system designer must view the whole architecture and consider all of the applicable security factors when designing a secure digital library. The nature of a security attack may differ according to the architecture of the digital library; a distributed digital library has more security weaknesses than a centralized digital library. Security attacks can be categorised as physical attacks and logical attacks. A physical attack involves hardware security where keys, locks, cards, and visitor monitoring is used. A logical attack involves an attack on the content or digital library system. We focus on the logical attacks and software security of digital libraries.

SECURITY ISSUES WITH DIGITAL LIBRARIES

According to the DELOS Reference Model there are 6 main concepts in a digital library universe: content, user, functionality, architecture, quality, and policy. Each of these concepts has security issues that affect it.

Content

The content of a digital library includes the information objects that a digital library provides to the users. Some of the security issues involved are integrity and access control. Integrity requires that each object/resource has not been altered or changed by an unauthorised person. Access control encompasses two security requirements. The first is authentication where the user must log into the system while the second is confidentiality, which means that the content of an object is inaccessible by a person unless they have authorisation. Not all digital libraries are free; often content is provided to digital library users for a certain fee, whereupon access control is needed to protect the content.

Further, some content is inappropriate for some users, or targeted to particular user groups; there are a whole host of such other reasons for access control. Logical attacks such as hacking and message tampering can affect the integrity and confidentiality of the content. Improved information access in digital libraries has raised many issues that affect the management of digital libraries. Content Management, or more specifically Digital Rights Management, refers to the protection of content from the different logical security attacks and issues relating to intellectual property rights and authenticity.

Digital Rights Management

DRM provides content protection by encrypting the content and associating it with a digital licence. The licence identifies the user allowed to view the content, lists the content of the product, and states the rights the user has to the resource in a computer readable format using a digital rights expression language (DREL) or extensible Rights Markup Language (XrML) that also describes constraints and conditions. There are 7 technologies used to provide DRM. Table summarises the DRM components and supporting technology.

Each of these components involves mechanisms used to provide DRM:

- *Encryption:* Encryption techniques such as symmetric and asymmetric ciphers can be used to provide access control; public-key encryption is used in payment systems that control how and by whom the content is used. Symmetric ciphers using DES, 3DES, AES, and RC4 algorithms require the use of a shared secret key to encrypt data before it is sent. At the receiver's end the cipher text is decrypted using the same secret key. Symmetric ciphers depend on both the sender and receiver knowing the shared key. Asymmetric ciphers use a pair of keys, public and private, for each of the sender and the receiver. The public keys of both the sender and the receiver are known but the private key is kept secret. If encryption is performed using the public key then only the private key can be used for decryption and vice versa.
- *Passwords:* Stored strings must be matched by users desiring access.
- *Watermarking:* Characters or images are added to reflect ownership. Steganography is used to conceal data inside audio, video, or images. Different watermarking techniques have different aims; some watermarks might be visible while others invisible. Some watermarks are reversible; it depends on the desired use of the watermark and what is being protected.
- *Digital Signature:* Asymmetric encryption can be used. Likewise, hash algorithms such as MD5 and SHA can be used to create a signature.

- *Digital Fingerprint:* Digital fingerprints are a more powerful technique involving digital signatures and watermarking. The creator of the content creates a unique copy of the content marked for each user; the marks are user-specific hence, called fingerprints. Should a user illegally distribute the content, the creator can use search robots to find those copies.
- *Copy Detection Systems:* Search engines also can help locate such copied objects. Copydetecting browsers can protect digital content too.
- *Payment Systems:* Users must divulge personal information to pay for content. Installing payment systems can help protect digital content.

There is no standard mechanism for providing DRM, mainly due to the lack of regulations, however there are various systems and protocols introduced to provide content management and support fair usage policies. There is a tradeoff between security and performance. Nadeem and Javed use a Pentium-4, 2.4 GHz machine running Microsoft Windows XP operating system, encrypt 20527 bytes to 2323398 bytes of data using DES, 3DES, and AES.

For 20527 bytes of data it took 2 seconds to encrypt using the DES algorithm and 4 seconds to encrypt using the AES algorithm. It can be seen that the more complex the encryption algorithm the longer it takes to encrypt the data. In another study, encrypting data with the RSA algorithm using a key size of 1024 took 0.08 milliseconds/operation on an Intel Core 2 1.83 GHz processor under Windows Vista in 32-bit mode, while using a key size of 2048 took 0.16 milliseconds/operation.

User

The User in a digital library refers to 'the various actors entitled to interact with digital libraries'. Digital libraries connect the different actors with the information they have and allow the users to consume old or generate new information. Security issues relating to the users of a digital library intersect with content issues. A main logical security issue relating to users and content is access control.

Different access control requirements arise for distributed systems to ensure both confidentiality and authentication:

- Access control must be applied and enforced at a distributed platform level, so should be scalable and available at various levels of granularity.
- Access control models should allow a varied definition of access rights depending on different information and must be dynamic where changes to policies are easily made and easy to manage.
- 'Access control models must allow high-level specification of access rights.'

Digital library users may need to be authenticated before they can access content. Global/universal identification may not suffice. A service provider that provides content based on a non-identity based criteria like age will not benefit from global identification because there is no way to verify the authenticated user's personal information. Usernames and passwords are not efficient ways to provide authentication. One of the most widely used authentication protocols is Kerberos.

It is a client–server model, which secures communication with servers on a local network. Developed at MIT in the 1980s to provide security across a large campus network, it is based on the Needham-Schroeder protocol and has now been standardised and included in many operating systems such as UNIX, Linux, Windows 2000, NT, XP, etc. Kerberos is used as an authentication protocol in cases where attackers monitor network traffic to intercept passwords. It secures communication, provides single sign on and mutual authentication, and does not send a user's password in the clear on an insecure network.

An alternative solution suitable for digital libraries is to represent information about an individual using credentials. Credentials are "abstract objects which contain statements expressing knowledge or information from a definite context." Credentials do not specify direct information about a client and their attributes, they describe the local environment and context in which the requests originate. Digital credentials can be used as a means of authentication in providing DL access control. Two agents can be used to assist in the management: a personal security assistant and a server security assistant, to manage digital credentials using a client/server model. The server must notify the client of the credentials required for the current request. The client then sends its credentials for authentication.

The client must have some trust of the server to give its credentials, which raises privacy issues. The personal security assistant is used to obtain credentials on behalf of the client, store the credentials, parse and interpret the required credentials, and manage the acceptance policies. A server security assistant is available to specify the credential acceptance policies and their usage. There is a tradeoff between flexibility and security that must be considered when choosing an access control model.

Access Matrix Model

This conceptual model specifies the rights that each subject possesses for each object. Actions on objects are allowed or denied based on the access rights specified.

There are 2 implementations of the AMM:

- An Access Control List provides a direct mapping of each object the subjects are allowed to access, and their usage right; and
- A Capability List defines the objects each subject is allowed to access and the usage rights.

Access control lists and capability lists are not suitable for distributed systems. Their limitations lead to multiple problems. ACL provides limited expressibility of policies. Any change in the policies will propagate in the system/application. Authentication in a system that uses ACL solely is a problem because using username and password in a distributed system is not practical.

In a distributed system, administration of the system should be decentralised by delegation to reduce the overhead. The owner of the object specifies a policy in ACL. If an overall policy is specified by an entity higher than the object owner, then conflicts may occur in the access rights. The number of administrative entities in a distributed system can be very large. Not all the administrators may have trust amongst themselves, resulting in incorrectly defined policies. For example, admin A may trust B but not C, however B may trust C. If A were to define policy for B then it would be implicitly applicable to C, causing problems.

Role-based Access Control

Role-based access control involves policies that regulate information access based on the activities the users perform. Such policies require the definition of roles in the system: "a set of actions and responsibilities associated with a particular working activity". Permissions are assigned to roles instead of individual users. Specifying user authorisation involves 2 steps: first assigning the user to a role, second defining the access control that the role has over certain objects. RBAC is easier to manage and is more extensible than ACL. However RBAC doesn't flexibly handle constraints, where a user with a specific role may need specific permission on an object.

An example of RBAC architecture addressing key limitations is OASIS, for use in distributed systems. Role management in OASIS is decentralised and service specific. OASIS is integrated with an event-based middleware that notifies applications of any environmental changes. Roles are parameterised by applications and services to define their client roles, and to enforce policies for role activation and service invocation within each session. Role membership certificates (RMC) are returned to each user on successful login, to be used as a credential to activate other roles. RBAC is suitable for use with digital libraries because it supports decentralised architectures and varying roles, however RBAC doesn't allow for the definition of different roles in a collaborative group.

Task-based Access Control

The Task-based access control model extends subject/object access control by allowing the definition of domains by task-based contextual information. Steps required to perform the task are used to define access control; the steps are associated with a protection state containing a set of permissions for each state, which change according to the task. TBAC uses dynamic management of permissions. TBAC systems are limited to defining contexts in relation to activities, tasks, or workflow progress. Since, it is implemented by recording usage and validity of permissions, therefore, TBAC requires a central access control module to manage permissions activation and deactivation in a just-in-time fashion.

Team-based Access Control

RBAC doesn't address cases where group members of different roles want to collaborate in a single group. The TMAC model defines collaboration by user context and object context. "User context provides a way of identifying specific users playing a role on a team at any given moment" while object context defines the objects required. TMAC offers the advantages of RBAC along with ability to specify fine-grained control on users and on object instances.

A scalable access control data structure can be used with large collections, applying concepts of team based access control, focusing mainly on the access control data structure, and employing an access control framework called Document Access Control Method (DACM) with a Document Storage System (DocSS). DACM allows the decentralised administration of privileges, the definition of different rule sets to control a single collection, and different delegation patterns as models. Current object access control policies use an array of rules to record the privileges each subject is allowed to each object.

This is impractical to manage in the large data collections found in digital libraries. DACM solves this problem by finding symmetries in a permission function to allow a brief expression without losing important distinctions.

Content-based Access Control

Another approach to access control models involves defining models according to content. This approach is applicable in digital libraries and distributed systems, where the access rights to the user are dynamic and may change with each login. Content-based access control policies are very well suited for digital libraries and distributed systems. Recent research has proposed different models; most use digital credentials for authentication, but vary in the definition/ storage of the policy.

An important content-based access control model introduces a contentbased access control system, Digital Library Authorisation System, that utilises the Digital Library Authorisation Model (DLAM). Subject, object, and privilege sets can't be used to define policies in digital libraries mainly because DLs are dynamic with large collections of data and subjects. It defines access control policies based on subject qualifications and characteristics. DLAM provides a means to specify the qualifications and characteristics of subjects. It uses content dependant and independent access control and allows the definition of policies with varied granularity.

Functionality

The concept of functionality encompasses the services that a Digital Library offers to its users. The minimum functions of a Digital Library include adding new objects to the library or searching and browsing the library and other functions relating to DL management. A security attack that can affect the functionality of the Digital Library is a Denial of Service attack, which can affect the performance of the system and prevent users from accessing the system.

Architecture

Digital libraries are complex forms of information systems, interoperable across different libraries and so require an architectural framework mapping content and functionality onto software and hardware components. There are various models for architecture, *e.g.*, client-server, peer-to-peer, and distributed. All these require the protection of the communication channels between 2 parties, where sensitive data might be transferred. Securing the connections involves different layers—Internet, transport, or application layer-depending on the architecture of the system. The distributed model is scalable and flexible.

It is useful when building a digital library with changing content from different sources and offers potential for increased reliability. The security requirements for a distributed digital library are challenging, since, the content and operations are decentralised. Fault tolerance and error recovery are issues that affect a distributed system. Replication is used to increase the availability of the system. While this approach solves problems with denial of service attacks, it complicates the protection of the content because a replica of the content exists.

The client-server model doesn't have the same security problems as a general distributed model, however, it presents a major security weakness, the server being a single point of failure. Attacks are concentrated on one server rather than on the multiple replicas of a distributed model.

Quality

The content and behaviour of a Digital Library is characterised and evaluated by quality parameters. Quality is a concept not only used to classify functionality and content, but also used with objects and services. Some of the parameters are automatically measured and are objective while others are considered subjective; some are measured through user evaluations.

Policy

Policy is the concept that represents the different regulations and conditions that govern the interaction between the Digital Library and users. Policy supports both extrinsic and intrinsic interactions and their definition and modification. Examples of security issues relating to policies include providing digital rights management, privacy, and confidentiality of the content and users, defining user behaviour, and collection delivery.

7

Promotion and Evaluation

Institutional Repositories

Facilitating Structure, Collaborations, Scholarly Communications, and Institutional Visibility

The advancement of information and communication technology (ICT)—Internet in particular—has caused enormous changes in the world we are living today. Many things are not what they used to be decades, or even years ago. Imagine how we communicated and shared information in the fifties, when computers were still 'archaic' and the Internet was still in its inception stage. Compare that to the numerous communication gadgets and the information overload that we have today. All those changes happened in only a little over fifty years. Libraries as information providers have also undergone massive changes due to their close association to the way people communicate, collect, manage, use, and share information.

Any advancement in ICT will have direct and indirect impacts on the ways libraries provide their collections and services to their user communities and society in general. Some advancements might be welcome by libraries. Others might be perceived as threats to the existence of libraries since, they are perceived as 'things' that would cause libraries to become obsolete, or at least redundant, amidst the new emerging technologies.

Some have also caused mixed reactions among librarians, who might 'love' and 'hate' them at the same time. Librarians usually love advancements in ICT since, they can help tremendously in the librarians' efforts to fulfill the information needs of their users. However librarians might also notice that many (or most?) of their traditional roles as librarians have been, or will be, taken away from them by those advancements. Digital libraries (DLs), which include all of its variants such as institutional repositories (IRs), is one of the most important changes in libraries triggered by advancements in ICT. DLs have caused fundamental changes in the way libraries operate.

It has also challenged the traditional roles of libraries and compelled them to redefine their roles in this new environment. Discussions in this stage are the results of the expansions and 'conversations' from several of my previous journal articles on IRs. However they will take into account as much as possible and where appropriate, recent developments and discussions about IRs. The discussions will also use Desa Informasi (Information Village)—an institutional repositories project at Petra Christian University (PCU) Library in Surabaya, Indonesia—as a study case. The project is not intended to serve as an example of a success in IRs implementation.

In fact, it is still far from an ideal implementation of IRs. It is being used solely for the purpose of sharing experiences gained from its execution. Naturally, perspectives raised in the discussion will be of an academic librarian in a developing country. The environment, where the project is being carried out—a medium-sized private university with mostly undergraduate students—will certainly offers certain influences into the discussions as well.

ICT ADVANCEMENTS AND THE FUTURE OF LIBRARIES

The rapid developments of ICT since, the birth of computers and the Internet has contributed so much in changing the way we live our daily life. They affect the way we do things, which includes the way we do our jobs. They even affect the way we relate to one another in terms of personal relationships, as well as professional ones. Almost everything we do in daily basis has something to do with ICT.

It ranges from simple stand-alone applications to collaborative and networked systems. Nowadays it's almost unimaginable to write an article without the help of a word processor application, online dictionary or thesaurus, reference management application, and online journal databases.

All these advancements have offered invaluable help for people from any professions in terms of working more effectively and productively. Some ICT advancements however can cause fundamental changes in the traditional roles and functions of certain professions. They fundamentally alter the ways in which people or institutions provide products and services. Libraries—especially academic libraries—and their librarians have been living through these inevitable, yet often subtle, transformations. Nowadays most librarians are familiar with—or at least aware of—approval plans, selector services, new acquisitions of library materials with embedded electronic bibliographic records, copy cataloging, self-check-in/out, Internet search engines, virtual reference services, etc.

All these roles and/or functions (acquisition, cataloging, reference, etc.) were traditionally the domains of (local) librarians. Local librarians used to have the authority over or in charge of performing these roles and/or functions. However the new environment affected or created by ICT advancements has created new 'arrangements', where these basic roles and/or functions are gradually being taken over by ICT, or at least transferred to other institutions outside the libraries. In short, traditional roles and/or functions of librarians are being challenged by the rapid technological changes, which usually also leads to social changes. Librarians need to 'redefine' their roles and/or functions in the new landscape of the future information society. Davenport stated something that I believe is a good response to the challenge.

She suggested that librarians should have "expanded, more collaborative roles in the creation and dissemination of knowledge," which will empower (academic) libraries to assume new role and/or function as learning space instead of information storehouse. It is now up to librarians on how to assume this 'new' role and/or function in the new landscape.

Digital libraries (DLs) and/or institutional repositories (IRs) offer opportunities for librarians and libraries to re-assert their influence in the creation and dissemination of knowledge. DLs/IRs is a strategic move for libraries to maintain their relevance in the new landscape of ICT-savvy society. However before going into any further discussions, we need to be on the same page on what we call digital libraries (DLs) and/or institutional repositories (IRs).

INSTITUTIONAL REPOSITORIES

IRs is one of the relatively new terms generated by advancements in ICT, one that needs to be defined to enable us to proceed with our discussion.

One of the pioneers in IRs—Clifford Lynch—gave one of the most fundamental definitions of IRs:

- "A university-based institutional repository is a set of services that a university offers to the members of its community for the management and dissemination of digital materials created by the institution and its community members. It is most essentially an organisational commitment to the stewardship of these digital materials, including long-term preservation where appropriate, as well as organisation and access or distribution."

It is worth to mention specifically that Lynch defined IRs as 'a set of services' instead of merely digital contents. Lynch also sees "institutional repositories as a species of digital library than a publishing platform," which is a sufficient ground for me to conclude that 'the terms IRs and DLs ... interchangeable'. Lynch's definition—'a set of services'—suggests his far reaching look into the future. However for the sake of flow of discussion, let's talk first about (digital) contents of IRs. There are several different views on what IRs should contain. These different views don't necessarily contradict one another. They rather define IRs contents from different scopes and perspectives, which in my opinion can complement one another.

McDowell gave a more technical classification of IRs contents by stating:

- "IR contents were classified into the following types: ETDs; e-prints (pre-or post-print articles); working papers and technical reports; conference proceedings and presentations; ejournals and e-books; learning objects; multimedia files (digital audio/video); datasets; pictures (images); digitized archival documents and university records (historical texts and primary sources); non-scholarly institutional publications; undergraduate student work; graduate student work (non-ETD); and course content (syllabi, assignments, lectures)."

Crow defined IRs contents more concisely as "scholarly; produced, submitted, or sponsored by an institution's faculty (and, optionally, students), or other authorised agents; non-ephemeral; and licensable in perpetuity".

In terms of contents of IRs, Lynch suggested that:

- "A mature and fully realised institutional repository will contain the intellectual works of faculty and students—both research and teaching materials—and also documentation of the activities of the institution itself in the form of records of events and performance and of the ongoing intellectual life of the institution."

It is interesting to notice that Lynch's definition doesn't limit IRs contents to "the intellectual works of faculty and students—both research and teaching materials" only. Instead it also encompasses "documentation of the activities of the institution itself in the form of records of events and performance and of the ongoing intellectual life of the institution". Desa Informasi (DI) adopts Lynch's definition for IRs contents and assumes that Crow's and McDowell's definitions as 'subsets of Lynch's' and summarises them into the characteristic of 'locally-produced' contents.

Desa Informasi then expands the definition to also include contents that have 'features of local entities'. Using parallel terminologies from the traditional (hardcopy) collections, the 'locallyproduced' contents are the equivalence of 'grey literature', while contents with 'features of local entities' are the equivalence of 'local collections'. The term 'local content' is a familiar term among Indonesian librarians in defining both characteristics, and it will be used in this stage to refer to contents with both characteristics. DI started off as a limited-in-scope of theses digitisation project to address the physical space limitation of PCU Library, which then evolved into an institutional repositories project. DI utilises a custom-made web-based application called iSPEKTRA to manage digital objects using modified Dublin Core metadata set.

Although "interoperability on a metadata level has clearly been the most active area in digital repositories ... spurred by the Open Access movement, numerous repositories exposed their metadata through standard protocols," iSPEKTRA has not yet addressed the interoperability issues in terms of compliance to Open Archives Initiatives—Protocol for Metadata Harvesting (OAI-PMH). It is a crucial issue that is being addressed along with the development of the new version of iSPEKTRA. DI divides its collections into Themes instead of one big collection in order to create 'added value' to the collections.

The main consideration is that "having several smaller thematic collections of interest to the communities is far better than having one big collection consisting of just about anything people can throw into the collection without any defining 'character' that binds them together".

The current DI collections are as follows:

- *Digital Theses:* Petra Christian University students' theses collection in digital format; mostly PDF documents. There are also an increasing number of multimedia resources generated by the students of Faculty of Art and Design.
- *eDIMENSI:* Digital version of articles from DIMENSI, scientific journals published by various academic departments of Petra Christian University.
- *Petra@rt Gallery:* Works of art by campus communities or works of art that are exhibited/

displayed at Petra Christian University campus; mostly photographs and digitised-images. The collection contains wonderful visual resources, capturing and immortalising the intrinsic knowledge and values of art in the works documented. Some of the wonderful themes are the Visual Poetry, Café Décor, Chairs of Indonesia, Destination Branded, Nusantara Bersatu, etc.

- *Petra iPoster:* Posters of events or issues related to Petra Christian niversity.
- *Petra Chronicle:* Historical documents related to Petra Christian University.

The collection themes clearly represent the 'locally-produced' definition of DI contents. One other collection that represents the definition of 'features of local entities' is the Surabaya Memory collection. It contains digital heritage resources on Surabaya city. Another newly-planned collection will be the 'Chinese in Indonesia' digital collection, which is intended to supplement the special collection of the same name.

This latest collection (still in planning stage as of the time of this book's publication) is created as support system for the newly-established Center for Chinese Indonesian Studies at Petra Christian Universities.

FACILITATING STRUCTURE AMIDST INFORMATION OVERLOAD AND CHAOS

As with most IRs, 'student work accounts for the largest percentage of items' in DI. Digital Theses is the largest collection in DI so far. This phenomenon happens in many institutions implementing IRs since, "ETDs are simply the lowest hanging fruit, and new submission batches can generally be counted on each semester". ETDs are also the 'preferred' contents since, they "raise the profiles of the students who author them, the faculty and departments who foster them, and the institutions that provide them to the world". The following tables will give readers a glimpse of DI collections.

Table. 7.1 Brealdown of Desa Informasi's Digital Collections by Themes

Collection Name/Theme	# of Records	# of Digital Objects	Total Size (bytes)
Digital Theses	12,618	134,268	170,284,316,475
eDIMENSI	809	809	282,689,311
Petra iPoster	120	244	365.416.831
Petra@rt Gallery	261	854	4,132,526,401
Surabaya Memory	258	657	402,415,694
Petra Chronicle	180	559	2,489,567,862
TOTAL	**14,246**	**137,391**	**177,956,932,574**

In their article titled "Size isn't everything: Sustainable repositories as evidenced by sustainable deposit profiles," Carr and Brody stipulated that 'sustained deposits' is a more accurate measurement than merely the size of IRs, since, it reflects 'community engagement.' They stated that "one of the measures of repository success should therefore be the university community's take-up of these services".

Table. 7.2 Breakdown of Desa Informasi's Digital Collections by Types of Document

Collection Name	# of Digital Objects				
	Text	Image	Moving Image/Video	Animation	Audio, etc.
Digital Theses	115,830	18,228	119	24	67
eDIMENSI	809	0	0	0	0
Petra iPoster	0	244	0	0	0
Petra@rt Gallery	57	797	0	0	0
Surabaya Memory	25	632	0	0	0
Petra Chronicle	160	399	0	0	0
TOTAL	116,881	20,300	119	24	67

They warned against using the size of IRs as the only indication of 'healthy' IRs. Referring to Davis and Connolly's 2007 article titled Institutional repositories: Evaluating the reasons for non-use of Cornell University's installation of

DSpace, they noticed that "a repository can exhibit respectable overall growth that is attributable mainly to special-case batch imports". Along this line of thinking, we should then analyse the deposit profile of DI to see any indication of its 'health.'

Table 7.3 shows the growth of digital resources in DI from 2005 up to 2010. Carr and Brody used daily deposit profile in their survey of IRs by utilising ROAR registry of Institutional Repositories. However since, such data is not available for DI, Table uses annual deposit profile instead.

Table. 7.3 Growth of Desa Informasi's Digital Collections

	2005/2006	2006/2007	2007/2008	2008/2009	2009/2010
# of Records	3,178	5,025	7,697	10,857	14,246
Growth from Previous Year	N/A	1,847	2,672	3,160	3,389
# of Digital Objects	N/A	39,438	68,510	98,092	137,391
Growth from PreviousYear	N/A	N/A	29,072	29,582	39,299

We can conclude from table that DI has a 'healthy' deposit profile since, the growth of its contents is sustainable. Table shows a steady growth in # of Records and Digital Objects every year. It is an indication of community engagement in supplying resources for DI. We can also conclude from our discussion so far that higher education institutions produced intellectual works in numerous subjects and formats besides the obvious scholarly works (theses and dissertations, journal articles, and research reports). Student works usually comprise the bulk of the works. Unfortunately most lecturers and academic departments don't have the 'sensitivity' or the expertise needed to identify these student works as intellectual outputs that can be re-used as learning resources.

They don't know how to collect, organise, manage, and re-use/serve these digital objects as learning resources. Davenport observed that "lack the organisation and structures that would allow campus departments to easily share such information". Based on my observations, most faculties only keep the digital version of the resources on CD Roms and stack them in cabinets. This practice will consequently make the resources hard to be found and re-used. It's as if faculties are lost amidst the chaotic and unstructured information overload. Academic libraries could and should jump into the scene to introduce some sense of structure into the seemingly chaotic information resources produced by students. IRs can be introduced as an elegant solution for the academic departments' need for organising these works and re-use them as learning resources.

JISC (Joint Information Systems Committee) suggested this approach when it reported that IRs "are increasingly expected to act as corporate information management tools (records management and content management systems) and data sharing platforms (*e.g.*, for the re-use of research data and learning objects)". This is one of the variations of IRs implementations and a common approach in Indonesian higher education libraries.

However libraries should not just offer the IRs platform as a solution and then leave the academic departments, faculties, and students on their own to figure out how to self-archive (uploading their works into the IRs) and help them organise those resources. Based on an article by Erickson, Rutherford, and Elliott, Salo warned against this approach when she reminded the readers that "the term 'self-archiving' has been taken too literal, abandoning faculty to their uncertainties and incapacities". Librarians should actively assume their 'new' role as IRs managers to increase the probability of a successful implementation of IRs by providing needed assistance to students and (especially) faculties in populating IRs. Libraries should do extra efforts to assist the academic departments, faculties, and students to get their works into IRs.

However in their efforts to populate IRs, it is of a strategic importance for libraries to always present the issue as the academic departments and lecturers' interests, not merely the libraries'. Mediated-deposit services was the method of choice for content acquisition for DI since, it was formally launched in 2005. Local conditions required it and the fact that librarians would be the ones in charge of managing the contents–including the metadata—sounded more promising in the long run.

The approach also asserts the role of librarians in providing some sense of structure into the whole collections. This choice turns out to be the right one since, it works so far, while the alternative doesn't look too promising. In her article Salo stated that "the notion that faculty members will actually push buttons and type metadata in order to deposit materials into IRs is an article of faith among repository-software developers. In practice, however, most deposits are third-party mediated, many by librarians, some by support staff or IT personnel". Salo's assertions and experience in DI prove that although mediated-deposit services might sound more 'expensive' and labour-intensive, it does offer more sustainability for IRs and more visibility to the role of librarians in the overall landscape of universitywide information management/organisation. Content acquisition strategy is different from one collection to the others, based on the nature of the contents.

For example, the content acquisition for Digital Theses is pretty straight forward since, it 'piggybacks' on the university-wide theses deposit policy, which mandates all graduating students to deposit their theses to the Library in hardcopy and softcopy format. Contents for Petrart Gallery on the other hand are much harder to acquire since, they are produced sporadically without any fixed-patterns. However it is crucial that content acquisition process establishes some kind of connections to the 'administrative systems of the university or the local communities it serves' as Liauw suggested, since, "otherwise the collection process will be too massive to manage sporadically and the sustainability of the flow of resources from the communities into the IRs will depend largely on fluctuating individual interests". Contents for eDIMENSI are acquired through formal cooperation with the university's research center, which acts as the publisher for

DIMENSI journals. This approach ensures 100 per cent incorporation of all articles published by the center into DI. Petra iPoster provides valuable lessons in its content acquisition effort and deserves a longer description.

It is a common practice in Indonesian universities for the Public Relations office to be in charge for approving posters that will be posted on campus premises. We would have thought that a formal cooperation with the Public Relations office would guarantee 100 per cent acquisition of posters at PCU by requiring poster-issuing units to provide the digital version of the submitted posters. However experience showed that it isn't as simple as that initial assumption. User behaviours play critical roles in this matter. Poster-issuing units usually don't have the digital version since, they outsource the design and printing process to outside vendors. It requires extra time and effort to get them from the vendors. Other reasons might simply be the reluctance of the poster-issuing unit to spend more time preparing the digital copy to be submitted to the Public Relations office, especially when people are usually under a tight deadline to put the posters up.

A request to provide an extra hardcopy poster as an alternative, instead of the digital version, was not successful either. We then noticed that another unit—the Campus Facility Management unit—is in charge for taking down 'expired' posters all across campus based on the expiry date stamped on each poster by the Public Relations office. We saw it as an opportunity to collect the posters for inclusion into Petra iPoster. So, instead of discarding the posters we merely ask the Campus Facility Management unit to send the posters to the Library.

This never-thought-of-before approach proves to work well since, it does not require any—or at least too much—disruption in the unit's daily operations. Aschenbrenner *et al.*, suggested this approach by saying that 'repositories become a natural part of the user's daily work environment'. The authors were referring to the overall aspects of IRs but the principal can be applied in a narrower scope to content acquisitions in IRs. We don't encounter too many difficulties in acquiring contents for Petra Chronicle since, most historical materials related to PCU will be deposited to the Library. The Library has had supports from various parties in developing Petra Chronicle and Petra iPoster since, the personal nature of the resources, which have certain appeals to the nostalgic aspects of various stakeholders.

The support only increases with the upcoming 50th Anniversary of PCU in 2011. In acquiring contents for IRs, librarians should actively come to the academic departments, lecturers, and students as someone who is offering an information/resources management system to address their needs for organising faculty and student works. IRs can be offered as the solution that will help in introducing and facilitating structure amidst the bulk and numerous different types of faculty and student works. Librarians will then be able to re-assert their role as information managers for their campus communities. Surabaya Memory (SM) presents another challenge in its content acquisition due to the nature of its contents that features 'local entities,' which translates into public participation in the content development.

Unlike contents for other collections in DI that are locally produced, contents for SM is developed by involving the campus communities as well as general public. There has been some level of public participation from individuals and organisations that lent their personal or institutional collections relating to the heritage and history of Surabaya city. However the current level of public participation is still not as well as expected. Liauw observed that the two main reasons for this lack of participation are "the lack of information-sharing culture and the sentimental/personal values of heritage-related resources to their owners or copyright holders." Bluntly put, "some people have been making money out of selling duplicates of old photographs and manuscripts".

On the other side, some individuals have been spending a lot of money to acquire old photographs and manuscripts into their personal collections. The money spent in acquiring those resources has become a big obstacle to share the resources—not even their digitised version—with the society. It's also a common knowledge that 'big collectors tend to collect for their own enjoyment". Facing such challenges, Liauw suggested two strategies to help alleviate the problem.

The first strategy is to collaborate with big collectors to hold exhibitions. When we have gained their trust it usually (but not always) is easier to solicit their participations by contributing some of their collections to SM. The second strategy is to "network with other heritage-based organisations to identify individuals with possession of cultural heritage materials". I would like to also add that it is very important to show to stakeholders (especially those big collectors) that the shared resources will benefit the society. Although content acquisition itself has posed many challenges, it is essential that we do not view any IRs projects only as a matter of populating it with the desired contents. McDowell offered another perspective on IRs.

He offered a definition from functional point of view, which defines IRs as:

- An institution-wide service. Faculty members of every academic unit must be able to submit, regardless of departmental affiliation.
- Intended to collect, preserve, and provide access to, among other things, faculty scholarly output in multiple formats.
- Must be actively taking submissions.

Although DI does fulfill the definition and has managed to reach some level of sustainability in content acquisition, it still falls short in providing services and interactions/ collaborations to its users, capitalising on the acquired contents. Regarding future directions for IRs, Furlough suggested that IRs (contents) should be 'integrated into instruction, reference and collection development". Based on the IRs, such as DI, has managed to fulfill its role to "serve as tangible indicators of a university's quality and to demonstrate the scientific, societal, and economic relevance of its research activities." Let's now examine the successfulness of IRs in fulfilling its other role to "provide a critical component in reforming the system of scholarly communication...reasserts control over scholarship by the academy, increases competition and reduces the monopoly power of journals".

FACILITATING SCHOLARLY COMMUNICATIONS

Although reforming scholarly communication system has been one of the 'two strategic issues' that IRs try to address, McDowell concluded that "IR has been relatively unsuccessful in fulfilling 'original' role.' This assertion was supported by his survey, which found that "the percentage of peer-reviewed works—pre-and post-prints, e-journal articles, and e-books—is considerably around 13 per cent". It is obvious IRs has been facing serious challenges in the scholarly communication arena.

There are several reasons why IRs is not the preferred choice for disseminating researches. Aschenbrenner *et al.*, observed that "journal publication patterns are already well in place and they are often (rightly or wrongly) considered the most reliable route to scientific credit". Foster added to that observation by identifying the current established system that "rewards faculty members with tenure and promotion based on their success at getting published in respected scholarly journals" as the main reason why 'professors do not have much incentive to put their material in an experimental online archive'.

There are also some faculties "who believe that self-archiving may threaten their rights over their work, their relationship with their favourite publishers, or their status in their disciplinary communities." This trend has led Salo to assert that "libraries whose support for repositories rests purely on hopes of collecting peerreviewed literature would be well-advised not to bother with them".

Another challenge in the scholarly communication arena comes from the fact that most IRs are functioning only as digital resources management system, without 'the more complex services on which users depend'. IRs might be useful and/or powerful for organising and managing digital resources, but "want something that will support the authoring process, not just the finished product". IRs also needs to strive to 'become a natural part of the user's daily work environment'. This might explain why IRs can achieve relative successes in acquiring contents from students, but not from faculties or peer-reviewed publication authors. Salo noticed that slight exceptions might apply for "younger scholars may be attracted to self-archiving as a way to game a prestige system otherwise stacked against them".

Besides all the shortcomings of IRs in the scholarly communication arena, I believe IRs has managed to reduce the total monopoly of conventional journal publishers. Many journal publishers have revised their publishing and copyright policies to allow authors to selfarchive in institutional or subject repositories. The new policies wouldn't have had materialised had it not been because of open access movement (or spirit) embodied in IRs. There are currently open access (book and journal) publishers offering alternatives to conventional publishers. More and more universities and research institutions are jumping into the open access (and IRs) bandwagon by instituting Open Access Mandates in their institutions.

Although in its current state IRs might not achieve big success in (radically) reforming scholarly communication, I believe that IRs has contributed—to certain extent—the efforts in "advancing the positive transformation of scholarly communication over the long term". The same challenge is faced by DI in acquiring journal articles from faculties. DI—as an IRs system—has not yet accommodated any authoring or collaborative process. In its current state, DI acquires contents for eDIMENSI (scientific journal articles) collections through a formal cooperation with the Research Center at PCU. The Research Center is the formal agency at PCU that manages the review, editorial, and publication processes of DIMENSI journals using the Open Journal System (OJS).

The cooperation allows the Library to batch download the newly published articles and feed them into DI. It might be the future direction to merge the two systems into a single platform, which will streamline much of the processes involved in both entities (Research Center and Library) and open up opportunities to create new collaborative features in the future.

FACILITATING COLLABORATIONS

An important aspect of IRs that is often overlooked is its potential as a collaborative platform for the campus communities. If we agree that IRs is, as Lynch stated, "a set of services that a university offers to the members of its community for the management and dissemination of digital materials created by the institution and its community members" then academic libraries have an invaluable asset in their hands.

This asset has a functions and/or roles that span traditional boundaries of campus communities, units, and academic disciplines. Due to this nature, academic libraries that implement and manage IRs will soon discover themselves introduced to a rich variety of local contents produced by different campus communities covering a wide range of academic disciplines. Cross-pollination or cross-fertilisation of knowledge is a natural consequence of exposures to such rich and diverse local contents. Contents produced by a campus community can be re-used as learning resources by other campus communities. Marketing or promotional efforts can be conducted by academic libraries to introduce these local contents to all academic departments and provide insights on possibilities of their uses for each department.

Libraries can also expand features in their IRs to be able to link to e-learning systems used on campus. The linking will enable students and faculties to access our local contents directly from the e-learning systems that they are using for teaching and learning, thus increasing exposures of the contents to various campus communities. These efforts will expose local contents from a specific campus community to a wider audience.

Thematic exhibitions will also provide rich exposures for students, who otherwise would have been 'confined' to their particular field of studies. The experience will enrich students' learning experience. Thematic exhibitions of local contents can sometimes create unique opportunities for inter-disciplinary conversations. Liauw told of an interesting story as an example of how thematic exhibitions can create such conversations.

A thematic onsite exhibition featuring photography documentary of Sedulur Sikep—an ethnic minority in Central Java, Indonesia—was held in 2006, displaying works of a student from Visual Communication Design Department. The exhibition sparked interests from other academic disciplines to conduct other researches on the ethnic minority. An English Department faculty was interested to conduct further study on the linguistic aspects of the ethnic minority. Another faculty from Interior Design Department expressed interests in doing further studies on the ornamental design on the ethnic's settlements.

This example shows that academic libraries should treat their local contents and exhibition spaces as assets to be used to facilitate collaborations and conversations across academic disciplines. Wider collaborations among different campus units and academic departments can be facilitated when academic libraries capitalise on their local contents in IRs to reach out to the society. Academic libraries can create and carry out various programmes and activities jointly with other campus communities. Surabaya Memory (SM) provided a good example on this aspect. Digital resources in SM have been used as part of the teaching and learning process by Architecture Department, Tourism and Leisure Management Department, and Hotel Management Department.

However SM has also become a collaborative platform for PCU Library and other campus units to reach out to the society in Surabaya city. Every May (anniversary of Surabaya) SM conducts thematic exhibitions in a mall in Surabaya. During the exhibition, which usually lasts four to ten days, various competitions, cultural performances, and heritage walks are held to celebrate the city's anniversary.

All these programmes and activities have been made possible by the collaborations between the Library and various academic departments. The Event Management course at

Hotel Management Department has been using SM as real world projects for its students. The students are assigned to help the Library in preparing and supervising the exhibition, looking for sponsors, creating events and performances during the exhibition, etc.

The Cultural Tourism course at Tourism and Leisure Management Department has also been using SM as real world projects for its students by conducting heritage walks throughout the year for campus communities as well as the general public. IRs can also serve as collaborative platform to build networks with various parties outside the university boundaries. SM has been functioning as a networking tool for PCU. Various co-operations and collaborations have been initiated between PCU communities and outside parties through SM.

Furthermore SM has served as a common platform for campus communities at PCU to reach out to the society. It is obvious from that IRs can facilitate collaborations if academic libraries are willing to go beyond merely populating their IRs with digital contents. Collaborations with various campus communities will strengthen the libraries' roles on campus and help libraries tremendously in advocating their services to the campus communities. Libraries can even increase the institutional visibility of the whole institution with their IRs projects.

FACILITATING INSTITUTIONAL VISIBILITY

Academic libraries have always contributed to the institutional visibility of their host institutions. They have unconsciously played 'silent' marketing role, promoting their host institutions in the process. Their unique nature as public spaces has allowed them to be visited by various members of the community, inside and outside of campus boundaries. Libraries are the very few institutions in the world where ordinary people would feel comfortable to visit even though they don't have any membership or institutional affiliation. Academic libraries should capitalise on this aspect to facilitate institutional visibility.

Before the advent of the Internet and DLs/IRs, this would mean providing their traditional collections and services, and physical spaces to the campus communities and the society. The Internet, open access movement, and DLs/IRs have provided new opportunities for academic libraries to raise their contributions to the facilitating of institutional visibility of their host institutions. Digital contents in IRs should be provided freely to enable a wider dissemination to the global audience, which in turn will translate into a significant increase in institutional visibility. There is no longer any physical barrier that limits the scope of the dissemination of the IRs' contents as in physical library collections. This is also the experience of DI. Table shows the web access profile for 'petra.ac.id' domain. Where Visitors Go on Petra.ac.id.

Table. 7.4 Domain Profile for 'petra.ac.id' from Alexa

Subdomain	Per Cent of Site Traffic
Digilib.petra.ac.id	59.6
Dewey.petra.ac.id	20.5
Petra.ac.id	5.1
Genesis.petra.ac.id	4.3
Careercenter.petra.ac.id	1.8
Puslit2.petra.ac.id	1.1
Fportfolio.petra.ac.id	1.1
It.petra.ac.id	0.7
Puslit.petra.ac.id	0.7
Communication.petra.ac.id	0.4
John.petra.ac.id	0.4

This is a very significant contribution that PCU Library–through DI–has made to the overall 'Internet marketing' of the university. The access statistics from Alexa is confirmed by the weblog of the DI server as shown in table. More opportunities to facilitate institutional visibility can be gained when we share metadata of our digital contents with other IRs. This can be achieved by utilising the OAIPMH or even a 'low-tech' approach by exporting the metadata and exchange them using spreadsheet application such as Microsoft Excel.

Table. 7.5 Web Access Statistics of Desa Informasi

Month	Unique Visitors	Number of Visits	Pages	Hits	Bandwidth
Sep-09	160,097	355,177	3,125,802	6,686,167	191.36 GB
Oct 2009	224,082	607,877	5,305,997	11,296,525	315.91 GB
Nov 2009	215,583	563,184	5,005,537	10,664,877	325.83 GB
Dec 2009	201,370	510,646	4,581,746	9,751,878	283.93 GB
Jan-10	212,415	538,796	4,538,643	9,769,348	295.05 GB
Feb-10	197,727	450,327	4,293,240	8,789,435	360.64 GB
Mar-10	247,483	615,001	5,058,876	10,573,688	431.89 GB
Apr-10	237,076	577,638	4,845,910	10,138,585	454.83 GB
May 2010	207,424	484,272	4,225,088	8,831,741	436.39 GB
Jun-10	199,156	454,782	3,975,456	8,281,444	496.72 GB
Jul-10	174,474	360,614	3,175,481	6,503,735	398.71 GB
Aug 2010	157,810	317,685	2,804,185	5,897,145	338.25 GB
	2,434,697	5,835,999	50,935,961	107,184,568	4,329,51GB

This approach is being utilised by DI while an upgrade to an OAI-PMH compliant system is still in progress. The Indonesian Ministry of National Education under its Directorate General of Higher Education has launched a collaborative programme to create a 'union catalog' of metadata for local contents from higher education institutions across Indonesia called Garuda. Networking opportunities like this provide increased visibility of our IRs and host institution. Rankings by independent organisations that measure web sites and online resources provide additional incentives for developing IRs.

One of them is the Ranking Web of World Universities that measures world universities' commitment to open access by looking at digital contents on their web sites. Using certain methodology it has managed to rank world universities based on several parameters. DI opens up its digital contents to be indexed by Google, which has enabled Webometrics to measure the 'Size' and 'Rich Files' stored in DI. Webometrics rankings are important for us in Indonesia since, they are being used by Directorate General of Higher Education as one of several metrics to measure performances of Indonesian higher education institutions. PCU has been ranked #5 along with big state universities in Indonesia. A good rank will surely contribute to the increased visibility of the host institutions. This fact strengthens the assertion that IRs serve as one of "meaningful indicators of an institution's academic quality ... thus increasing the institution's visibility, status, and public value".

DEVELOPING AND USING A GUIDE TO ASSESS LEARNING RESOURCE QUALITY IN EDUCATIONAL DIGITAL LIBRARIES

The democratisation of content creation via ubiquitous Internet tools and infrastructure has fueled an explosion of user-generated digital content in the commercial and educational markets. Federal agencies in the United States, such as the National Science Foundation, are actively seeking ways to integrate teachers and learners into the education cyber-infrastructure. The overall purpose of this education cyberinfrastructure is to connect people with information and with web-based tools to improve productivity, teaching, and learning. By connecting teachers and learners with tools, they become co-creators of educational content. Educational digital libraries, part of this cyberinfrastructure, have been created as places to deposit and disseminate educational content, which often takes the form of online learning resources of varying levels of granularity.

Digital library content can be created easily and deposited rapidly, placing it outside the peer review processes typically employed by publishers and professional societies, but it is unclear whether teachers are using high quality online learning resources in the classroom. To date, educational digital library developers, catalogers, teachers and school administrators have depended on one or a combination of the following proxies to establish an imprimatur of content quality: the reputation and oversight of a funding organisation, the credentials of the content creator, or the collection development policies of specific digital libraries.

However, the definition of 'quality'for organisations like those often reflects internal policies and goals, resulting in reviews or judgements that are not comparable across institutions. Further blurring the boundaries between creator-reviewer, teacher-learner and publisherconsumer, many sites employing user ratings and comment tools, such as YouTube, Flickr, iTunesU, and ccMixter provide an alternative to the evolving education cyber-infrastructure, creating a rich and diverse environment for disseminating user-generated educational content. Most educational digital libraries do not rely on even a quasi-review for assessing the quality of the content created for, or by, their users as the above sites do.

However, in the omnipresent climate of accountability within the U.S., K-12 education system at the federal, state and local levels, education digital libraries are being challenged to prove their value. For these reasons, it is useful, if not necessary, to develop a method to review the quality of online education resources. And, since, social networking tools make sharing a by-product of content creation, it is necessary to develop a standardised set of measures that can be employed across a range of education digital library environments while leveraging existing and emerging social and technical networks to enrich, facilitate, and automate the review process.

This stage describes the development of a guide to assess the quality of educational learning resources within the context of the Instructional Architect, a web-based content-authoring tool for K-12 teachers in the United States. We describe the motivation for developing this Quality Guide, the process for creating it by synthesising the rubrics of other education digital libraries, and the results of testing and using the Guide with K-12 teachers in the context of professional development workshops.

Analyses of its usability and reliability indicate that the Quality Guide influences how teachers design instructional activities using online learning resources. But, defining 'quality' remains a difficult task since, the perception of quality is dependent on a reviewer's, or user's, purpose for the learning resources and context of their use. Over the past 10-15 years, as part of the many global initiatives created to provide access to online educational resources, educational digital libraries in the United States have been developed for K-12 and higher education audiences with support from state and federal agencies: from private foundations, and from universities.

These institutions funded projects create, or provide access to, curricula that integrates online educational resources and training programmes to empower teachers to incorporate learning technologies into their daily preparation and practice and, ultimately, to design their own learning resources. Educational digital library developers have gathered online learning resources of varying levels of granularity (*e.g.*, from images to entire lessons) and of varying sources of authorship (*e.g.*, grant-funded subject matter experts; K-12 teachers; graduate students) into central online portals to enable discovery and re-use by other educators. While traditional libraries use collection development plans to guide acquisitions that are based on knowledge of their users, educational digital libraries acquire resources created as a result of projects with museums, practicing teachers, researchers and from Internet users.

The challenge is to balance collecting and providing access to many online learning resources while maintaining a level of resource quality, cataloging, and curation that distinguishes educational digital libraries from generic Internet search engines and non-educational social software. However, it is often as difficult for teachers and learners to define quality as it is for the courts to define pornography. As U.S., Supreme Court Justice Potter Steward once noted, 'I know it when I see it." The problem (or the solution?) lies in the perspective of users who are confronted with a variety of resources of indeterminate origin.

For school administrators, teachers, and learners, a high quality resource could consist of an entire lesson that meets several state standards; a web-based animation that accurately depicts a science concept. Grappling with the idea of 'quality', several education digital libraries have already created rubrics to assess their content. As we tried to apply these criteria to the content in the Instructional Architect, we observed that portions of each rubric were applicable in different settings, and other portions were specific to each digital library with little room for re-use outside of the original context. As such, our goals were:

- To synthesise the various dimensions of existing rubrics in order to identify a standardised set of criteria that could potentially be used by any digital library with online educational resources; and
- To create a guide that could be used to assess the quality of materials in the Instructional Architect projects.

This stage briefly describes our process for developing the standardised set of assessment criteria; evaluating its utility and usability with middle school science and math teachers; developing a Quality Guide for use with Instructional Architect projects; testing its reliability; and, exploring how the Guide could foster teachers' skills in designing learning resources.

PREVIOUS RESEARCH

Many education digital library builders have developed rubrics to help assess the quality of online educational resources generated by teachers, faculty and learners. However, the motivations and methods for implementing the rubrics vary as do the implied assumptions about the value of the results for each education digital library. Established publishing houses and professional societies institute peer review processes to maintain a reputation for producing quality publications thereby increasing subscriptions and membership.

For newly-funded education digital libraries, under pressure to prove their value, rubrics and a process to measure quality, were created to first establish a reputation with users. Similarly, other education digital libraries used rubrics to support access to high quality resources in a digital library or repository because use of a collection development policy for inclusion of quality resources adds value and buy-in from peer reviewers and users. Still other sites developed a rubric to guide authors in creating high quality online resources by gathering feedback from target users. The methods by which education digital libraries collected data using rubrics and how they used that information also varied. Muramatsu and Agogino used a rubric to gather feedback from targeted users to inform collection development, while Recker, Walker, and Lawless gathered data through automated mechanisms to provide teachers with suggestions based on resources they had previously viewed and used. Establishing peer review panels and processes was not a *de facto* choice for every education digital library. Enlisting users-as-builders, or reviewers-as-builders, is a characteristic of the grass-roots environment in which many education digital libraries evolved over the last decade in the U.S.

However, many digital library developers found that gathering reviews from users was difficult, though providing incentives, in the form of awards or other methods was one way to increase acceptance and adoption of the rubric and review process and of the education digital library in general. The process of creating and testing an assessment rubric can be time consuming. Many rubric creators believe it is important to map out stakeholders and end-users, review previous work by other digital libraries and learn how to gather data. Testing a rubric with users, for formative evaluation, further refines the rubric, yielding usability information as well as real time feedback from target users which ultimately assists with the process of implementing the rubric with a larger group of users.

CONTEXT

The Instructional Architect

The Instructional Architect is a simple, web-based authoring tool designed to help K-12 teachers find, design, and use online learning resources in their classrooms. When using the Instructional Architect, teachers search for and save links to online learning resources from the Web and educational digital libraries such as the National Science Digital Library. Resources that can be linked include online content, RSS feeds and podcasts. Once resources are gathered users then create 'Instructional Architect projects' that contain instructional objectives, activities, and assessments. The resources are either embedded into the project or link out to web-based resources.

In this way, teachers create Instructional Architect projects that customise resources to their local context. Figure shows an Instructional Architect project and an accompanying resource.

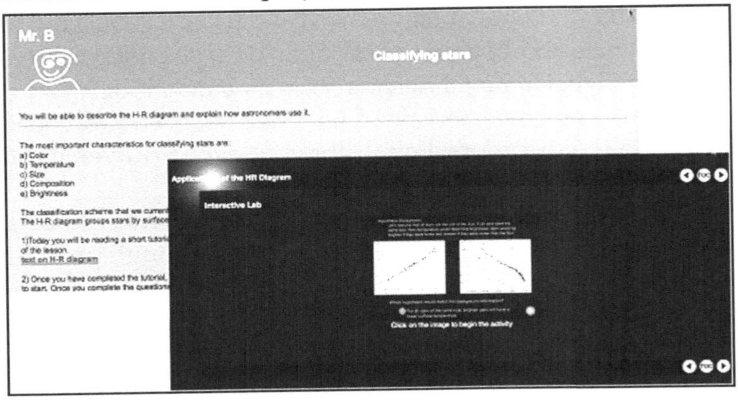

Fig. 7.1 Example of an Instructional Architect Project Created by Mr. B and Related Resource

Initially the majority of users were K-12 teachers in the U.S., who participated in professional development workshops from 2005-2009. Recently, the Instructional Architect system has garnered more widespread usage and spread 'virally' to teachers not directly attending these workshops. Table 7.6 shows statistics on Instructional Architect usage and growth in the number of Instructional Architect projects and resources over the last 12 months.

Table. 7.6 Instructional Architect Usage Data

Data	N	12-month growth in Per cent
Registered users	5,300	23
Instructional Architect projects created	11,500	37
Online learning resources used	52,100	67
Visits to Instructional Architect project (since, 8/2006)	1 million	64

Before any of the abundant Instructional Architect projects created by users can be ingested into educational digital libraries, like the National Science Digital Library, to become part of the education cyberinfrastructure, they need to be evaluated for quality. To support this outcome, the Instructional Architect projects must be reviewed with a rubric that is reliable across multiple sites, a process that is scalable across the thousands of IA projects, and that has useful results for end-users, reviewers, and digital library developers.

METHOD

Synthesising Existing Rubrics and Creating the Quality Guide

Following the recommendations for establishing a rubric to assess content, we began with a literature review in the disciplines of computer science, library and information science, education, and digital libraries. We selected only articles that included or referenced rubrics used to review online educational resources.

The literature review yielded articles with descriptions of 12 rubrics. In keeping with our first goal, our initial plan was to identify review criteria at the most granular level and then do a frequency analysis to identify broad topics that applied across criteria.

These would then become the foundational criteria. Accordingly, we un-bundled the rubrics and identified over 200 review criteria, some of which included only one or two words and sometimes no definition.

However, when conducting our frequency analysis, we found it difficult to group similar review criteria because:

- None of the rubrics used a standard vocabulary for their review criteria;
- The definitions for criteria contained multiple concepts that defied easy categorisation; and
- Some criteria were so contextualised to their site that they became virtually meaningless when viewed out of context from the whole rubric.

These factors also made it difficult to create topic areas before and after the frequency analysis. Given the challenges of our initial approach, we revised our methods and used a card sort technique. Card sorts are typically employed as a user-centered design approach for assessing web site structure. This process has participants sort a series of cards, each labelled with a piece of content or functionality into groups that make sense to them.

This technique allows input from several experts, with the consensus between them resolving ambiguities in and across the review criteria. In preparing the initial list of over 200 review criteria for sorting, we realised that some of the most granular criteria, especially those without definitions, would prove difficult to sort, appearing as so much noise to study participants. Therefore, we culled the list to include only criteria from the literature that included a definition and that would make sense when read outside the context of its original use. Our intention was not to represent criteria as they had been used within a particular review process, but to use the criteria as presented in the literature.

The result was that 104 review criteria remained for use in the card sort exercise. The card sort methodology recommends using seven to ten participants. Our sorting exercise included 10 participants who were graduate students, professors from instructional technology and education, and academic librarians. We presented the participants with a spreadsheet containing the review criteria, criteria definitions, and the source rubric or citation.

We chose the 'open sort' method and asked participants to sort the review criteria into groups of their own choosing within a spreadsheet and to provide their own titles for the groups. Participants were allowed to place criteria in more than one group as long as they indicated which criteria-group pairing represented their highest priority.

Each of the ten participants created an average of nearly 13 groups into which they individually sorted the 104 review criteria. One participant sorted criteria into multiple groups but did not indicate a top priority, so rather than guessing at the intention, the results were not included. Ultimately, we analysed the nine result sets containing an average of 11 groups per participant. A detailed analysis yielded six elements from the 11 groups.

These became the foundational set of criteria, which were standardised to the point where they could be used by any digital library with online education resources, thereby accomplishing our first goal.

Table. 7.7 Standardised Set of Criteria with Definitions

Standardised Criteria	Definitions and R eferences
Interface Design and Accessibility	The resource is attractive. The resource is easy to navigate. The resource contains no advertising. The resource contains links that work. The resource is designed to accommodate disabled and mobile learners.
Technical Reliability	The resource uses multimedia that work. The resource clearly identifies the supporting technical resources required. The resource contains help features.
Content	Resource content is accurate. Resource content is complete. Resource content is impartial. Resource content is clearly written. Resources content is maintained.
Pedagogy	The resource is engaging. The reource is motivating. The resource is interactive. The resources includes assessment(s) (Ohio Resource Center). The resource provides feedback. The resource supports learners proceeding at their own pace. The resource supports introductory, reinforcing, or summative activities.

(Contd...)

Administrative	The resource contains direct and explicit links to state or national educational teaching standards. The resource contains information about ist author or creator, e-mail, site domain, role. The resource is described by current metadata.
Other	The resource requires a fee for access. The resources overall rating/confidence level.

Table 7.7 shows the six elements, or standardised criteria, developed by study participants in the card sort exercise. Corresponding definitions and the references for them are also displayed.

The definitions (*e.g.*, Resource content is accurate) are statements from the original 12 rubrics that participants associated with the standardised criteria. Using these foundational criteria, we then began to address the second goal of creating a guide that could be used to assess the quality of materials in the Instructional Architect projects.

☆☆☆☆☆	Interface Design Definition: Dynamic, Visually Pleasing Aesthetics, Standards, Accessibility, Navigation, Good User Interface
☆☆☆☆☆	Accessibility Definition: Technical Reliability, Reusability,Usability Design, Reliability, Adaptability ADA
☆☆☆☆☆	Content Definition: Accuracy, Organization, Quality, Completeness, Currency, Value, Interdisciplinary
☆☆☆☆☆	Pedagogy Definition: Instruction Methods, Design Methods, Learning Goals, Anticipated Outcomes, Motivation, Engagement
☆☆☆☆☆	Administrative Definition: Authority, Authorship, Metadata, Advertising, Credibility
☆☆☆☆☆	Overall Rating

Fig. 7.2 Prototype of Foundational Criteria and Definitions

Figure 7.2 shows the prototype of the foundational criteria and definitions in beta form before it was designed to be more user-friendly and visually appealing. This subsequently became the first version of the Instructional Architect Quality Guide, and included five Likert scale star ratings for each criterion, as these are widely used by rating systems, and less-detailed definitions of criteria.

Testing the Instructional Architect Quality Guide

Twenty-eight participants were recruited to test the first version of the Instructional Architect Quality Guide. They were part of a cohort of U.S., K-12 teachers in an online graduate programme, and they completed required activities as part of an online course.

Testing the Quality Guide was directed by the following research questions:

- What is the student's view of using technology in a classroom.
- How do teachers assess an online educational resource before and after using the Quality Guide.
- Using the Quality Guide, how helpful are conducting and receiving peer reviews for the student and,
- What changes should be made to the Instructional Architect Quality Guide based on student use and feedback.

Data Sources

The participants took part in an online learning module in the context of learning how to use the Instructional Architect and the Quality Guide. They completed pre-and post-online surveys, which used a combination of open-ended and Likert-scale questions. Surveys measured the extent of participants' experience and classroom practice in using online educational resources; their attitudes about online educational resources and technology in general and their use in a classroom; and, strategies for evaluating an online educational resource.

Within the learning module, participants were placed in small groups of 4-5 participants, and they evaluated one another's Instructional Architect projects using the Quality Guide. Conversations about these evaluations were posted in a BlackBoard discussion forum and collected for analysis by the researchers. Lastly, participants wrote a reflection paper describing their experience using the Instructional Architect, how they used online educational resources in an instructional situation, difficulties and successes in designing and implementing their project, what they learned by reviewing their peers' Instructional Architect projects and by using the Quality Guide, and how they could improve their Instructional Architect project.

RESULTS

Research question one used data from the pre-and post-survey Likert items. Effect sizes were calculated on questions relating to participants' attitude, experience with and use of online educational resources and technology in their classrooms in order to understand changes in participants' pedagogical choices and activities in their classrooms. An effect size (dw) shows a magnitude of change and is considered small at 0.2 detectable by an expert looking closely at the phenomenon, medium at 0.5, and large at 0.8 detectable by an untrained observer. Larger effect sizes equate to larger impacts due to the intervention. Small, but positive changes, statistically significant at $p < 0.05$, were shown from the pre-test to the post-test as teachers reported that they knew how to effectively teach with technology in the classroom ($dw = 0.28$, $p < 0.05$), and they knew how to effectively use technology in their classroom ($dw = 0.42$, $p < 0.05$).

From this we know that after participating in the learning module, teachers began to overcome initial barriers of using technology in the classroom and could now focus on making better pedagogical decisions about the type of learning resources they could create. We then used a qualitative analysis to address research question two with the understanding that participants had learned how to use online educational resources.

Using a constant comparative analysis, data from the reflection papers, discussion boards, and one question in the pre-and post-survey were mapped into themes and analysed. Participants reported in the pre-survey that when evaluating online educational resources they looked for fit with the curriculum, accuracy, ease of use, currency, text readability, and recommendations by others. After completing this course module, participants added in their post-survey comments that they looked for: content quality, distractions on the resource pages, credibility of the site, and engagement.

Many of the criteria they added were items listed in the Quality Guide. Thus, it appeared that use of the Quality Guide helped refine participants' approach to designing online learning resources, in the form of Instructional Architect projects. To answer research question three, the comments from the discussion boards in Blackboard where participants posted their evaluations of their peers' Instructional Architect projects were used. Some participants commented on the readability and text clarity of the Instructional Architect project, and many caught spelling errors. One participant commented after receiving some feedback, "I have learned that having a peer read through my projects can be very valuable.

They catch mistakes that I do not see." Overall, 53 per cent of the participants reported that providing and receiving feedback from their peers via reviews was valuable. Two additional themes surfaced from analyses of the discussion boards during the process of peer evaluation that related to re-use of other teachers' Instructional Architect projects and ideas. *First,* participants asked if they could use an Instructional Architect project they reviewed, or said they planned to use it in their classroom. The *second* theme was that participants learned what others had done and wanted to implement the same idea in their project. A participant commented that, "Completing a peer review gives us an opportunity to see other creations and improve our programmes as we see fit."

The *final* data collection point included participants' reflection papers. Participants were asked to report on their instructional situation, successes and difficulties, what they learned from their peers and using the Quality Guide, and how they could improve their Instructional Architect project. Three areas of learning were repeatedly reported in the reflection papers: what they learned by reviewing peer work; what they learned for their own work; and, the value of re-using Instructional Architect projects. Similar ideas were also expressed throughout the discussion boards and survey answers.

Reliability and Improvements

Version one of the Quality Guide was tested for reliability in order to answer research question four. Peer ratings of Instructional Architect projects using the Guide, provided by the students in the online graduate course, and were used for this analysis. The Quality Guide criteria were scored on a scale of 0-4, where zero or one star is low and four or five stars is high (*e.g.*, very clear). Means and standard deviations were run for each question.

Number	Criteria	Rating
1	Content Accuracy	Very Inaccurarte · Somewhat Inaccurate · Not Enough Information · Somewhat Accurate · Very Accurate Comments:
2	Text Clarity	Very Unclear · Somewhat Unclear · Not Enough Information · Somewhat Clear · Very Clear Comments:
3	Links in Project	No Links Work · Some Links don't Work · Not Enough Information · Some Links Work · All Links Work Comments:
4	Project Completeness: Includes the state Standard Learning Goal, Assesment, etc.	Very Incomplete · Somewhat Incomplete · Not Enough Information · Somewhat Complete · very Complete Comments:
5	The Project:(Circle One)	a. Provides a Resorce List b. Teacher a Concept c. Reinforces a Concepts d. Provider a Summary of Content With a Learning Activity e. Don't Know f. Does Somthing else (Describe below)
6	Overall Rating of the Project	Meets no criteria · Meets Very Little Criteria · Meets Some Criteria · Meets Criteria · Exceed Criteria Comments:

Fig. 7.3 First Version of the Instructional Architect Quality Guide

Criteria one through four and six of the Quality Guide were analysed using an intra-class correlation. Criteria five was not analysed as it asks for a classification on what the Instructional Architect project is doing (*e.g.,* teaching a new concept, reinforcing a concept, etc). Table shows the intraclass correlation values for each question analysed. A close look at the data shows that the teachers generally rated their peers at an average of 2 or more (3 or more stars on the Quality Guide) for any of the criteria on the Guide. This could possibly be attributed to the fact that educators as a whole tend to provide high ratings for their peer, a phenomenon observed in prior work.

Table. Means and Standard Deviations for Criteria 1-4, 6 of the Instructional Architect Quality Guide.

S.No.	Criteria	Mean	Standard Deviation
1	Content accuracy	2.50	1.13
2	Text clarity	2.34	0.98
3	Links in project	3.30	0.83
4	Project completeness	2.14	1.50
6	Overall rating	3.22	1.84

As a result of the high ratings, the full range of the scale was not used, and slight departures were magnified in the intraclass correlation. The negative values indicate that there was more variation between projects than there was between raters. As is shown in the low intraclass correlation, agreement on those ratings was never high, and in most cases was non-existent.

Table. 7.9 Intraclass Correlation (ICC) Values for Criteria 1-4, 6 of the Instructional Architect Quality Guide

S.No.	Criteria	Intraclass Correlation
1	Content accuracy	0
2	Text clarity	-0.129
3	Links in project	0.031
4	Project completeness	-0.89
6	Overall rating	-0.129

The reliability analysis suggests that the scale needs more explanation for each item and that the scale should encompass either a broader range or a dichotomous rating (yes or no). Improvements made to the Quality Guide as a result of this testing included adding more detailed definitions of the review criteria, re-arranging the order of criteria, and modifying scoring instructions. As a result of this testing, improvements were made to create the final version of the Quality Guide, which is currently used to inform and support individual teachers as they create Instructional Architect projects.

Instructional Architect™

Use the Following Indicators to Inform Your Choices When Designing or Reviewing IA Projects.

Accuracy
Information is Credible, Truthful, Reliable, Current

Very Incomplete	Incomplete	Accurate	Very Accurate
Comments:			

Text Clarity
Appropriate Grade Level, Length, and Amount (as Concise as Needed)

Very Unclear	Unclear	Clear	Very Clear
Comment:			

Links in Project
Work and go to the Correct Page

All Links Fail	Most Links Fail	Most Links Work	All Links Work
Comments:			

Project Completeness
Includes the State Standard, Objectives, Learning Goal, Assessment, or an Example

Very Incomplete	Incomplete	Complete	Very Complete
Comments:			

The Project

Provides a Resource List	Teaches a Concept	Reinforces a Concept	Provides a Summary of Content	Other
Comments:				

Overall

Meets no Criteria	Meets Some Criteria	Meets all Criteria	Exceeds criteria
Comments:			

Utah State University DL NSDL

Fig. 7.4 Final Version of the Instructional Architect Quality Guide

Bibliography

Albanese, A.: *Revolution or Evolution: Trends in Electronic Scholarly Publishing, India: Library Journal,* 2001.

Biggs, M.: *Information Overload and Information Seekers, UK: The Reference Librarian,* 1999.

D'Esposito, J. E., & Gardner, R. M.: *University Students' Perceptions of the Internet: An Exploratory Study,* USA: Journal of Academic Librarianship, 1999.

Davis, P.: *The Effect of the Web on Undergraduate Citation Behaviour,* UK: *Research Libraries* Press 2002.

Diedrichs, C. P.: *Library Collections, Acquisitions, and Technical Services,* NJ: Information Today, 2001.

Duggan, A., Hess, B., Morgan, D., Kim, S., & Wilson, K.: *Measuring Students' Attitude Toward Educational Use of the Internet, USA:* American Educational Research Association, 2000.

Eason, K. D., Yu, L., & Harker, S.: *The Use and Usefulness of Functions in Electronic Journals,* NJ: Information Today, 2000.

Fenichel, C. H.: *The Process of Searching Online Bibliographic Databases,* London: Open University Press, 2001.

Grimes, D. J. & Boening, C. H.: *Worries with the Web: A Look at Student Use of Web Resources,* New York: Academic Press, 2001.

Harter, S. P. & Hert, C. A.: *Evaluation of Information Retrieval Systems: Approaches, Issues, and Methods,* New York: Wiley Press, 2000.

Hawkins, D.: *Online Bibliographic Search Strategy Development*, Chicago: American Marketing Association, 2003.

Herring, S. D.: *Faculty Acceptance of the World Wide Web for Student Research*, London: Academic Press, 2001.

Hunter, R. N.: *Successes and Failures of Patrons Searching the Online Catalog at a Large Academic Library*, Brisbane: Australian Academic Press, 2003.

Kling, R., & McKim, G.: *Field Differences in the Shaping of Electronic Media in Supporting Library Administration*, England: Allyn & Bacon Press, 2000.

Lynch, M. J.: *Reference Interviews in Public Libraries*, New York: Cambridge University Press, 2003.

McBride, K. B., & Dickstein, R.: *The Web Demands Critical Reading by Students: The Chronicle Of Higher Education*, London: Academic Press, 2004.

McLuhan, M.: *Understanding Media: The Extensions of Man*. New York: McGraw-Hill, 2001.

Mercado, H.: *Library Instruction and Online Database Searching*, Brisbane: Australian Academic Press, 2003.

Peters, T. A.: *An Analysis of the Transaction Log of an Online Public Access Catalog*, London: Intermediate Technology Publications, 2004.

Pettigrew, K. E., Fidel, R., & Bruce, H.: *Conceptual Frameworks in Information Behaviour*, New York: Plenum Publication, 2001.

Pullinger, D. J.: *Academics and the New Information Environment: The Impact of Local Factors on Use of Electronic Journals*, UK: Cambridge, 2003.

Index